PURE-LAND ZEN
ZEN PURE-LAND

Letters from Patriarch Yin Kuang

PURE-LAND ZEN
ZEN PURE-LAND

Letters from Patriarch Yin Kuang

Translated by Master Thích Thiền Tâm, *et al*
Forrest Smith, *editor*

This book is a translation of selected passages from the letters of Elder Master Yin Kuang, the Thirteenth Patriarch of Pure Land. The original Chinese titles are *Yin Kuang Fa Shih Wen Ch'ao* and *Yin Kuang Ta Shih Chia Yen Lu.* The Vietnamese version is entitled *Lá Thư Tịnh Độ*, Thích Thiền Tâm, translator.

First edition: 1992

**Sutra Translation Committee of the
United States and Canada**

Dharma Master Lok To, Director
2611 Davidson Ave.
Bronx, N.Y. 10468 (USA)
Tel. (718) 584-0621

Printed in the United States of America

The supreme and endless blessings
of Samantabhadra's deeds,
I now universally transfer.
May every living being, drowning
and adrift,
Soon return to the Land of Limitless
Light!

The Vows of Samantabhadra

About the Author

The life of the Pure Land Patriarch Yin Kuang (1861-1940), which covers one of the most eventful periods for East Asia, spans the Chinese Revolution of 1911 and two world wars.

> The revolution of 1911 that toppled the Manchu dynasty and established the Republic of China also brought in its wake a number of problems for the Buddhist sangha. Following the political revolution, an intellectual climate was ushered in that was unfriendly to the interests of Buddhism ... The attack and criticism against Buddhism ... resulted in a number of discriminatory measures, such as special taxes and contributions being levied on temples, monasteries being appropriated for use as barracks and police stations, tenants on temple lands being encouraged not to pay rent, and Buddhist images being destroyed ... (K.K.S. Ch'en, *Buddhism in China*, p. 455.)

Against this backdrop, two monks rose to lead the resurgence of Buddhism: Master T'ai Hsu, who was instrumental in the revival of the Mind-Only school and Master Yin Kuang, later to become the Thirteenth Patriarch of Pure Land.

> The monk mainly responsible for instilling new life and meaning into ... [the practice of Buddha Recitation and

the chanting of sutras was Master] Yin Kuang ... who, after his conversion to Pure Land pietism, concentrated on living a pure religious life based on faith, devotion and holiness ... [Master] Yin Kuang carried on his teachings mainly in the provinces of Kiangsu and Chekiang, where he gained numerous followers and disciples ... These efforts by [Master] Yin Kuang and his followers brought about an extensive revival of the Pure Land school. Lotus Societies, Nien-fo [Buddha Recitation] Societies, and others of a similar nature sprang up all over China. (Ibid., p. 460.)

The compendium of Master Yin Kuang's letters -- excerpts of which are translated in this book -- represents a broad cross-section of the Master's thought and forms a prized collection of inspirational writings cherished throughout the Mahayana world. Scarcely a Mahayana temple can be found anywhere without several different editions of these letters.

Diệu Phụng
Minh Thành
P.D. Leigh

Festival of
Amitabha Buddha
Shepherd Park
Hartford, CT: 1992

Contents

1   Preface
7   Introduction
        The Pure Land Tradition

Translations

19   *Letters from Patriarch Yin Kuang*

        General Buddhism
        Zen and Pure Land
        Pure Land Practice

219   Appendix: *Avatamsaka Sutra,
                        chapter 40*

235   Editors' Glossary
263   Bibliography

Acknowledgements

We respectfully acknowledge the assistance and support of the following good spiritual advisors, without whom this book could not have been produced. Our gratitude goes first to Dharma Master Lok To (Bronx, New York) and Dharma Master Thích Đức Niệm (Sepulveda, California). Their encouragement, advice, long-distance telephone clarification of difficult passages and, toward the end, gentle prodding, directly led to the production of this book. Thanks also go to Cheng Chien Bhikshu, who read the penultimate draft as well as to Rev. Thích Minh Đức, Rev. Charles O'Hara and Rev. Thích Huệ Minh, all of whom clarified important points and helped sharpen the focus of the text and notes.

In the translation of this book, as with the other volumes in this Pure Land series, we have been assisted by a number of lay Buddhists, whom we shall list in the order of our temporal association with them: Upasaka Lee Tsu-ku (always cheerful and helpful, albeit in a low-keyed, almost Zen-like manner); Upasaka Dương Đình Hỷ (Zen-enthusiast cum firm believer in the Bodhisattva Kuan Yin; scientist cum sinologist at heart); Upasika/Upasaka Michelle and Bruce Kou (may their deepest wish to work full time for the Dharma, parental obligations notwithstanding, be realized); Upasika Lily Wang (East Brunswick -- home of rush computer delivery); Upasika Lien Smith (a model Buddhist, practitioner of the dana paramita); Upasaka Larsen Raleigh (afflictions are Bodhi, the ordinary Mind is the Way); Upasaka Ming-Yee Wang (a friend in the Dharma, a true kalyanamitra); and Dr. Fang Wong (beautiful calligraphy is more than art, it is Mind).

Finally, we are greatly indebted to Dr. C.T. Shen, who, with a friend, kindly went through the whole manuscript and to Prof. Taitetsu Unno, who provided much-needed encouragement and feedback in the initial stage of translation. Last but not least, our editor, Prof. Forrest Smith, formerly of the University of Eastern Illinois, read and re-read the whole manuscript. Externalists like Prof. Smith are one in ten million in this Dharma-Ending Age!

Preface

After the death of the historical Buddha, His teachings spread in two main directions, southward (Theravada tradition) and eastward into China, Vietnam, Korea, Japan (Mahayana tradition). In East Asia, these teachings developed into ten different schools, several of which have remained particularly important to this day: Zen, Tantric and Pure Land. Pure Land is by far the most widespread form of Buddhism in East Asia.[1]

All these schools teach the same basic truth: "Do not what is evil, do what is good, keep your mind pure."[2] True to this spirit, the Pure Land approach is simple and straightforward. Through *mindfulness of the Buddha*[3] (i.e. Buddha Recitation), the practitioner can calm his mind and achieve samadhi and wisdom.[4] After rebirth in the Pure Land (i.e., in the *all-encompassing Mind* and/or the transcendental Land of Amitabha Buddha), he will eventually attain Buddhahood.[5] This is also the core teaching, the very essence, of Zen and all other Mahayana schools.[6] As D.T. Suzuki has pointed out, "the psychological effects of the repetition of the holy name are close to the effects of Zen meditation."[7]

But why do we have to calm the mind and attain Buddhahood? It is because in the wasteland of Birth and Death, subject to the three poisons of greed, anger and delusion, we truly undergo immense suffering.[8] Echoing this conclusion, an American psychologist made this observation about the motivation of Western

Buddhists:

> Probably the majority of non-Orientals who become
> practicing Buddhists do so because of an overriding need
> for relief from suffering. Sometimes the suffering is
> physical, but more often it is emotional and often
> psychosomatic. The individual practicing meditation,
> chanting, or any kind of Buddhist "self-cultivation" is
> motivated by a need for symptomatic relief, mitigation of
> anxiety and depression, reduction of hostility ... (Emma
> McCloy Layman, *Buddhism in America*, p. 269.)

This is precisely why the Buddha, when preaching
the Four Noble Truths to Kaundinya and his friends,
taught them first the Truth of Suffering. The letters of
Master Yin Kuang address this issue squarely. If you are
suffering *and* if you realistically discover that you have
only average motivation, fortitude and self-discipline,
then Pure Land is for you. Pure Land is about suffering
and the *liberation* from suffering. "Said the Buddha: 'As
the sea has one savour, salt, so my Teaching has one
savour, deliverance from suffering.'"[9]

o

oo

This book consists of excerpts of selected letters by
Master Yin Kuang, with notes and Glossary prepared by
the Van Hien Study Group. The reader's indulgence for
possible errors and omissions is requested. Each letter
can be considered a unit in itself and important
explanatory notes are repeated for the convenience of
the reader. Please note that in this text, the expressions
"Buddha Recitation" and "Buddha's name" refer
specifically to Amitabha Buddha. We have included in
an appendix "The Practices and Vows of the Bodhisattva
Samantabhadra" (*Avatamsaka Sutra*, ch. 40) as Master
Yin Kuang frequently lectured on it to foster Pure Land
practice. Caveats: "wisdom lies beyond and the beyond

lies within"[10] ... "as soon as something is expressed in words, the true meaning is already lost."[11]

Here, then, are the letters of Master Yin Kuang. We hope the Western reader will enjoy and benefit from them, as several generations of Eastern readers have. As a Zen Master has written in another context, "read them once, read them twice and look for the same thing that Bodhidharma brought to China: look for the print of the Mind."[12]

Van Hien Study Group
Festival of the Bodhisattva Samantabhadra
New York: 1992

---

(1) "The Pure Land School is presently the school of Buddhism in China and Japan that has the most followers." (*The Shambhala Dictionary of Buddhism and Zen*, p. 174.) "The Pure Land school is the largest in modern Japan." (Christmas Humphreys, *The Buddhist Way of Life*, p. 157.)

(2) See the *Dhammapada Sutra,* verse 183.

(3) See Introduction to this book (para. D) and the following advice from the eminent 16th century Zen Master Chu Hung to a lay disciple:

This [Pure Land] Path is the most primal and the most subtle and wondrous. It is also the simplest. Because it is simple, those of high intelligence overlook it.

Birth and death are not apart from a single moment of mindfulness. Consequently all the myriad worldly and world-transcending teachings and methods are not apart from a single moment of mindfulness. Right now take this moment of mindfulness, and be mindful of buddha, remember buddha, recite the buddha-name. How close and cutting! What pure essential energy, so solid and real! If you see through where this mindfulness arises, this is the Amitabha of our inherent nature. This is the meaning of the patriarch coming from the West [the meaning of Zen]. (J.C. Cleary, *Pure Land, Pure Mind*, unpub. manuscript.)

(4) The relationship between samadhi and wisdom (or between samatha and vipasyana) is a crucial point in

Buddhism. In the Theravada tradition, the differences between them are emphasized; samadhi and wisdom are considered entirely separate facets of cultivation. In the Mahayana tradition (Zen, Avatamsaka, Pure Land), however, samadhi and wisdom are considered indivisible; there is complete interpenetration of all dharmas. Moreover, wisdom is not something external to be "obtained" through practice; it is inherent in all sentient beings. It is as though we have lost a pearl at the bottom of a lake. When there is no wind and the water is calm, the pearl naturally becomes visible. To recover the wisdom-pearl, the practitioner has only to calm the turbid waters of his mind. Thus, to cultivate samadhi is to achieve wisdom.

(5) See the following quote from D.T. Suzuki:

> Some of our readers may be led to think that the sole object of the Pure Land devotees is to be born in Amida's Land of Bliss and Purity ... But the fact is that the birth itself ... is not the object, but to attain enlightenment in the country of Amida where conditions are such as to ensure a ready realization of the true Buddhist life ... If we can say so, to be born in the Pure Land is the means to the end; for Buddhism in whatever form is the religion of enlightenment and emancipation. (*The Eastern Buddhist*, Vol. 3, No. 4, p. 321.)

Please note an important point: the Pure Land is a projection of the mind, a mental construct but it is also real -- to the same extent that our world and everything around it are real. See also Introduction, Note 10.

(6) At the ultimate level, Zen and Pure Land lead to the same goal, Buddhahood. However, at the common, everyday level, an important difference lies in the "issue" of rebirth in the Pure Land. Although both Zen and Pure Land cultivators recite the Buddha's name in their daily practice, Zen followers do not seek rebirth in the Pure Land. (See, for example, *Ch'an Newsletter*, no. 92, May 1992, p. 5.) This apparent difference is, however, easily reconciled when we understand the truth of Self-Nature Amitabha, Mind- Only Pure Land. As the *Vimalakirti Sutra* states: "When the mind is pure, the Buddha land is pure." Rebirth in the Pure Land is rebirth in our pure mind.

(7) Quoted from Heinrich Dumoulin, *Zen Buddhism*, p. 286.

See also the following passages:

> Dr. Suzuki is generally associated with the Zen school, so it is often a matter of surprise to hear that he translated many Pure Land Buddhist texts into English and nourished a belief that Pure Land rather than Zen might be the form of Buddhism most suitable for Westerners. (John Snelling, *The Buddhist Handbook*, p. 216.)

> Most Buddhists in the world, by far the vast majority, practice a Faith or devotional form of worship. Dr. D.T. Suzuki strongly believed that the direction American Buddhism would take was towards Shin Buddhism [Pure Land] and its practice of Faith. It may turn out at this time that most Westerners, originally seeking personal enlightenment, will find themselves choosing a devotional path. (Ryushin Sarah Grayson in *Butsumon*, Fall 1989.)

(8) See Glossary, "Eight sufferings." To illustrate the point that suffering is an inevitable part of our world, consider the example, adapted from the sutras, of worms feeding on rotten apples. The worms are running hither and yon among the apples, each worm "elbowing" the others for a better spot, a larger piece of the rotten matter. They all feel their actions necessary and desirable. They all seem very busy and very happy. To us humans, however, theirs is indeed a pitiable lot. The human condition is the same when seen from the viewpoint of celestials, Bodhisattvas and Buddhas -- such a pitiful sight indeed, whether of beggars or presidential hopefuls!

(9) Quoted in Christmas Humphreys, *The Buddhist Way of Life*, p. 52.

(10) Ibid., p. 153.

(11) This an important teaching in Buddhism. Truth is beyond words and can be attained only through determined study and practice, with practice as the central factor. The various Buddhist methods are like fingers pointing to the moon -- to the Self-Nature, the Buddha within.

(12) Red Pine, *The Zen Teaching of Bodhidharma*, p. xvii.

From all delusions, karma, and demon-states,
Amid all worldly paths, I will be freed,
As the lotus does not touch the water,
As sun and moon do not stop in space.

The Vows of Samantabhadra

Introduction

The Pure Land Tradition

The goal of all Buddhist practice is to achieve
Enlightenment and transcend the cycle of Birth and
Death -- that is, to attain Buddhahood. In the
Mahayana tradition, the precondition for Buddhahood is
the Bodhi Mind, the aspiration to achieve
Enlightenment for the benefit of all sentient beings,
oneself included.[1]

Since sentient beings are of different spiritual
capacities and inclinations, many levels of teaching and
numerous methods were devised in order to reach
everyone. Traditionally, the sutras speak of 84,000, i.e.,
an infinite number, depending on the circumstances, the
times and the target audience. All these methods are
expedients -- different medicines for different
individuals with different illnesses at different times --
but all are intrinsically *perfect and complete*.[2] Within
each method, the success or failure of an individual's
cultivation depends on his depth of practice and
understanding, that is, on his mind.

A) Self-power, other-power

Throughout history, the Patriarchs have elaborated
various systems to categorize Dharma methods and the
sutras in which they are expounded. One convenient

division is into methods based on self-effort (*self-power*) and those that rely on the assistance of the Buddhas and Bodhisattvas (*other-power*).[3] This distinction is, of course, merely for heuristic purposes, as the Truth is, ultimately, one and indivisible: Self-power *is* other-power, other-power *is* self-power.[4]

Traditionally, most Buddhist schools and methods take the *self-power* approach: progress along the path of Enlightenment is achieved only through intense and sustained personal effort. Because of the dedication and effort involved, schools of this self-power, self-effort tradition all have a distinct monastic bias. The laity has generally played only a supportive role, with the most spiritually advanced ideally joining the Order of monks and nuns. Best known of these traditions are Theravada and Zen.

Parallel to this, particularly following the development of Mahayana thought and the rise of lay Buddhism, a more flexible tradition eventually arose, combining self-power with *other-power* -- the assistance and support provided by the Buddhas and Bodhisattvas to sincere seekers of the Way. Most representative of this tradition are the Tantric and Pure Land schools. However, unlike the former (or Zen), Pure Land does not stress the master-disciple relationship and de-emphasizes the role of sub-schools, gurus and rituals. Moreover, the main aim of Pure Land -- rebirth in the Land of Ultimate Bliss through the power of Amitabha Buddha's Vows -- is an attainable goal, though to be understood at several levels. Therein lies the appeal and strength of Pure Land.[5]

B) Pure Land in a Nutshell

Pure Land, like all Mahayana schools, requires first

and foremost the development of the Bodhi Mind,[6] the aspiration to attain Buddhahood for the benefit of all sentient beings. From this starting point, the main tenets of the school can be understood at two main levels, the transcendental and the popular -- depending on the background and the capacities of the cultivator.

i) At the transcendental level, i.e., for cultivators of the highest spiritual capacity, the Pure Land method, like other methods, reverts the ordinary, deluded mind to the Self-Nature True Mind.[7] In the process, wisdom and Buddhahood are eventually attained. This is exemplified by the following advice of the eminent Zen Master Chu Hung (Jap. Shuko), one of the three "Dragon-Elephants" of Ming Buddhism:

> Right now you simply must recite the buddha-name with purity and illumination. Purity means reciting the buddha-name without any other thoughts. Illumination means reflecting back as you recite the buddha-name. Purity is *sammata*, "stopping." Illumination is *vipasyana*, "observing." Unify your mindfulness of buddha through buddha-name recitation, and stopping and observing are both present. (J.C. Cleary, *Pure Land, Pure Mind,* unpub. manuscript.)

As stated in the treatise *Buddhism of Wisdom and Faith:*

> If we have the roots and the temperament of Mahayana followers, we should naturally understand that the goal of Buddha Recitation is to achieve Buddhahood ... Why is it that the goal of Buddha Recitation is to become a Buddha? -- It is because, as we begin reciting, the past, present and future have lost their distinction, marks exist but they have been left behind, form is emptiness, thought is the same as No-Thought, the realm of the Original Nature "apart from thought" of the Tathagata has been penetrated. This state is Buddhahood, what else could it be?

This transcendent form of Pure Land is practiced by those of the highest spiritual capacities: "this Mind is the Buddha ... when the Mind is pure, the Buddha land is pure ... to recite the Buddha's name is to recite the Mind." Thus, at the transcendental level, Pure Land is identical to Zen, Pure Land *is* Zen.[8]

ii) In its popular form, i.e., for ordinary practitioners in this Degenerate Age, some twenty-six centuries after the death of the historical Buddha, Pure Land involves seeking rebirth in the Land of Amitabha Buddha. This is achieved within one lifetime through the practice of Buddha Recitation with sincere faith and vows, leading to one-pointedness of mind or samadhi.

> The devotees of this school venerated Amitabha Buddha and sought not outright Nirvana but rebirth in the ... "Pure Land" of Amitabha, also called Sukhavati. In that idyllic environment, no new negative karmic accumulations would be created and all existing ones would evaporate. Nirvana would be therefore just a short step away. (J. Snelling, *The Buddhist Handbook*, p. 133-4.)

Thus, at the popular level, the Pure Land of Amitabha Buddha is an ideal training ground, an ideal environment where the practitioner is reborn thanks to the power of Amitabha Buddha's Vows (other-power).[9] No longer subject to retrogression, having left Birth and Death behind forever, the cultivator can now focus all his efforts toward the ultimate aim of Buddhahood. This aspect of Pure Land is the form under which the school is popularly known.[10]

In its totality, Pure Land reflects the highest teaching of Buddhism as expressed in the *Avatamsaka Sutra*: mutual identity and interpenetration, the simplest method contains the ultimate and the ultimate is found in the simplest.[11]

c) Transference of Merit

Central to the Pure Land tradition is the figure of Amitabha Buddha, who came to exemplify the Bodhisattva ideal and the doctrine of transfer or dedication of merit. This is particularly apparent in the life story of the Bodhisattva Dharmakara,[12] the future Amitabha Buddha, as related in the sutras.

The Mahayana idea of the Buddha being able to impart his power to others marks one of those epoch-making deviations which set off the Mahayana from so-called ... original Buddhism ... The Mahayanist accumulates stocks of merit not only for the material of their own enlightenment but for the general cultivation of merit which can be shared equally by their fellow-beings, animate or inanimate. This is the true of meaning of Parinamana, that is, turning one's merit over to others for their spiritual interest. (D.T. Suzuki, tr., *The Lankavatara Sutra*, p. xix.)

The rationale for such conduct, which on the surface appears to run counter to the law of Cause and Effect, may be explained in the following passage concerning one of the three Pure Land sages, the Bodhisattva Avalokitesvara (Kuan Yin):

Some of us may ask whether the effect of karma can be reverted by repeating the name of Kuan-Yin. This question is tied up with that of rebirth in Sukhavati [the Pure Land] and it may be answered by saying that invocation of Kuan-Yin's name forms another cause which will right away offset the previous karma. We know, for example, that if there is a dark, heavy cloud above, the chances are that it will rain. But we also know that if a strong wind should blow, the cloud will be carried away somewhere else and we will not feel the rain. Similarly, the addition of one big factor can alter the whole course of karma ...

It is only by accepting the idea of life as one whole that both Theravadins and Mahayanists can advocate the practice of transference of merit to others. With the case of Kuan-Yin then, by calling on Her name we identify ourselves with Her and as a result of this identification Her merits flow over to us. These merits which are now ours then counterbalance our bad karma and save us from calamity. The law of cause and effect still stands good. All that has happened is that a powerful and immensely good karma has overshadowed the weaker one ... (Lecture on Kuan-Yin by Tech Eng Soon - Penang Buddhist Association, c. 1960. Pamphlet.)

This concept of transference of merit, which presupposes a receptive mind on the part of the cultivator, is emphasized in Pure Land. However, the concept also exists, albeit in embryonic form, in the Theravada tradition, as exemplified in the beautiful story of the Venerable Angulimala.[13]

D) Faith and Mind

Faith is an important component of Pure Land Buddhism.[14] However, wisdom or Mind also plays a crucial, if less visible, role. This interrelationship is clearly illustrated in the *Meditation Sutra*: the worst sinner, guilty of matricide and parricide, etc. may still achieve rebirth in the Pure Land if, on the verge of death, he recites the Buddha's name one to ten times with utmost faith and sincerity.

This passage can be understood at two levels. At the *level of everyday life*, just as the worst criminal once genuinely reformed is no longer a threat to society and may be pardoned, the sinner once truly repentant may, through the vow-power of Amitabha Buddha, achieve rebirth in the Pure Land -- albeit at the *lowest* possible grade. Thus, Pure Land offers hope to everyone; yet at the same time, the law of Cause and Effect remains valid.

At the *higher level of principle or Mind*, as the Sixth Patriarch taught in the *Platform Sutra:*

A foolish passing thought makes one an ordinary man, while an enlightened second thought makes one a Buddha.

Therefore, once the sinner repents and recites the Buddha's name with utmost sincerity and one-pointedness of mind, *at that very moment* he becomes an awakened person silently merging into the stream of the Sages -- can Buddhahood then be far away? As the *Meditation Sutra* states: "the Land of Amitabha Buddha is not far from here!"

o
oo

This, then, is the Pure Land tradition, harmonizing everyday practice and the transcendental, self-power and other-power. This tradition is, by all accounts, one of the pillars of the great Mahayana edifice, that lofty tradition of the great Bodhisattvas Avalokitesvara and Samantabhadra -- so much so that Pure Land has been, for centuries, one of the most enduring and widespread forms of Buddhism in Asia.[15]

Van Hien Study Group
Festival of the Bodhisattva Kuan-Yin
Village of Rye Brook, autumn 1992

---

(1) See the following passage, by the late founder of the Buddhist Lodge and Buddhist Society (London), on the true goal of all Buddhist practice:

In the West, the need for some guidance in mind-development was made acute ... by a sudden spate of books which were, whatever the motive of their authors, dangerous in the extreme. No word was said in them of the sole right motive for mind-development, the enlightenment of the meditator for the benefit of all mankind, and the reader was led to believe that it was quite legitimate to study and practice mindfulness, and the higher stages which ensue, for the benefit of business efficiency and the advancement of personal prestige. In these circumstances, *Concentration and Meditation*, ... was compiled and published by the [British] Buddhist Society, with constant stress on the importance of right motive, and ample warning of the dangers, from a headache to insanity, which lie in wait for those who trifle with the greatest force on earth, the human mind. (Christmas Humphreys, *The Buddhist Way of Life*, p. 100.)

(2) See the following passage from D.T. Suzuki:

Buddhist theology has a fine comprehensive theory to explain the manifold types of experience in Buddhism, which look so contradictory to each other. In fact the history of Chinese Buddhism is a series of attempts to reconcile the diverse schools ... Various ways of classification and reconciliation were offered, and ... their conclusion was this: Buddhism supplies us with so many gates to enter into the truth because of such a variety of human characters and temperaments and environments due to diversities of karma. This is plainly depicted and taught by the Buddha himself when he says that the same water drunk by the cow and the cobra turns in one case into nourishing milk and in the other into deadly poison, and that medicine is to be given according to disease. This is called the doctrine of [skillful] means ... *(The Eastern Buddhist*, Vol. 4, No. 2, p. 121.)

(3) Other-power: "Invisible assistance -- provided by the Buddhas and Bodhisattvas of Healing -- can be a potent aid in this process [of elimination of greed, anger and delusion]. This assistance often is described as stemming from the force of their fundamental vows." (Raoul Birnbaum, *The Healing Buddha*, p. xv.) This power, is, of course, common to all Buddhas and Bodhisattvas.

(4) See the following passage from D.T. Suzuki:

Jiriki (self-power) is the ... [wisdom] aspect of enlightenment and tariki (other-power) is the ... [Great Compassion] aspect of the same. By [wisdom] we transcend the principle of individuation, and by [Great Compassion] we descend into a world of particulars. The one goes upwards while the other comes downwards, but this is our intellectual way of understanding and interpreting enlightenment, in whose movement however there is no such twofold direction discernible. *(The*

Eastern Buddhist, Vol. 3. No. 4, p. 314.)

On the important point of other-power and self-power, see Letter 13, Note 12.

(5) As a historical perspective, the roots of Pure Land go back to Ancient India, albeit the tradition was not emphasized there:

> Although a cult dedicated to Amitabha Buddha worship did arise in India, piety toward this Buddha seems to have been merely one of many practices of early Mahayana Buddhism. (Elizabeth ten Grotenhuis, in Joji Okazaki, *Pure Land Buddhist Painting*, p. 14.)

When Mahayana Buddhism spread to China, however, Pure Land ideas found fertile ground for development. In the fourth century, the movement crystallized with the formation of the Lotus Society, founded by Master Hui Yuan (334-416), the first Pure Land Patriarch. The school was formalized under the Patriarchs T'an Luan (Jap. Donran) and Shan Tao (Jap. Zendo). Master Shan Tao's teachings, in particular, greatly influenced the development of Japanese Pure Land, associated with Honen Shonin (Jodo school) and his disciple, Shinran Shonin (Jodo Shinshu school) in the 12th and 13th centuries.

Note: An early form of Buddha Recitation can be found in the *Nikayas* of the Pali Canon:

> In the *Nikayas*, the Buddha ... advised his disciples to think of him and his virtues as if they saw his body before their eyes, whereby they would be enabled to accumulate merit and attain Nirvana or be saved from transmigrating in the evil paths ... (D.T. Suzuki, *The Eastern Buddhist*, Vol. 3, No. 4, p. 317.)

(6) See the following passage on Bodhisattva practice, taken from the well-known "Practices and Vows of the Bodhisattva Samantabhadra":

> Because of living beings, they bring forth great compassion. From great compassion the Bodhi Mind is born; and because of the Bodhi Mind, they accomplish Supreme, Perfect Enlightenment. (*Avatamsaka Sutra*, ch. 40. See Appendix.)

(7) The ordinary, deluded mind (thought) includes feelings, impressions, conceptions, consciousness, etc. The Self-Nature True Mind is the fundamental nature, the Original Face, reality, the Buddha Nature, etc. As an example, the Self-Nature True Mind is to the ordinary mind what water is to waves -- the two cannot be dissociated. They are the same but they are also different. See also Letter 17, Note 11 on this important point.

(8) See the following passage from D.T. Suzuki:

> We observe that even the extremely devotional form of Buddhist life as revealed in the [Pure Land] begins in its last stage of "spiritual rest" ... to approach the Zen type. Indeed here lies the unity of Buddhist experience throughout its varied expressions. (D.T. Suzuki, *The Eastern Buddhi⌐ᵗ*, Vol. 4, No. 2, p. 121.)

(9) The text of the Primal (Eighteenth) Vow is as follows:

> If, after my obtaining Buddhahood, all beings in the ten quarters should desire in sincerity and trustfulness to be born in my country, and if they should not be born by only thinking of me for ten times ... may I not attain the highest enlightenment. (*Meditation Sutra*, quoted by Elizabeth ten Grotenhuis, op. cit., p. 15.)

(10) On the related question of whether the Pure Land exists or is Mind-Only, see the words of the eminent Zen Master Chu Hung (16th century):

> Some people say that the Pure Land is nothing but mind, that there is no Pure Land of Ultimate Bliss beyond the trillions of worlds of the cosmos. This talk of mind-only has its source in the words of the sutras, and it is true, not false. But those who quote it in this sense are misunderstanding its meaning.
>
> Mind equals object: there are no objects beyond mind. Objects equal mind: there is no mind beyond objects. Since objects are wholly mind, why must we cling to mind and dismiss objects? Those who dismiss objects when they talk of mind have not comprehended mind. (J.C. Cleary, *Pure Land, Pure Mind*.)

Please note that understanding the dual nature of the Pure Land, as Mind-Only and as a separate entity, requires practice -- not intellectual reasoning.

In secular western thought awareness of psychological projection as a source of supernatural being has served to demythologize demons, goblins, angels and saints and rob them of their power. The Bardo Thodol [Tibetan Book of the Dead], however, speaks of the deities as "projections" but never as "mere projections." The deities are present and must be dealt with religiously ... not just by intellectual insight." (D.G. Dawe in *The Perennial Dictionary of World Religions*, p. 93.)

(11) This is clearly shown in the *Avatamsaka Sutra*, particularly chapter 26 which describes the last phases of practice of a Bodhisattva before final Buddhahood. In that chapter, it is taught that in each and every single stage, the actions of the Bodhisattva "never go beyond Nien Fo" [Buddha Recitation]:

This is a summary of the tenth stage of enlightening beings, called Cloud of Teaching ... Whatever acts they undertake, whether through giving, or kind speech, or beneficial action, or cooperation, it is all never apart from thoughts of Buddha [Buddha Recitation], the Teaching, the Community ... (Thomas Cleary, tr., *The Flower Ornament Scripture*, Vol. II, p. 111.)

(12) See the following passage:

The [*Longer Amitabha Sutra*] ... which was in existence before a.d. 200, describes a discourse offered by the Buddha Sakyamuni ... in response to questions of his disciple Ananda. Sakyamuni tells the story of the Bodhisattva Dharmakara, who had for eons past been deeply moved by the suffering of sentient beings and who had determined to establish a Land of Bliss where all beings could experience emancipation from their pain ... In the presence of the eighty-first Buddha of the past, Lokesvararaja, Dharmakara made forty-eight vows relating to this Paradise, and promised that he would not accept enlightenment if he could not achieve his goals ... When, after countless ages, Dharmakara achieved enlightenment and became a Buddha, the conditions of his [18th] vow were fulfilled: he became the Lord of Sukhavati, the Western Paradise, where the faithful will be reborn in bliss, there to progress through stages of increasing awareness until they finally achieve enlightenment. (Elizabeth ten Grotenhuis, in Joji Okazaki, *Pure Land Buddhist Painting*, p. 14-15.)

(13) The life story of the Venerable Angulimala is one of the most moving accounts in the Theravada canon. After killing ninety-nine persons, Angulimala was converted by the Buddha, repented his evil ways and joined the Order:

One day as he went on his round for alms he saw a woman in labor. Moved by compassion, he reported this pathetic woman's suffering to the Buddha. He then advised him to pronounce the following words of truth, which later became known as the Angulimala Paritta (Mantra) ...

"Sister, since my birth in the Arya clan [i,e., since my ordination] I know not that I consciously destroyed the life of any living being. By this truth may you be whole and may your child be whole."

He went to the presence of the suffering sister ... and uttered these words. Instantly, she delivered the child with ease. (Narada Maha Thera, *The Buddha and His Teaching*, p. 124.)

(14) Faith is an important element in all Buddhist traditions, but it is particularly so in Pure Land. See the following passage from the *Avatamsaka Sutra*, which almost all Mahayana monks and nuns can recite by heart:

Faith is the basis of the path, the mother of virtues,
Nourishing and growing all good ways ...
Faith can increase knowledge and virtue;
Faith can assure arrival at enlightenment.

(Thomas Cleary, tr. *The Flower Ornament Scripture*, vol. 1, p. 331.)

(15) The strength and pervasiveness of Pure Land is such that its main practice, Buddha Recitation, is found in both the Tantric and Zen schools. In Pure Land, Buddha Recitation is practiced for the purpose of achieving rebirth in the Land of Amitabha Buddha. In the Tantric school, the aim is to destroy evil karma and afflictions, obtain protection against demons and generate blessings and wisdom in the current lifetime. In Zen, the koan of Buddha Recitation is meant to sever delusive thought and realize the Self-Nature True Mind. The ultimate goal of all three schools is, of course, the same: to achieve Enlightenment and Buddhahood.

Letters from Patriarch
Yin Kuang

I will be a good doctor for the sick and suffering. I will lead those who have lost their way to the right road. I will be a bright light for those in the dark night, and cause the poor and destitute to uncover hidden treasures. The Bodhisattva impartially benefits all living beings in this manner.

The Vows of Samantabhadra

*
**

Letter 1.
Turn Afflictions into Bodhi[1]

Since we last met, six years have gone by in a flash. During that time, not only have the snow and dew undergone change, the destiny of our nation has been profoundly transformed as well. The evanescence of life is truly something we all deeply mourn![2]

I am pleased to learn from your letter that you have not neglected your Pure Land practice. However, you indicated that you are not at peace in body and mind. Could this be the result of financial difficulties or chronic illness?

If you suffer financial hardship, I suggest you retreat a step. You should reflect thus: "although there are many in this world more fortunate than I, those who are less well off are hardly few in number. I should seek only to escape hunger and cold; why dream of riches and honor?"

Moreover, if you are content and at peace with your circumstances and surroundings, you can even turn afflictions into Bodhi (Enlightenment),[3] not to mention grief into peace and joy!

If you suffer chronic illness, you should reflect deeply that this body is the very source of suffering,[4] develop a revulsion toward it and strive to cultivate the

Pure Land path, determined to achieve rebirth in the Land of Ultimate Bliss. The Buddhas view suffering as their teacher,[5] thus achieving Ultimate Enlightenment. Likewise, you should consider illness as medicine,[6] to escape Birth and Death.

You should realize that human beings are bound by all kinds of karmic afflictions. Without the sufferings of poverty and illness, they will, by nature, pursue the world of sight and sound, fame and profit, finding it difficult to let go.[7] Who would then willingly turn around to watch and ponder the state of perdition to come?[8]

The sage Mencius once said:

> Those who will be entrusted with great tasks should first endure hardship both in body and mind, suffering hunger and destitution or failure in their undertakings. Only then will they be able to forge their character, develop patience and endurance and attain outstanding abilities, beyond the ken of the multitude.

Therefore, you should realize that human character is usually forged in adversity. If adversity cannot be avoided, you should remain at peace and practice forbearance.

Moreover, in speaking of great tasks, the sage Mencius was referring merely to mundane undertakings. Even so, enduring hardship is necessary for success -- how much more so when lowly beings such as ourselves undertake the great dual task of achieving Buddhahood and rescuing sentient beings! If you are not tested to a certain extent by financial hardship and disease, your worldly delusions will know no bounds and your Pure Land practice will be difficult to perfect. With your Mind-mirror[9] clouded, you will revolve for many eons in the evil realms -- not knowing when you will ever achieve liberation!

The ancients have said:

If it were not for a period of penetrating cold, the plum blossom could never develop its exquisite perfume!

This is the meaning of what I said earlier.

o

oo

You should persevere in reciting the Buddha's name, to eradicate past karma swiftly and avoid developing a mind of afflictions, resenting the Heavens, blaming your fellow beings, considering the law of Cause and Effect as a fairy tale and rejecting the Buddhas and their teachings as ineffective. You should know that from time immemorial, we have all created immeasurable evil karma. As the *Avatamsaka Sutra* states:

If evil karma had physical form, the empty space of the ten directions could not contain it.

Thus, how can haphazard, intermittent cultivation possibly annihilate all afflictions and obstructions?

Sakyamuni Buddha and Amitabha Buddha, out of compassion for sentient beings who lack the strength to rid themselves of evil karma, specifically taught the method of "relying on the Buddha's power to take their residual karma along to the Pure Land."[10] Such compassionate action is all-encompassing; even our obligations to the Heavens or to our parents cannot be compared to it -- not even on a scale of ten thousand to one. Therefore, you should engage in earnest repentance, seeking the Buddhas' assistance in eradicating past karma and achieving peace and tranquillity of body and mind.

o
oo

If illness and suffering become unbearable, in addition to reciting the Buddha's name morning and night and dedicating the merits toward rebirth in the Pure Land, you should call wholeheartedly upon the Bodhisattva Kuan Yin (Avalokitesvara). With Her silent vow to rescue sentient beings, the Bodhisattva appears throughout the worlds of the ten directions. If in time of crisis, a person can keep reciting Her name and revere Her, She will respond according to the circumstances, enabling him to escape suffering and achieve happiness.[11]

o
oo

Although Buddha Recitation is simple, it is very deep and encompassing.[12] The most important thing is to be utterly sincere and earnest, for only then will your thoughts merge with those of Amitabha Buddha and will you reap true benefits in this very life. If you are lazy and lax, lacking even the least bit of reverence and awe, you may sow the seeds of future liberation but you must still bear the inconceivably evil karma stemming from disrespect and over-familiarity.[13] Even if, thanks to residual merits, you escape the evil realms and are reborn in the celestial or human realms, you will still find it difficult to join the Ocean-Wide Lotus Assembly![14]

Nowadays, there are quite a number of scholars who study Buddhism. However, almost all of them simply read the words of the sutras and commentaries seeking arguments and rationalizations to prove that they are versed in the Dharma. Those with the sincerity and devotion to cultivate according to the Dharma are few indeed! I have always said that to reap the real benefit of the Dharma, you should approach it with a truly reverent mind. One-tenth of reverence and devotion annihilates one-tenth of afflictions and evil karma, and increases merit and wisdom by one-tenth -- and this applies to two-tenths, three-tenths or total reverence and devotion.

Conversely, the more lax and disrespectful you are, the more obstructions and evil karma you develop, resulting in a corresponding decrease in merit and wisdom. How sad it is! When you meet with other laymen, you should counsel them along these lines. This would be a great Dharma gift.

o

oo

If you can penetrate the profound, subtle meaning of the Pure Land method, so much the better. However, even if you are not entirely clear about certain aspects of it, you should still believe firmly in the words of the Buddhas and the Patriarchs. You must not harbor doubts. To doubt is to turn your back on Buddha Amitabha, distancing yourself from Him, making it difficult to be in communion with Him and be "received and guided" at the time of death. The ancients have taught:

> Only the Buddhas can truly fathom the ultimate meaning of Pure Land; even those Bodhisattvas who have achieved near equality with the Buddhas cannot grasp it completely.

If even the highest level Bodhisattvas cannot fully understand the Pure Land method, how can we expect to assess it with our own limited minds and capacities without falling into error? Intelligent persons, these days, may study the Dharma, but since they have not been in the company of fully enlightened sages, they almost always emphasize theory and noumenon[15] (principle) while rejecting "phenomenal" cultivation[16] as well as the law of Cause and Effect. Little do they realize that without phenomenal cultivation and belief in Cause and Effect, theory and noumenon cease to exist.

There are also certain individuals of great talent and ability, whose writings can astound the gods. However, their actions are no different from those of the dullards in the marketplace. The root cause is their rejection of phenomenal cultivation and Cause and Effect. This grave error is repeated by other people; it is a case of betraying the Dharma with one's body (actions).[17] The depth of such offenses and transgressions is immeasurable! Witnessing this, those endowed with profound wisdom can only sigh in pity and compassion ...

An Elder Master once said:

Those who skillfully discourse on Mind and Self-Nature surely can never reject Cause and Effect; those who believe deeply in Cause and Effect naturally understand the Mind and Self-Nature in depth. This is a natural development.

The Master's words are a truth that has withstood the test of time, a needle pricking the heads of those with delusive wisdom.[18]

Last autumn, during your esteemed brother's visit to P'u T'o Mountain, I brought up these "sincere, respectful" points. However, I wonder whether he has taken them as the sincere, earnest words they were meant to be?

NOTES TO LETTER 1

(1) Letter to Teng Po-ch'eng. (Chinese ed. Vol. I, p. 37; VN

ed., p. 7)

(2) Sakyamuni Buddha established three Dharma "seals," or criteria, to determine the genuineness of Buddhist teachings, namely, impermanence, suffering, no-self. A fourth seal, emptiness, was later extrapolated from the sutras. Thus, the truth of impermanence is basic to Buddhism ... After seeing a corpse, the young prince Siddhartha (Sakyamuni Buddha) decided to leave the royal life to become an ascetic.

An interesting corollary of the concept of Dharma seals is that much of the current speculation about whether or not this or that sutra is genuine is, in a sense, moot. A sutra is a sutra not necessarily because it ostensibly contains the words of the Buddhas but because the ideas expressed in it conform to the Dharma seals. An example of this is the *Platform Sutra*, which records the words of the Sixth Patriarch of Zen.

(3) This is a key Mahayana concept, particularly emphasized in Zen. At the level of noumenon, or principle, afflictions and Enlightenment have the same intrinsic nature. To cultivate is to turn afflictions into Enlightenment.

In the *Platform Sutra*, second chapter, the Sixth Patriarch stated that "sentient beings are Buddhas, afflictions are Bodhi."

A foolish passing thought makes one an ordinary man, while an enlightened second thought makes one a Buddha. A passing thought that clings to sense-objects is [defilement and affliction] while a second thought that frees one from attachment is Bodhi. ("The Sutra of Hui Neng," p. 28 in A.F. Price and Wong Mou-Lam, tr. *The Diamond Sutra and the Sutra of Hui Neng.*)

In the same line of thought, see the following paragraph on the identity of samsara and Nirvana as products of the mind:

In the Mahayana, samsara refers to the phenomenal world and is considered to be essentially identical with nirvana. The essential unity of samsara and nirvana is based on the view that everything is a mental representation, and thus samsara and nirvana are ... labels without real substance, i.e., they are empty. To the extent that one does not relate to the phenomenal aspect of the world but rather its true nature, samsara and nirvana are not different from one another. (*Shambhala Dictionary of Buddhism and Zen*, p. 184.)

In other words, the ideal cultivator is not out to slay dragons, but is rather a consummate statesman converting opponents into friends. Both friends and opponents are, after all, taxpayers and voters. Likewise, the cultivator's aim is to turn afflictions into Bodhi, for, while afflictions and Bodhi are different at the phenomenon level, they are intrinsically the same at the noumenon (ultimate) level. Both are mind-made.

(4) See the following passage concerning the *Vimalakirti Sutra:*

> The sage Vimalakirti discussed the experience of illness at great length ... With many visitors assembled to inquire after his health, the infirm sage took the opportunity to speak out against the human body and its limitations.
>
> "O, virtuous ones, the wise do not rely upon the body. It is like a mass of froth which cannot be grasped, like a bubble which bursts in an instant. The body is like a flame arising from the thirst of love ... like a shadow, appearing as a result of karma. It is like an echo, responding to causes and conditions ... The body does not act of itself; but it is spun around by the force of the winds of passion."
>
> His own face gaunt and creased by illness, vividly impressing upon visitors the transitory nature of earthly existence, Vimalakirti then urged them to seek the Buddha-body. (Raoul Birnbaum, *The Healing Buddha*, p. 13.)

It should be clear that although the Buddhas taught that the human body is a skin-bag filled with excrement, theirs is not a pessimistic view of life, but a realistic one. They recognized the need to use the body as a means to Enlightenment. Thus, one important injunction to monks and laymen is never to entertain the thought of suicide.

(5) See the following two passages on the significance of adversity and suffering:

> Every suffering is a buddha-seed, because suffering impels mortals to seek wisdom. But you can only say that suffering gives rise to buddhahood. You can't say that suffering is buddhahood. Your body and mind are the field. Suffering is the seed, wisdom the sprout, and buddhahood the grain. ("The Wake-up Sermon" in Red Pine, tr. *The*

Zen Teaching of Bodhidharma, p. 63.)

A Pure Land treatise on the Buddha Remembrance Samadhi has explained the "ten practices of non-seeking" to eliminate the ten major obstacles encountered by practitioners on the path to Enlightenment. These ten major obstacles encompass all obstructions and impediments. Therefore if we have a good grasp of the ten non-seeking practices, all obstacles will disappear. These ten practices [include]:

1. We should not wish that our bodies be always free of diseases and ailments, because a disease-free body is prone to desire and lust. This leads to precept-breaking and retrogression.

2. We should not wish that our lives be free of all misfortune and adversity, lest we be prone to pride and arrogance. This leads us to be disdainful and overbearing towards everyone else ... (Master Thích Thiền Tâm, *Buddhism of Wisdom and Faith*, sect. 65, p. 269.)

(6) See the following passage on the role of illness, in particular:

Similar to Vimilakirti's concept and to Sakyamuni's fundamental teachings, an illness when properly dealt with can serve as a major event that propels one onwards towards higher spiritual attainment. In the case of healings by [the Medicine Buddha], the sincere act of faith by the ill person results in healings granted. During the healing process, insight arises that causes the person to reform the patterns of his deeds, words and thoughts, so that they accord with the quest for Enlightenment. (Raoul Birnbaum, *The Healing Buddha*, p. 69.)

(7) See also the following passage on the need to escape Birth and Death:

But why do we need to escape from the cycle of birth and death? It is because, in the wasteland of birth and death, we truly undergo immense pain and suffering. If students of Buddhism do not sincerely meditate on this truth of suffering, they cannot achieve results despite all their scholarship, as they do not experience fear or seek liberation. The sutras say: "If the fearful mind does not come easily, the sincere mind cannot spring forth easily." This is the reason why the Buddha, when preaching the Four Noble Truths to the five monks led by Kaundinya, taught them first the Truth of Suffering. According to this truth, we should observe the suffering of the human condition. Only then will we have a clearer idea as to why we must swiftly escape the cycle of birth and death. (Master Thích Thiền Tâm, *Buddhism of Wisdom and Faith*, sect. 4, p. 14.)

(8) Master Yin Kuang is referring here to the concept of the "third lifetime" associated with rebirth. In the first lifetime,

the practitioner engages in wholesome actions which bring blessings (wealth, power, authority, etc.) in the second lifetime. Since wealth and power tend to corrupt, he is likely to create evil karma, resulting in retribution in the third lifetime. Thus, wholesome deeds in the first lifetime are considered potential "enemies" of the third lifetime.

(9) Mind-mirror. Buddhist sutras commonly compare the Self-Nature to a mirror. The Mind-mirror of the Buddhas is bright, empty and still; the Mind-mirror of sentient beings is dull and clouded. However, the intrinsic nature of both mirrors (brightness) is the same. If sentient beings can wipe their Mind-mirror completely clean, they will return to their Self-Nature -- the nature of the Buddhas. This is the basis of gradual cultivation, as taught in most Buddhist schools.

(10) The following passage explains how sentient beings burdened with heavy karma may achieve rebirth in the Pure Land:

> There is a parable in the *Questions of King Milinda Sutra*:
>
> > "A minute grain of sand, dropped on the surface of the water, will sink immediately. On the other hand, a block of stone, however large and heavy, can easily be moved from place to place by boat. The same is true of the Pure Land practitioner. However light his karma may be, if he is not rescued by Amitabha Buddha, he must revolve in the cycle of birth and death. With the help of the Buddha, his karma, however heavy, will not prevent his rebirth in the Pure Land."
>
> We can see from this passage that, thanks to "other-power," the Pure Land method can help the practitioner "bring his karma along" to the Pure Land. The huge block of stone represents the weight of heavy karma, the boat symbolizes the power of Amitabha Buddha's Vows. Therefore, the cultivator should not think that residual greed, anger and delusion will prevent him from being reborn ... (Master Thích Thiên Tâm, *Buddhism of Wisdom and Faith*, sect. 68 A, p. 284.)

(11) See the following passage:

> In the Buddhism of faith, Kuan-Yin is a refuge and protector, who "suffers vicariously in the hells out of great compassion." Reflectively, however, Kuan-Yin exemplifies the compassion of one who knows that, "in some way, all suffering is his own suffering, and all sentient beings the disguises of his own inmost nature." "A skylark wounded in the wing, a

churubim does cease to sing." The Bodhisattva is sick because his fellow-being is sick. (C.N. Tay, *Kuan-Yin: The Cult of Half Asia.*)

(12) Pure Land teaching, at the higher level, includes both *sammata* and *vipasyana*. See Introduction, sect. B.

See also the following passage:

The Pure Land method is not reserved for people with low or moderate capacities alone; it embraces those of the highest capacities as well. Sentient beings of middling and low capacities who recite the Buddha's name will be able to rid themselves of afflictions and karmic obstacles and develop merit, virtue and wisdom, leading in time to the state of concentration. Depending on the amount of effort they exert, they will be reborn within the nine lotus grades of the Land of Ultimate Bliss. Those of high capacities, on the other hand, enter deeply into the sphere of concentration and wisdom as soon as they begin uttering the Buddha's name. Whether walking, standing, lying down or sitting, they are always in the "Buddha Remembrance Samadhi." After death they will be reborn in the highest grade. (Master Thích Thiên Tâm, *Buddhism of Wisdom and Faith*, sect. 18, p. 73.)

(13) This strong statement underlines the crucial role of the mind in Buddhist practice. Without a reverent, pure mind as a starting point, no practice can succeed and the door is open to all kinds of transgressions and evil karma ... everything stems from the mind.

(14) Ocean-Wide Lotus Assembly. The Lotus Assembly represents the gathering of Buddha Amitabha, the Bodhisattvas, the sages and saints and all other superior beings in the Land of Ultimate Bliss. This Assembly is "Ocean-Wide" as the participants are infinite in number -- spreading as far and wide as the ocean. The term Ocean-Wide Assembly is associated with the *Avatamsaka Sutra*, a text particularly prized by the Pure Land and Zen schools alike.

(15) Noumenon/Nature: the essence of things in themselves, while phenomena or marks are the forms and characteristics of those things. For example, the phenomenal aspect of the precept not to take life is literally not to kill any sentient being. The essence, or noumenal aspect of that precept is to foster compassion: it is because of compassion that we refrain

from taking life. See also the following:

> The noumenon is the doctrine underlying any phenomenal event. For example, in principle a tree has the potential to become a house. Before the house is built, it has that noumenal aspect. Once built, the house itself is the phenomenon, which appears because of the noumenon. In principle, we can all realize Buddhahood, but we have not phenomenally done so. If we have Faith, Vows and Hold the Name, we will arrive at the phenomenon of Buddhahood, just as the tree can be made into a house. (Master Hsuan Hua, *A General Explanation of the Buddha Speaks of Amitabha Sutra.*, p. 26.)

(16) "Phenomenal" cultivation. Refers typically to concrete acts, such as keeping the precepts, bowing, making offerings to the Buddhas, lighting incense, fingering the rosary, etc., as well as oral recitation.

(17) Betraying the Dharma with one's body: There are many ways to teach the Dharma. For instance, one can lecture on compassion or teach it by personal example. If one talks about compassion while at the same time acting in a mean, non-compassionate way, one is said to be betraying the Dharma with one's body. That is, one is acting in a way that is not consonant with the teachings of the Buddhas.

(18) Delusive wisdom: "Wisdom" that does not lead to the ultimate goal of Enlightenment and Buddhahood.

*
**

Letter 2.
A Pure Mind in a Pure Land[1]

How delighted I was to receive and read your letter! The sage Ch'u Po-yu,[2] upon reaching his fiftieth birthday, looked back and realized the errors he was still committing at age forty-nine. When nearing seventy, Confucius expressed the wish to survive much longer in order to study the *Book of Changes* in depth and thus avoid major transgressions.

The scholarship of these sages had reached the highest level of mind and thought. Today's scholars like to study chapter by chapter, with few showing concern for the issue of rectifying mind and thought. Thus, they peruse books all day long without understanding the true intent of the sages, their words and actions differing from those of the sages as greatly as day from night or square from round. There is no possible correspondence. We are not even speaking here of the transgressions of mind and thought; if these transgressions were enumerated, they would be countless![3]

Buddhist sutras teach followers to practice repentance constantly in order to annihilate delusion and achieve Buddhahood. Thus, even the Bodhisattva Maitreya, who has attained the level of Equal Enlightenment, still pays respect to the Buddhas of the ten directions during the six periods of the day,[4] so as to wipe out delusion and attain the Dharma Body. If this is true for the Bodhisattva Maitreya, what can we say of common beings filled with heavy karmic afflictions?

If you do not feel shame and remorse, your Self-Nature may be the same as the Buddhas', but it is hidden by afflictions and evil karma and cannot manifest itself. Just like a precious mirror which has been covered with dust for eons, not only does it not reflect light, even its reflecting nature is hidden. If you realize that the mirror already possesses the nature of brightness and strive ceaselessly to clean it, the light reflected will gradually increase until it reaches maximum radiance. The mirror can then become, once more, something of value in the world.

You should realize that the potential for reflection

is inherent in the mirror and is not the result of polishing. If it were not so, a brick or rock would also gleam when polished. Yet, you should also realize that although the brightness is inherent in the mirror, without polishing, the day would never come when it would gleam.[5]

The Mind-Nature of sentient beings is similar. Although it is *intrinsically* identical to that of the Buddhas, [it is clouded]. Thus, if sentient beings do not mend their ways,[5] from evil to wholesome, and turn their backs on worldly dusts[6] "to merge with Enlightenment," their inherently virtuous nature cannot appear. Such a mind-consciousness, inherently possessing the Buddha Nature in full but busily creating evil karma and suffering -- mired in Birth and Death for many eons -- is no different from a dark house filled with treasures. You not only cannot make use of the treasures, you may, in fact, suffer further loss. Is this not lamentable?

Pure Land is precisely the sublime method enabling the practitioner to turn his back on worldly dusts to merge with Enlightenment and return to the source (the Mind). Laymen bound up in mundane affairs cannot easily find the time to attend retreats, practice meditation and recite the sutras. This method is, therefore, very suitable for you. Each person can pay respect to the Buddhas and recite sutras or Buddha Amitabha's name according to individual circumstances and capacities, dedicating the merits thus accrued to rebirth in the Pure Land. In addition to your regular cultivation sessions, you should practice Buddha Recitation when walking or standing, reclining or sitting, speaking or remaining silent, eating or dressing, throughout the day, wherever you may be.[7]

When venerating the Buddhas in clean places, you may recite either aloud or silently. In dirty places (such as washrooms) or in circumstances that do not call for reverence (such as sleeping or bathing) you should just recite silently. To recite aloud when reclining is not only disrespectful, it also wastes breath, leading in time to illness.[8] Silent recitation brings the same blessings and virtues as vocal recitation, as long as it is distinct, earnest and not subject to distractions.

You already know that you must confess your transgressions and practice repentance. This is very much in accord with the Pure Land method because "when the mind is pure, the Buddha lands are pure."[9] However, once having repented, you should change your ways and practice wholesome deeds, lest your repentance consist of empty words bringing no real benefit. This is also true if you wish to be free of external attachments in order to concentrate on Buddha Recitation and reach one-pointedness of mind. No extraordinary method is required: you should paste the single word "death" on your forehead or dangle it from your eyebrows,[10] always keeping the following thoughts in mind:

Since time immemorial I have created untold, immeasurable evil karma; if such karma had form, the empty space of the ten directions could not contain it.[11] Thanks to good conditions, I have been reborn in a human body and have, in addition, had the opportunity to hear the Dharma. However, given my evil karma, I must now recite the Buddha's name singlemindedly, seeking rebirth in the Pure Land. Otherwise, when my breath has ceased, [I am bound to endure the sufferings of hell, hungry ghosts and animality]. After recovering a human body, I would lack intelligence and be deluded, prone to create evil karma, unable to perform good deeds readily. In no time, I would sink once again into the evil realms. With my residual bad karma from previous lives still not repaid, I would commit new evil karma, constantly revolving along the six paths throughout eons as numerous as motes of dust, hopelessly lost in the immense sea of suffering, not knowing how to reach the shore.

If you always reflect on these points, your cultivation will be focussed. Take the example of the two notorious men[12] who -- on the verge of death -- witnessed the marks of hell appear, whereupon they recited the Buddha's name several times *with utmost sincerity and devotion.* Immediately, they saw Amitabha Buddha coming to "receive and guide" them back to the Pure Land.[13] This beneficial feature exists only in the Pure Land method, out of all the countless methods taught by Sakyamuni Buddha throughout His teaching career. Therefore, I have always said that "if the nine realms of sentient beings do not practice this method, they cannot easily perfect the fruits of Enlightenment, while if the Buddhas of the ten directions abandon this method, they cannot benefit the masses far and wide."

o

oo

If you have utmost Faith[14] and cultivate earnestly, seeking escape from Birth and Death, then even though you still have not escaped the evil, deluded world, you will not remain long in the Saha World either. While you may not have reached the Pure Land yet, you will soon be a new guest in the Realm of Ultimate Bliss.

From now on, when you meet virtuous persons, do your utmost to emulate them; when you encounter an opportunity to practice good deeds, do not hesitate. How can you have the heart to procrastinate, lest the error of one moment lead to ten thousand lifetimes of regret?[15] Surely those with high aspirations cannot tolerate being "walking corpses," running aimlessly while alive and simply decaying after death, along with the grass and trees. Redouble your efforts and exert yourself!

o
oo

Finally, while the key to rebirth in the Pure Land is singlemindedness, you, as a layman, still have your parents and your family. Although you should not unduly seek wealth and honor, you should still fulfill your family obligations -- for to cultivate the Dharma is not to abandon everything.[16] If you could let go of everything and still manage to provide for your parents and family, that would be all to the good. Otherwise, it would be contrary not only to human morality but also to the Dharma. This is something you should also realize.

As a filial son, you should counsel your parents concerning cultivation, so that they may practice Buddha Recitation and seek rebirth in the Pure Land. If they can practice with faith, they will surely achieve rebirth. Once reborn, they will transcend the mundane and enter sagehood, escape Birth and Death, join the Ocean-wide Assembly, be close to Amitabha Buddha and eventually achieve Buddhahood. Mundane filiality cannot be compared with such an achievement!

If anyone were to advise others to cultivate the Pure Land method, the merits and virtues from such teaching would be entirely his. In the future, such an individual would surely be reborn in the upper lotus grades.[17]

NOTES TO LETTER 2

(1) Another letter to Teng Po-ch'eng. (Chinese ed. Vol. I, p. 41; VN ed., p. 10)

(2) Ch'u Po-yu: a disciple of Confucius, known for this very example.
Book of Changes: a Taoist classic, used particularly in

divination.

(3) In this connection, a Zen Master once discovered that "ten thousand" thoughts had crossed his mind from the time he woke up to the time he slipped on his shoes. In the case of ordinary persons, most, if not all, of these thoughts would be within the realm of greed, anger and delusion and would, therefore, be transgressions.

(4) Six periods of the day: all the time, the day being divided into six periods of four hours each.

(5) This is a most important point. To cultivate is to uncover that Self-Nature, the Mind-Nature, always bright and all-encompassing -- to awaken.

(6) Worldly dusts: a metaphor for all the mundane things that can cloud our bright Self-Nature. These include form, sound, smell, taste, touch, dharmas (external opinions and views). These dusts correspond to the five senses and the discriminating, everyday mind (the sixth sense in Buddhism).

(7) Buddha Recitation involves a number of practices, including visualizing Amitabha Buddha's features, contemplating an image of the Buddha, etc. In these letters, Master Yin Kuang is usually referring to the most popular practice, oral recitation of the Buddha's name.

Buddha Recitation centers on the mind; even when speaking of other things or even during sleep, the thought of Buddha Amitabha should remain in your mind. This practice is akin to meditating on a koan in Zen. As the Sixth Patriarch said, when a practitioner has a wholesome thought, he is at that moment a Buddha (that is, an enlightened being). Ideally, therefore, he should be filled with wholesome thoughts i.e., be mindful of Amitabha Buddha, at all times.

(8) Some practitioners, during retreats, may recite up to one hundred thousand times per day (an ideal benchmark); hence this warning from Master Yin Kuang.

Reciting aloud when bathing is considered disrespectful

because the practitioner is nude. In East Asian custom, respect is demonstrated by covering the body. This is contrasted with the Indian custom, reflected in the sutras, of showing respect by baring the right shoulder. This difference is seen today in the dress of Theravada and Mahayana monks, respectively.

(9) This is one of the fundamental concepts of Buddhism, particularly emphasized in Zen and in Buddha Recitation at the noumenon level. See Introduction, sect. D and the following passage from the *Vimalakirti Sutra:*

> Therefore, Ratna-rasi, if a Bodhisattva wants to win the Pure Land he should purify his mind, and because of his pure mind the Buddha land is pure." (Charles Luk, tr. *The Vimalakirti Nirdesa Sutra*, p. 13.)

(10) See the following passage:

> The first principle of Ch'an [Zen] practice is to empty one's mind. One must first paste the two words "life-death" on the forehead, and regard them as seriously as if one owed a debt of a million taels. In day or night, while drinking or eating, traveling or staying at home, sitting or lying, entertaining friends, in a quiet moment or at a noisy hour, you must hold on to the ... [koan]. (Zen Master Han-Shan Te-Ch'ing, in Sung-peng Hsu, *A Buddhist Leader in Ming China*, p. 130.)

(11) This passage is taken from the *Avatamsaka Sutra*:

> Moreover, good man, to "repent misdeeds and mental hindrances" is explained like this: the Bodhisattva reflects, "from beginningless kalpas in the past, I have created measureless and boundless evil karma, with my body, mouth, and mind, because of greed, hatred, and stupidity. If this evil karma had a substance and form, all of empty space could not contain it." (Hsuan Hua (Master), tr., *Flower Adornment Sutra*, ch. 40, p. 69.)

(12) Two notorious men. This refers to two men, Chang Shan-ho and Chang Chung-k'uei, mentioned repeatedly in Pure Land commentaries. The latter made his living slaughtering animals, thus violating the most fundamental Buddhist precept -- not to kill.

(13) See *Meditation Sutra*, Sixteenth Meditation. The two operative phrases here are "on the verge of death" and "utmost sincerity and devotion." When a wicked person, on his deathbed, senses evil omens arising from his subconscious and

he sees no possible alternative, a mind of utter sincerity and devotion is sometimes possible. Such a frame of mind is practically impossible to develop in the course of everyday life. The following story provides a good illustration of this point.

There was once a Zen monk meditating on a deserted mountain far away from all human habitation. Because of the rigors of the climate and the isolation of the place, he found it difficult to concentrate. His mind constantly wandered toward life in the village down below. One evening, as he was seated lost in errant thought, he had the sensation that he was being watched. He slowly turned his head, and lo and behold, there was a tiger crouched in the bushes behind him! One false move and the tiger would pounce on him. He had no choice but to remain ramrod straight, in singleminded concentration. When dawn broke, the tiger, fearful of the light of day, gave up this cat-and-mouse game and disappeared. The next two evenings, the monk, faithful to his vow, resumed his meditation at the appointed time and place. The tiger returned and the scene repeated itself each evening. When daylight came on the third day, the monk, after three nights of *singleminded concentration*, experienced a Great Awakening, collapsed and died. At his funeral, it was reported that a tiger was seen watching and wailing in the distance.

As to how the karma of a lifetime can be dissipated in an instant, let us picture a house which has been boarded up for generations. All it takes for the darkness to disappear is to open a window and let the sun in (Great Awakening). The key point is how to enter the house, open that window and keep it open at all times. See also Introduction, sect. D.

(14) The key words here are "utmost faith." According to a well-known Elder Master, Tzu Chao, the Pure Land practitioner faces three points of doubt at the time of death:

1) Fearing that his past karma is heavy and his period of cultivation short, and that, therefore, he may not be reborn;

2) Fearing that he has not yet fulfilled his vows nor eliminated greed,

anger and delusion, and that, therefore, he may not be reborn;

3) Fearing that, even though he has recited the Buddha's name, Buddha Amitabha may not come, and that, therefore, he may not be reborn. (Thích Thiên Tâm, *Buddhism of Wisdom and Faith*, p. 281.)

(15) Everything centers on the mind -- the compass of all our actions ... "A miss is as good as a mile."

(16) See the following passage, which reflects the deep pragmatism of the Buddhist Order:

King Suddhodana [Buddha Sakyamuni's father] was deeply grieved to hear of the unexpected ordination of his beloved grandson. He approached the Buddha and, in humbly requesting him not to ordain anyone without the prior consent of the parents, said, "When the Lord renounced the world it was a cause of great pain to me. It was so when Nanda [another son of the King] renounced it and especially so in the case of Rahula [son of the Buddha]. The love of a father towards a son cuts through the skin, the flesh, the sinew, the bone and the marrow. Grant, Lord, the request that the noble ones may not confer ordination on a son without the permission of his parents."

The Buddha readily granted the request, and made it a vinaya rule [rule of discipline]. (Narada Maha Thera, *The Buddha and His Teachings*, p. 72.)

(17) Lotus grades. In Pure Land Buddhism the practitioner can be reborn after death within one of nine grades. These grades depend on his level of mental concentration during practice. See *Meditation Sutra*, 14th to 16th Meditations.

*
**

Letter 3.
The True Mark Vehicle has no Marks[1]

It is very difficult indeed to respond to the important questions raised in your letter. Why? It is because your aspirations are lofty while my knowledge is limited and meager. Loftiness and meagerness cannot meet; therefore, my teaching will not be appropriate to your needs!

However, in the True Mark Single Vehicle, the marks of loftiness and meagerness cannot be found. Within this Vehicle, whether the marks are lofty or limited depends on how they are conceived. Loftiness and meagerness always possess in full the nature of the Dharma Realm.[2] Moreover, the meagerness to which I refer encompasses all the dharmas of the ten realms.

The Pure Land Patriarch Shan Tao[3] has said:

If you wish to study "meaning," [understand the Dharma] you should study all dharmas, from the mundane level to the level of the Buddhas. However, if you want to engage in "practice," you should choose a method compatible with the truth as well as your own capacities and level and then concentrate on it earnestly.[4] Only then can you reap benefits swiftly. Otherwise, even if you spend many eons, you will still be unable to escape Birth and Death.[5]

This being so, there is no better method than to recite the Buddha's name with a mind of Faith and Vows, seeking rebirth in the Pure Land. If you wish to go deeper, you should carefully peruse the *Commentary on the Essential Points of the Amitabha Sutra* and other Pure Land sutras and treatises.[6]

o
oo

Buddhism is an open method within the ten Dharma Realms -- everyone *should* practice it and anyone *can* practice it. Because they do not fully understand its true nature, some Confucian scholars blindly criticize Buddhism ... However, the evil karma resulting from maligning the Dharma pales before the karma of vilifying it with one's own body![7] These days, some individuals, mouthing Mahayana teachings, consider themselves awakened to the Way. They say: "I am [intrinsically] a Buddha, why recite the Buddha's name? Afflictions are Bodhi, what is the need to sever them? Lust, anger and delusion are precepts, concentration and wisdom, why sever lust, anger and delusion?"[8]

Their words are as lofty as the heavenly clouds, but their actions, upon close examination, are as low as the underworld! Such persons may be considered the enemies of Buddhism. Their evil karma is ten thousand times worse than that of persons who malign Buddhism through mere ignorance of the Dharma.[9] While their efforts in studying the Dharma are not entirely wasted, these can only constitute the seeds of liberation in the future. Their transgressions, on the other hand -- the vilification of the Dharma with their bodies -- will assuredly result in retribution along the evil paths for countless eons to come.

You should study Mahayana sutras and commentaries to ensure that your understanding is broad and complete. As far as cultivation is concerned, you should concentrate on Faith, Vows and oral recitation.

NOTES TO LETTER 3

(1) Letter to the layman Teng Hsin-an. (Chinese ed. Vol. I, p. 44; VN ed., p. 13)

(2) See Glossary for this important term.

(3) Shan Tao (613-681): one of the three early Patriarchs of the Pure Land school. His teachings are particularly reflected

in the Jodo and Jodo Shinshu schools in Japan.

(4) The key idea here is to concentrate one's efforts on one method in order to achieve success.

> We may take up any Dharma for practice as long as it is agreeable to our interest and inclination, and since every Dharma is perfect and complete, therefore in the course of cultivation, we should not think of changing from one Dharma to another, nor should we think that a certain Dharma may be superior or inferior to the others. As no medicine may be called ... bad as long as it can cure, likewise, no Dharma may be said to be ... low as long as it is adaptable to its followers. (Hsu Heng Chi, *What's Buddhism?*, p. 62.)

(5) See the following quote:

> The Buddha Dharma is a moral and philosophical system which expounds a unique path to Enlightenment, and is not a subject to be studied from a mere academic standpoint ... Mere learning is of no avail without actual practice; the learned man who does not practice the Dharma, the Buddha says, is like a colorful flower without scent. (Narada Maha Thera, *The Buddha and His Teachings*, p. vii.)

In the *Avatamsaka Sutra*, Sakyamuni Buddha compared individuals who study and verbalize (but do not practice) to those who count other people's money day in and day out while remaining destitute themselves.

(6) Many of the Pure Land commentaries are not yet available in Western languages. However, the main points of Pure Land doctrine are discussed at length in a recent publication, *Buddhism of Wisdom and Faith* (Master Thích Thiên Tâm), available in major university libraries and from the Sutra Translation Committee, 2611 Davidson Avenue, Bronx, NY 10468, USA (tel. (718) 584-0621). The International Buddhist Monastic Institute, 9250 Columbus Avenue, Sepulveda CA 91343, USA (tel. (818) 893-5317) may also be contacted.

(7) Vilifying (betraying) the Dharma with one's body. There are many ways to teach the Dharma. For instance, one can lecture on compassion or teach it by personal example. However, if one lectures on compassion while at the same time acting in a non-compassionate way, one is said to be

betraying the Dharma with one's body.

(8) For an explanation of why ordinary persons should not blindly borrow the words of the sages or emulate their extraordinary actions, see the following passage concerning Kumarajiva, the renowned T'ang Dynasty monk (who translated some thirty-five sutras into Chinese):

> When Kumarajiva went to China in the fourth century of this era, the Chinese Emperor thought that such a wise person ought to have descendents, so that his wisdom would carry on. He gave concubines to Kumarajiva, and since they were a royal gift, Kumarajiva had no choice but to accept them. Afterwards, his disciples asked, "Can we have relations with women too?"
>
> Kumarajiva said, "Sure, but first, let me show you something." He took a handful of needles and ate them as easily as if they were noodles. When he finished, he said, "If you can do that, then you can have relations with women." (Master Sheng-yen, *The Sword of Wisdom*, p. 229.)

(9) In this letter, Master Yin Kuang is presumably contrasting those who have some knowledge of Buddhism but have not mastered it (thus confusing theory and practice) with those who have no knowledge of Buddhism at all. (A little bit of knowledge is a dangerous thing!)

*
**

Letter 4.
The Jewelled Net of Indra[1]

From your letter, I can see that you are concentrating on reciting the Buddha's name, bowing to the *Lotus Sutra* and trying to reduce your transgressions, but you have not yet achieved success. You are thinking of following a special method to review your progress day by day. All these actions demonstrate that your cultivation in recent days is truly aimed at self-improvement, unlike those who attempt to deceive others with external displays to achieve renown. This being so, nothing could be better. I truly rejoice in your actions.

o
oo

A mind of sincerity and respect is the key to Pure Land cultivation. With utter sincerity and respect, even though you are only an ordinary being whose virtues are not yet perfected, you will achieve unimaginable results!

Conversely, without sincerity, bowing and reciting are no different from performing on stage, singing and prancing. Although you may be displaying the external signs of suffering, joy, compassion and other emotions, they are all make-believe because they do not spring from the depth of your mind. Any blessings or virtues that may result are but the *deluded* merits of the human and celestial realms, and these are precisely the basis of evil karma and the seeds of immense suffering in the future.[2] You should explain this to all your friends and colleagues, enjoining them to cultivate sincerely, so as to spread the benefits widely ...

You should not think that the merits and virtues of reciting the name of or visualizing *one* Buddha are less encompassing than those received from reciting the name of or meditating on *many* Buddhas. You should realize that Amitabha Buddha is the Dharma Realm Treasury Body. All the virtues of the Buddhas in the ten directions of the Dharma Realm are fully encompassed in Amitabha Buddha. This is like the jewelled net of Indra,[3] where thousands and thousands of jewels are fully reflected in one jewel, the image of one jewel is reflected in thousands and thousands of jewels, and each and every jewel encompasses every other, in perfect, unimpeded fashion.

o

oo

To great sages who have cultivated for a long time, widely varying conditions and environments do not matter; in fact, the more diverse they are, the more focussed the minds of these sages become. For beginners, on the other hand, if conditions and environments are varied, the mind-consciousness grows confused and unfocussed. Those with heavy obstructions and shallow wisdom may even, at times, be afflicted by demons.[4] For this reason, Buddha Sakyamuni and the Patriarchs all enjoined us to recite the Buddha's name singlemindedly until achieving samadhi -- at which time hundreds of thousands of Dharma methods and countless sublime meanings will manifest themselves in full. To exemplify this truth, the ancients have said:

> To bathe in the great ocean is to use the waters of hundreds of rivers ...

NOTES TO LETTER 4

(1) Letter to the layman Kao Shao-lin. (Chinese ed. Vol. I, p. 49; VN ed., p. 14)

(2) This paragraph touches on a subtle Buddhist teaching. Any good action leads to merit and virtue. The difference is in the level. Good actions performed with utter sincerity and with no thought of giver, receiver and gift accrue boundless merit and virtue outside the realm of Birth and Death (referred to as "Non-outflow merit and virtue"). Conversely, good actions performed without sincerity, for gain or fame, lead to merit and virtue "with outflow," i.e., limited and within

samsara.

Such tainted merit and virtue accumulated within the current lifetime may lead to rebirth within the human realm, in a position of wealth, power and authority (second lifetime). Since power tends to corrupt, the individual then creates evil karma, resulting in retribution in the third lifetime. Therefore, these merits and virtues are considered deluded.

(3) Dharma Realm: see Glossary.

Jewelled Net of Indra: one of the most beautiful and profound metaphors in the Mahayana tradition. It is associated with the *Avatamsaka Sutra*, with its conception of unity and interdependence:

> Far away in the heavenly abode of the great god Indra, there is a wonderful net which has been hung by some cunning artificer in such a manner that it stretches out infinitely in all directions. In accordance with the extravagant tastes of deities, the artificer has hung a single glittering jewel in each "eye" of the net, and since the net itself is infinite in dimension, the jewels are infinite in number. There hang the jewels, glittering like stars of the first magnitude, a wonderful sight to behold. If we now arbitrarily select one of these jewels for inspection and look closely at it, we will discover that in its polished surface there are reflected *all* the other jewels in the net, infinite in number. Not only that, but each of the jewels reflected in this one jewel is also reflecting all the other jewels, so that there is an infinite reflecting process occurring. The Hua-Yen [Avatamsaka] school has been fond of this image, mentioned many times in its literature, because it symbolizes a cosmos in which there is an infinitely repeated interrelationship among all the members of the cosmos. This relationship is said to be one of simultaneous *mutual identity* and *mutual intercausality*. (Francis H. Cook, *Hua-Yen Buddhism*, p. 2.)

(4) Demons (Skrt, Mara): evil influences which hinder cultivation. These can take an infinite number of forms, including evil beings or mental states, such as hallucinations. See the following gatha on Mara as the Demon of Lust, taken from the *Therigatha*, a collection of poems by the earliest Buddhist nuns:

[Mara]:

Come on, Khema!
Both of us are young

and you are beautiful.
Let us enjoy each other!
It will be like the music of a symphony.

[Khema]:

... Pleasures of the senses are
swords and stakes.
The elements of mind and body
are a chopping block for them.
What you call
delight
is not delight for me.

Everywhere the love of pleasure
is destroyed,
The great dark
is torn apart,
and Death,
you too are destroyed.
(Susan Murcott, *The First Buddhist Women*, p. 65.)

*
**

Letter 5.
The Ten Thousand Dharmas have no True Nature[1]

From your letter, I learned that in recent days you have engaged in earnest cultivation, examining yourself, mending your ways and following the path of the sages, with no desire for empty fame. I am very happy indeed!

To follow in the footsteps of the Buddhas and sages and escape Birth and Death, you should first develop an attitude of shame and repentance, abandon evil ways, perform wholesome deeds, keep the precepts and practice self-restraint. You should aim for the truth and practice to your utmost ability. Otherwise, there is deceit within deceit. Thus, understanding is not difficult; practice is the real difficulty![2] Many intelligent persons merely verbalize but fail to practice. They therefore waste an entire lifetime, spoiling a visit to the jewelled mountain and returning empty-handed. What a great pity! Their deluded thoughts flare up unchecked because they are not earnest in maintaining correct thought. If they would only concentrate on one realm, deluded thoughts would be converted into "correct wisdom."[3] Therefore, as the saying goes:

> If the king rules wisely, rebels and bandits will become like his own sons; if he rules unwisely, even his closest friends will turn into enemies.

o

oo

As common beings, who among us is not afflicted by delusion and evil karma? However, if you take precautions in your daily life, afflictions will not flare up whenever you meet with adverse circumstances. Even if they do arise, you will be aware of and eradicate them. The conditions leading to afflictions are numerous. Most powerful among them are *wealth, lust and unusual adversities.*

If you realize that ill-gotten gains are more dangerous than venomous snakes, you will not desire them when you see them. On the other hand, to assist fellow beings is precisely to lay the foundation for our own future merit and virtue. Knowing this, whenever those in need seek your help, you should not be stingy and refuse, developing afflictions in the process.

As for lustful thoughts, when you come across women as beautiful as flowers or precious gems, even women of pleasure and courtesans, you should view

them as your own sisters and, with a compassionate
mind, seek to rescue them. In this way, you will not be
moved by beautiful forms or swayed by lustful thoughts.
Within the family, husbands and wives should respect
one another as guests ...

When encountering adverse circumstances, you
should develop thoughts of compassion, forgiving those
who do not realize their mistakes and avoiding disputes.
You should think: "in my previous lives, I have caused
suffering and hurt sentient beings on many occasions. If
I meet with adversity today, it is merely the repayment of
previous debts." Thinking thus, you become naturally
content and do not develop a mind of anger and
vengefulness.

However, these methods are for those of low
capacities. In the case of sages who have cultivated for a
long time, all afflictions become the "shining Mind
Store," the ten thousand dharmas have always been
without True Nature[4] and the adverse or beneficial
consequences of all actions depend on the individual
alone.

o
oo

Faith, Vows and Practice form the cornerstone of
the Buddha Recitation method. If these three
conditions are fulfilled, rebirth in the Pure Land will be
achieved. You should pay particular attention to Faith
and Vows, and wish wholeheartedly to achieve rebirth in
the Pure Land ... [and not as a celestial being or a
Dharma Master, however awakened, as these are still
within the realm of Birth and Death]. Only then will
your Faith and Vows reach Amitabha Buddha so that
His Compassionate Vow may embrace you. In this

connection, Elder Master Ou I has said:

> Achieving rebirth in the Pure Land depends entirely on Faith and Vows, while the level of rebirth depends on the depth of practice.

This is a truth as solid as steel -- even if a thousand Buddhas were to appear on earth, it would not change.[5] Only by firmly believing in this truth will you have a destiny in the Western Pure Land.

o
oo

If you experience difficulty in reaching one-pointedness of mind, you should focus your mind and recite with care. The main criteria of such concentration are utter sincerity and earnestness. It is very difficult to achieve one-pointedness of mind without utter sincerity. However, sincerity is not enough. You should next listen attentively to the recitation. Whether or not recitation is performed aloud, it should originate from the mind. It then proceeds from the mouth and enters the ears (even if you recite silently, the marks of oral recitation still exist in the mind). With mind and mouth reciting clearly, the ears hearing clearly and the mind thus concentrated, deluded thoughts will cease by themselves.[6]

o
oo

You have now reached your fifties. If you wish to attain liberation in this very life, you should concentrate on the Pure Land method. The *Diamond Sutra* and the *Lotus Sutra*[7] should be temporarily set aside, until such time as you fully possess the Pure Land principles and achieve one-pointedness of mind through Buddha

Recitation. If you spend time studying while you are trying to engage in cultivation, you may not have the time or the energy. Thus, you will achieve neither and lose the benefits of both.[8]

NOTES TO LETTER 5

(1) Another letter to the layman Kao Shao-lin. (Chinese ed. Vol. I, p. 55; VN ed., p. 17)

(2) Practice is a cardinal point in Buddhist cultivation. A story concerning the famous T'ang Dynasty official and poet Po Chu-i illustrates this point.

One day, the official, passing along the road, saw a Zen monk seated on the branch of a tree preaching the Dharma. The following dialogue ensued: Official: "Old man, what are you doing up in that tree, in such a precarious position? One misstep, and you will fall to your death!" Monk: "I dare say, Your Lordship, that your own position is even more precarious. If I make a misstep, I alone may suffer; if you, as a high-ranking official, make a mistake in judgement, it can cost the lives of thousands." Po Chu-I, seated in his ornate sedan chair, was puzzled. He reflected for a moment before the parallel dawned on him. He then responded: "Not a bad reply. I'll tell you what. If you can explain the essence of Buddhism to me in one sentence, I'll become your disciple. Otherwise, we will go our separate ways, never to meet again." Monk: "What an easy question! Listen! The essence of Buddhism is to do no evil, do what is good and keep your mind pure." Official: "Is that all there is to it? Even a child of eight realizes that!" Monk: "True, a child of eight may realize it, but even a man of eighty cannot practice these injunctions!"

(3) Correct wisdom: knowing that the purpose of cultivation is to escape Birth and Death and achieve Buddhahood, not to be reborn as celestials or privileged human beings. This is the opposite of "delusive wisdom."

(4) True Nature = Original Nature = Self-Nature = Buddha

Nature = True Mind = Original Face, etc. See Glossary, "Buddha Nature."

(5) All Buddhist teachings are expedients. Sages and saints who propagate a method direct all teachings toward that method.

(6) One-pointedness of mind: singleminded focus, particularly on the name of Amitabha Buddha. According to Pure Land teaching, this is an essential condition for rebirth at a high lotus grade. See also the following passage:

> The Method of Hearing is in keeping with the fundamental principle that if one sense-organ is intensely concentrated, all the other five sense-organs would be also held still automatically. This is the most fundamental tenet of the reciting method, as said in the *Surangama Sutra*: "when the six sense-organs [mind included] are simultaneously held in concentration, there will be every pure thought in succession."
> (Hsu Heng Chi, *What's Buddhism*, p. 56.)

(7) The *Diamond Sutra* and the *Lotus Sutra* (see Glossary) are the fundamental texts of two Buddhist schools other than Pure Land, namely, Zen and T'ien T'ai, respectively. As Buddhist teachings are medicines that should be adapted to the needs of the individual patient, these sutras may be unsuitable remedies for certain cultivators beset, for example, by illness or advanced age.

(8) Buddhism deals with calming the mind, "reining in the wandering, monkey mind," keeping it pure, empty and still. The more one reads and studies about Buddhism, the more one engages in discrimination and the more agitated the mind becomes. Therefore, studying sutras and commentaries, while desirable, may not be the best method for everyone and is not a substitute for practice. This is particularly true of persons of advanced age.

*
**

Letter 6.
Faith, Vows and Practice[1]

The true intention of Buddha Sakyamuni, when he appeared in the world to preach the Dharma and rescue sentient beings, was for all beings to escape Birth and Death and attain Enlightenment immediately. However, because sentient beings were all of differing capacities and thus could not entirely meet His transcendental expectations, the All-Compassionate Being resorted to one expedient teaching after another, all of them adapted to the individual capacities of sentient beings.

To those of the highest capacities, the Great Sage taught the path of the Buddhas, showing them the Self-Nature directly so that they might attain Buddhahood in one lifetime -- as in the case of the youth Sudhana in the *Avatamsaka Sutra* or the Dragon Maid in the *Lotus Sutra*.[2] To those of more modest capacities, the Buddha taught the Bodhisattva, Pratyeka Buddha and Arhat paths, so that they might reach Buddhahood through step-by-step cultivation. To those of still lower capacities, the Buddha taught the Five Precepts and the Ten Virtues.

o
oo

These methods, high or low, some leading to swift liberation, others to gradual liberation, are all different. However, they all require self-power and deep cultivation to escape from the cycle of Birth and Death and reach the Self-Nature. If even a trace *delusion of views* or *delusion of thought*[3] remains, the roots of Birth and Death cannot be extirpated.[4] This being the case, even if the cultivator's power of concentration and wisdom is profound, he will continue to revolve in the cycle of Birth and Death. Only at the level of the Arhats are the roots of Birth and Death completely severed.

However, transcending Birth and Death is merely the small fruit of the Arhats; the cultivator must still aim for the path of Great Bodhi, relying on his Vow to be reborn in the worlds of the ten directions. He may then cultivate the six paramitas and the ten thousand conducts, in order to achieve Buddhahood and rescue sentient beings ...[5] [In this manner, he will gradually achieve the 52 different stages of Bodhisattvahood, up to the level of Wonderful Enlightenment, before finally reaching Buddhahood.]

o
oo

Although Buddha Sakyamuni expounded countless methods throughout His entire teaching career, they are all based upon the various stages of Bodhisattvahood mentioned above.

Thus, the Zen tradition points directly to the Self-Mind, seeing one's Nature and achieving Buddhahood. This is a perfect, direct shortcut. However, we are speaking here from the viewpoint of the inherent Dharma Body (that is, principle or noumenon), bypassing phenomenal cultivation and attainment grounded in the law of Cause and Effect. If we were to consider the different levels of cultivation and achievement, there would be no difference between Zen and the Sutra Studies method.

However, in the midst of this Dharma-Ending Age, there are very few good spiritual advisors,[6] while the capacities of sentient beings are limited. It is difficult enough to find someone who is *awakened to the Way,* not to mention one who has truly *attained Enlightenment!*[7] Thus, knowing that sentient beings would find it extremely difficult to achieve liberation by relying on *self-power* alone, Sakyamuni Buddha taught, in addition to other methods, the special approach of Pure Land. With this method, as long as their Faith and Vows are true and earnest, even those who have committed the Five Grave Offenses or the Ten Evil Acts, may, on the verge of death, when the marks of hell appear, follow the advice of a good spiritual advisor and recite the Buddha's name one to ten times.[8] Then, thanks to the compassionate power of Amitabha Buddha, even they will be received and guided to the Pure Land -- not to mention those who practice wholesome deeds and do not commit transgressions!

The more diligently the cultivator engages in wholesome conduct and the deeper his power of concentration, the higher his level of rebirth will be. He will see Amitabha Buddha soon after rebirth and be able to hear the wonderful Dharma. Therefore, even those who have awakened to the Way, severed delusion and attained the truth should dedicate all merits toward rebirth in the Pure Land, seeking perfect attainment of the Dharma Body and swift attainment of Buddhahood.[9]

o
oo

Other methods depend on the capacities of the practitioner. If they lead only to limited attainment [such as Arhatship], those of high capacities need not practice them. If they lead to great attainment, those of limited capacities cannot cultivate them. Only the Pure

Land method embraces practitioners of all three capacities, high, moderate and low. Supremely lofty beings, such as the Bodhisattvas Avalokitesvara, Mahasthamaprapta, Manjusri and Samantabhadra, cannot transcend it,[10] while those of low capacities, who have committed the Five Grave Offenses or the Ten Evil Deeds and have sown the seeds of the Never-Ending Hell, can still participate in it. If Sakyamuni Buddha had not taught this method, the majority of sentient beings in the Dharma-Ending Age could not hope to escape the cycle of Birth and Death.[11]

o

oo

Despite its loftiness, the Pure Land Dharma Door is a very easy method of cultivation. For this reason, not only do ordinary beings find it difficult to believe, but cultivators of the Two Vehicles (Theravada followers) also harbor doubts.[12] This applies even to Bodhisattvas at the "expedient level." Only those who have sown the wholesome seeds of Pure Land in previous lives as well as the higher level Bodhisattvas can truly have firm and deep Faith in it.

A newborn prince,[13] who has not yet proven his talents and virtues, is still above the ministers in nobility and honor, thanks to the power of his royal lineage. Likewise, those who practice Buddha Recitation with full Faith and Vows, though they may be ordinary beings, belong to a lineage superior to that of the disciples of the Two Vehicles. This is because they have learned to cast their earthly minds into the sea of Enlightenment -- silently in tune with the wonderful Way.[14] Thanks to Amitabha Buddha's power, they will swiftly attain the level of non-retrogression.

In discussing the Pure Land method, you should

make a general comparison of the ease and difficulty of *other power* vs. *self-power*, as employed in this and other methods, respectively. Otherwise, even if you do not doubt the Dharma, you will doubt yourself, and even a trace of doubt becomes an obstacle. In such a case, even if you engage in cultivation you will not reap the full benefit -- not to mention what will happen if you do not cultivate. For this reason, Faith is the first criterion.[15] You should firmly believe that the Saha World is a place of suffering, the Western Pure Land a realm of joy ... As is said in the *Smaller Amitabha Sutra:*

> Shariputra: Why is that land called Utmost Happiness? The beings of that land experience no suffering; they only know every kind of joy; therefore it is called Utmost Happiness. (Hozen Seki, *Amida-kyo*, p. 18.)

You should be wary and not attempt to reason with the mind of an ordinary being, lest you mistakenly think that "all the wonderful, extraordinary events beyond common understanding that occur in the Western Pure Land are myths representing the Mind Dharma, rather than a true environment."[16] With this misunderstanding, you lose the benefit of rebirth in the Pure Land. This is a major error, so be careful!

o
oo

Once you realize that the Saha World is a place of suffering[17] while the Pure Land is a place of joy, you should develop true, earnest Vows, resolving to leave the Saha World and return to the Land of Ultimate Bliss. Such Vows are no different from those of a person who has fallen into an excrement pit and seeks to escape swiftly, or of a prisoner who yearns for his native village. Such hopes and desires should be utterly sincere, because your own strength cannot free you from your predicament.

Sentient beings in the Saha World, facing circumstances that accord or fail to accord with their wishes, often develop the mind of greed, anger and delusion, create the karma of killing, stealing and lust, and tarnish the bright, spotless Self-Nature -- this is a filthy bottomless pit. Having created evil karma, they must endure suffering through many lifetimes along the evil paths -- this is a drawn out imprisonment.

Untold eons ago, Amitabha Buddha made forty-eight Vows to rescue sentient beings. One of the Vows [the eighteenth] stated:

If, after my obtaining Buddhahood, all beings in the ten quarters should desire in sincerity and trustfulness to be born in my country, and if they should not be born by only thinking of me ten times ..., may I not attain the highest Enlightenment. (Joji Okazaki, *Pure Land Buddhist Painting*, p. 15.)

Although Amitabha Buddha, the Compassionate One, made such a Vow, if sentient beings do not seek His help, there is little He can do. However, anyone who recites His name with utter sincerity, vowing to leave the Saha World behind, will be welcomed and escorted to the Pure Land. Amitabha Buddha has great power; He can rescue sentient beings from the excrement pit and the prison of the defiled world, guide them to the Land of Ultimate Bliss, and help them enter the realms of the Buddhas to assume the prerogatives and functions of the Tathagatas (Buddhas).

o
oo

Rebirth in the Western Land thus requires, first of all, deep Faith and fervent Vows. Without these conditions, even if you were to cultivate, you could not obtain a response from Amitabha Buddha. You would merely reap the blessings of the human and celestial realms and sow the seeds of liberation in the future. Anyone who fulfills the conditions of Faith and Vows is assured of rebirth in the Pure Land. When Elder Master Yung Ming stated that "out of ten thousand who cultivate, ten thousand will achieve rebirth," he was referring to those with full Faith and Vows. Once you have deep Faith and earnest Vows, you should practice Buddha Recitation as your principal method, guided by your Faith and Vows. These three components [Faith, Vows, Practice] are precisely the main tenets of Pure Land -- lack of any one of these conditions will prevent you from achieving rebirth in the Land of Ultimate Bliss.[18]

o

oo

The form of Buddha Recitation Practice depends on the circumstances of each individual -- there is no single set way ... If the cultivator is very busy, having no free time, he should set aside a specific period in the early morning. After washing up, he should bow three times to the Buddha in front of his altar (if he has one). Then, standing erect, he should join his palms and singlemindedly recite the words "Na Mo Amitabha Buddha" as many times as he can in one stretch, each stretch counting as one recitation. He should recite thus for ten stretches, and then utter the following stanza:

I vow that, along with other Pure Land
              cultivators,
I will be reborn in the Land of Ultimate Bliss,
See the Buddha, escape Birth and Death,
And rescue all, as the Buddha does.

After reciting this stanza, he should bow three times

before retiring.

If he does not have an altar, he can face west with palms joined, reciting according to the above method. This is the Ten Recitations Method which Elder Master Tzu Wen established for rulers and officials who are too busy with affairs of state to engage in cultivation. Why recite in one stretch? It is because sentient beings have scattered, unsettled minds and are thus unable to practice assiduously. This recitation method relies on the breath to concentrate the mind. However, the number of utterances is dependent on the length of the breath span. There should be no effort or constraint, as this would lead to fatigue ... Since recitation with a scattered mind cannot easily lead to rebirth in the Pure Land, this method helps focus the mind. While the recitations are few in number, the virtues accrued are profound and rebirth is assured.

o
oo

Moreover, the practitioner should maintain a virtuous and forgiving mind in all circumstances,[19] guard against mistakes in each of his thoughts, be willing to recognize mistakes, correct his transgressions and gladly perform good actions -- only then will he be in accord with Buddha Amitabha. Failure to do so indicates that his mind is still obstructed and thus not consonant with the mind of the Buddha. This makes it difficult for the two to interact. Furthermore, when bowing, reciting Mahayana sutras or accomplishing various wholesome deeds, he should dedicate all the resulting merits to rebirth in the Pure Land. He should not dedicate only the merits of Buddha Recitation itself, while transferring incidental merits[20] toward worldly blessings. In the latter case he would not be singleminded, making rebirth in the Pure Land very difficult to achieve.

o
oo

The Pure Land method is extolled in numerous Mahayana sutras.[21] Theravada sutras, on the other hand, do not mention it at all. Those who are not versed in the Dharma and reject Buddha Recitation as a "self-benefit" method are speaking thoughtlessly.[22] Do not listen to them.

NOTES TO LETTER 6

(1) Letter to the layman Ch'en Hsi-chou. (Chinese ed. Vol. I, p. 59; VN ed., p. 20)

(2) Avatamsaka Sutra; Lotus Sutra: see Glossary.

The youth Sudhana represents the ideal seeker of the Way and it was to him and through him that the Bodhisattva Samantabhadra taught his Ten Great Vows. (See Appendix.) The Dragon Maid refers to the daughter of the King of the sea dragons in the *Lotus Sutra* (ch. 12). She achieved Buddhahood right in front of the Assembly.

(3) Delusion of views; delusion of thought: see Glossary.

(4) This point is explained well in the following passage:

> We should know, furthermore, that to escape birth and death, we must sever delusions of views and thought. However, according to the ancients, "blocking delusions of views is as difficult as blocking a raging stream coming from forty miles away." Why, then, even mention eliminating all delusions of thought? Thus, if we want to achieve liberation in this Dharma-Ending Age, the most appropriate method is Buddha Recitation. This is because, through this method, the cultivator, after utilizing his self-power to the utmost, receives additional assistance from other-power. Even though his karma and delusions are not yet extinguished, he can, through Amitabha Buddha's power of welcoming and escorting, "take his residual karma along" to the Pure Land. Once reborn, he will no longer retrogress and will have

transcended birth and death forever! ... (Master Thích Thiên Tâm, *Buddhism of Wisdom and Faith*, sect. 54, p. 226.)

(5) Paramitas; ten thousand conducts: see Glossary.

(6) Good spiritual advisors: i.e., gurus, virtuous friends, wise people. In the *Avatamsaka Sutra,* each spiritual advisor of the youth Sudhana (the ideal seeker of the Way) takes on a different form but thcy all flow from the Bodhisattva Manjusri, the personification of wisdom. Thus, wisdom is of paramount importance in choosing a spiritual advisor. Both guru and student should exercise wisdom in choosing one another. See Glossary.

(7) A Zen story illustrates the distinction between awakening to the Way (Great Awakening) and attaining Enlightenment:

To make sure that his disciple would reach the great ocean and not be misled by smaller bodies of water, a Master explained the difference between rivers, lakes and seas, the characteristics of fresh water, salt water, etc. Finally, he took the disciple to the highest mountain peak in the area and pointed to the ocean in the distance. For the first time, glimpsing the ocean with his own eyes, the disciple experienced a Great Awakening. However, only after he followed the long, tortuous path and actually reached the ocean, tasting its waters, did he achieve Enlightenment.

(8) See *Meditation Sutra*, Sixteenth Meditation. The two operative phrases here are "on the verge of death" and "true and earnest." When a wicked person, on his deathbed, senses evil omens arising from his subconscious and he sees no possible alternative, a mind of utter sincerity and devotion is sometimes possible. Such a frame of mind is practically impossible to develop in the course of everyday life. The following story provides a good illustration of this point.

There was once a Zen monk meditating on a deserted mountain far away from all human habitation. Because of the rigors of the climate and the isolation of the place, he found it difficult to concentrate. His mind constantly wandered toward life in the village down below. One evening, as he was seated lost in errant thought, he had the sensation that he was being watched. He slowly turned his head, and lo and behold, there was a tiger crouched in the bushes behind him! One false move and the tiger would pounce on him. He had no choice but to remain ramrod straight, in singleminded concentration. When dawn broke, the tiger, fearful of the light of day, gave up this cat-and-mouse game and disappeared. The next two evenings, the monk, faithful to his vow, resumed his meditation at the appointed time and place. The tiger returned and the scene repeated itself each evening. When daylight came on the third day, the monk, after three nights of *singleminded concentration*, experienced a Great Awakening, collapsed and died. At his funeral, it was reported that a tiger was seen watching and wailing in the distance.

As to how the karma of a lifetime can be dissipated in an instant, let us picture a house which has been boarded up for generations. All it takes for the darkness to disappear is to open a window and let the sun in (Great Awakening). The key point is how to enter the house, open that window and keep it open at all times. See also Introduction, sect. D.

(9) See the following passage:

> Nothing prevents people who study Zen and who investigate inherent mind moment to moment from taking vows to be reborn in the Land of Ultimate Bliss when their lives here are over.

> Why is this? Though one may have an awakening by studying Zen, if one is as yet unable to abide in the eternal quiescent light like the buddhas, and is still not free of subsequent existence like the arhats, then when this physical body is used up, one is sure to be reborn. (Zen Master Chu Hung in J.C. Cleary, *Pure Land, Pure Mind.*)

(10) See Appendix to this book, *Avatamsaka Sutra*, Ch. 40, "The Practices and Vows of the Bodhisattva Samantabhadra."

(11) Dharma-Ending Age: see Glossary.

(12) Unlike Mahayana schools, the Theravada tradition does not recognize Amitabha Buddha, the Bodhisattva Avalokitesvara, etc. or the Pure Land. Theravadins believe only in Sakyamuni Buddha, the Bodhisattva Maitreya and a

few other Buddhas -- leaving out almost all of the transhistorical Buddhas and Bodhisattvas of the Mahayana tradition.

(13) This well-known example is taken from the *Avatamsaka Sutra:*

> Just as a newborn prince is not inferior to fully grown ministers, because of his superior birth, a beginning enlightening being, born in the family of the enlightened spiritual kings, is not inferior to Buddhist disciples with long experience in religious practice, because of the superiority of universal compassion of the aspiration for enlightenment. (Thomas Cleary, tr. *The Flower Ornament Scripture*, vol. III, p. 362.)

(14) This image alludes to the concept of merit transference practiced by Bodhisattvas -- to cast one's earthly mind and earthly merits into the sea of Enlightenment. A small merit, when dedicated to all sentient beings, becomes infinite, as are sentient beings themselves. A modern parallel would be using a million dollars to buy a mansion for one's family versus contributing it to a university or a hospital where that same amount of money will benefit countless generations to come. See also Introduction, Section C.

(15) Faith is an important element in all Buddhist traditions, but it is particularly so in Pure Land. See the following passage from the *Avatamsaka Sutra*, which almost all Mahayana monks and nuns can recite by heart:

> Faith is the basis of the path, the mother of virtues,
> Nourishing and growing all good ways ...
> Faith can increase knowledge and virtue;
> Faith can assure arrival at enlightenment.
> (Thomas Cleary, tr. *The Flower Ornament Scripture*, vol. 1, p.331.)

(16) See the Introduction to *Pure Land Buddhism: Dialogues with Ancient Masters:*

> Is not Pure Land teaching too close to traditional Western beliefs in a personal God, saints, sinners and Paradise? Answer. A person asleep and dreaming finds the scenes in his dreams very real; these scenes exist for him. Likewise, the Pure Land, saints, sinners, everything "exists" at the mundane level, albeit in an illusory, dream-like way. At the absolute level, however, everything, including the Pure Land and Amitabha Buddha, is Mind-Only, a product of our mind. This key Mahayana teaching is reflected in the paradox "True Emptiness Wonderful

Existence!" (p. 3)

On this important issue, see also the words of the
eminent Zen Master Chu Hung (16th century):

> Some people say that the Pure Land is nothing but mind, that there is no
> Pure Land of Ultimate Bliss beyond the trillions of worlds of the cosmos.
> This talk of mind-only has its source in the words of the sutras, and it is
> true, not false. But those who quote it in this sense are
> misunderstanding its meaning.

> Mind equals object: there are no objects beyond mind. Objects equal
> mind: there is no mind beyond objects. Since objects are wholly mind,
> why must we cling to mind and dismiss objects? Those who dismiss
> objects when they talk of mind have not comprehended mind. (J.C.
> Cleary, *Pure Land, Pure Mind.*)

(17) Sufferings: see Glossary, "Eight Sufferings."

(18) All Buddhist teachings are expedients, dividing the one
and indivisible Truth into many parts. Faith, Vows and
Practice, although three, are really one. Thus, it can be said
that rebirth in the Pure Land depends on three conditions or
two conditions or even one condition, as the one contains all
and all is contained in the one. The lower the capacity of a
practitioner, the more conditions he is taught to fulfill.

(19) See the following passage:

> What we are today comes from our thoughts of yesterday, and our
> present thoughts build our life of tomorrow: our life is the creation of
> our mind.

> If a man speaks or acts with a pure mind, joy follows him as his own
> shadow. (Juan Mascaró, tr., *The Dhammapada*, p. 35.)

(20) Incidental merits. Merits accrued from performing
wholesome actions (sundry practices) other than Buddha
Recitation (main practice). Caveat: Buddha Recitation
should always be accompanied by the Vow for rebirth.

(21) In addition to the three Pure Land sutras, these include
some 200 sutras and commentaries, such as the *Avatamsaka,
Surangama, Lotus* and *Prajnaparamita Sutras*, etc. (J.P.

Malalasekera, *Encyclopedia of Buddhism*.) The *Treatise on the Awakening of the Faith* specifically recommends Buddha Recitation:

> Next, suppose there is a man who learns this [Mahayana] teaching for the first time and wishes to seek the correct faith but lacks courage and strength. Because he lives in this world of suffering, he fears that he will not always be able to meet the Buddhas and honor them personally, and that, faith being difficult to perfect, he will be inclined to fall back.
>
> He should know that the Tathagathas have an excellent expedient means by which they can protect his faith: that is, through the strength of wholehearted meditation-recitation on the Buddha, he will in fulfillment of his wishes be able to be born in the Buddha-land beyond, to see the Buddha always, and to be forever separated from the evil states of existence.
>
> It is as the sutra says: "If a man meditates wholly on Amitabha Buddha in the world of the Western Paradise and wishes to be born in that world, directing all the goodness he has cultivated toward that goal, then he will be born there." Because he will see the Buddha at all times, he will never fall back ... [If a cultivator follows this path], he will be able to be born there in the end because he abides in the correct samadhi." (Asvaghosha, *The Awakening of the Faith*, p. 102.)

(22) See Introduction to this book. Development of the Bodhi Mind, the aspiration to rescue oneself and others, is a *sine qua non* of Pure Land practice.

*
**

Letter 7.
The <u>Brahma Net Sutra</u> and the Precepts[1]

I have made my home on P'u T'o Mountain[2] for some twenty years now, and during the entire time have not engaged in personal contact with lay people. Recently, when Master Fu Yen visited our mountain, he approached me in the meditation hut on several occasions within the space of ten days to talk about your fidelity and moral integrity, exhibiting deep concern each time. On these occasions, I advanced the opinion that although your integrity is praiseworthy, you do not know how to cultivate properly.

I also said that, time permitting, I would write a letter of advice to you explaining the main lines of the Pure Land method, so that you could, according to your strength and conditions, step onto the Pure Land path. Upon hearing this, Master Fu Yen expressed his approval and wholeheartedly requested me to do so. This is the genesis of my letter to you today.

o

oo

The Dharma already exists in full in the minds of all sentient beings -- both clergy and lay persons can uphold it. However, the lot of women entails many restrictions. If you leave your native village to travel afar, you may well be subjected to oppression and assault.[3] Therefore, you had better stay home, keep the precepts and recite the Buddha's name, determined to seek rebirth in the Western Pure Land. There is no need to leave your native place to become a nun. Extensive travel to various temples and other holy places to seek out great masters with whom to study the sutras in depth should be left to men. For women to follow this course is not advisable. You should strive to practice the Pure Land method, reciting the Buddha's name assiduously. If you succeed in gathering your six faculties together and engage in pure recitation without interruption, you can attain samadhi as a matter of course, in this very life. Why, then, worry about not reaching the higher lotus grades at the time of death?[4]

Even if you do not reach samadhi, you will still achieve rebirth [in a lower lotus grade], be part of the

Ocean-Wide Assembly, close to Amitabha Buddha; you will gradually return to the True Self-Nature and naturally understand the various teachings. Then, just like an image in a mirror, you will appear in the Saha World without leaving the Pure Land, to rescue sentient beings through countless expedients, helping them all to reach the Pure Land and attain the Tolerance of Non-Birth (insight into the non- origination of all things).[5] This will not be turning your back on your present firm determination to cultivate. In fact, you will deserve to be called a green lotus blossom, born amid fire, a true woman of character!

o
oo

The most fundamental criterion of Buddha Recitation is the determination to be reborn in the Pure Land. Therefore, its motto is "Faith, Vows and Practice." "Faith" means believing that the Saha World is filled with the eight sufferings, while the Pure Land is a realm of boundless joy!

Once you have firm Faith, you should vow to leave the Saha World, like a prisoner desperate to leave his jail, and resolve to achieve rebirth in the Pure Land, like a traveller longing for his native place.[6]

As someone who has not achieved rebirth in the Pure Land, even if you were presented with the jewelled throne of the god-king Brahma, you should consider it as a cause and condition of perdition, without a single thought of longing. Likewise, wishes such as "rebirth as a male,[7] entering the clergy early in life, attaining great intelligence, great spiritual powers ..."[8] should all be considered tortuous paths of cultivation which can only bring you back to your starting point. Abandon all these thoughts and seek only to achieve rebirth in the Pure

Land at the time of death. Once reborn, you will naturally escape the cycle of Birth and Death, transcend the human world, enter the realm of the sages, reach the stage of non-retrogression and attain the stage of Non-Birth. At that time, when you look back, you will discover that the royal throne in the human and celestial realms, even rebirth as a high-ranking monk, are but tiresome occurrences that last for many eons with no liberation in sight. You will then realize that compared to your present lotus grade, those aspirations are no different from a flickering flame versus a rainbow, or an anthill versus a mountain!

Thus, the Pure Land practitioner certainly should not seek the blessings and merits of the celestial and human realms, not even rebirth as a high-ranking monk. Just a trace of such thinking constitutes a lack of deep Faith and earnest Vows. Such thoughts place a barrier between you and the Vows of Amitabha Buddha -- preventing you from achieving rebirth in the Pure Land.[9] This is a great pity, a great waste, indeed! How could you have the heart to exchange the unimaginably sublime Pure Land for mundane happiness -- so that when all the blessings have been exhausted, you would sink once more into the cycle of Birth and Death, dragged by the current of karmic delusion, subject to untold suffering?

If poison is mixed with butter, the delicious butter becomes lethal. Practicing Pure Land without the right frame of mind brings similar harm. You must extirpate such wrong thoughts in order to enjoy fully the benefits of the Pure Land method.[10]

o

oo

Once having developed deep Faith and earnest

Vows, you should hold fast to the words "Amitabha Buddha." Regardless of the occasion, whether walking or standing, sitting or reclining, speaking or remaining silent, moving about, meditating, dressing, eating, even when in the privy, you should keep the words "Amitabha Buddha" firmly in mind. You should exert yourself until the recitations are constantly before you, the *whole Buddha* is Mind, Mind and Buddha are *one* -- reciting to the ultimate point where all mundane feelings are forgotten. At that time, the mind being empty, the Buddha appears. During this life you can attain the Buddha Remembrance Samadhi and at the time of death achieve rebirth in the uppermost grades.

Cultivating in this way may be considered as exercising your abilities to the utmost. In daily life, the merits accrued from the smallest wholesome deeds, as well as the virtues garnered from Buddha Recitation and Sutra Recital, should all be dedicated to rebirth in the Pure Land. All actions then become practices which facilitate rebirth -- not unlike deriving soil from dust and sand or the ocean from the rivers and streams. The depth and breadth of such Buddha Recitation is immense.

You should, furthermore, develop the Bodhi Mind,[11] vow to rescue sentient beings and dedicate the merits and virtues of cultivation to repayment of the four great debts in the Triple Realm, as well as to sentient beings in the Dharma Realm. This creates a far-reaching Dharma affinity with all sentient beings, like oil poured on fire or rain falling on new seedlings, so that you will achieve early success in your Mahayana practice. If you miss this point, your Pure Land practice will become the grasping, self-benefit approach common to humans and lower level sages [Arhats and Pratyeka Buddhas]. While your method of cultivation may be sublime, the benefits received will be extremely low level and limited.

o

oo

When reciting the Buddha's name, you should gather your thoughts together. Recitation originates in the mind and is channelled through the mouth, each phrase, each word, clearly enunciated. You should also listen clearly, impressing the words in your mind. If the faculty of hearing is under control, the other faculties are also held in check and cannot chase after external dusts. As a result, one-pointedness of mind is swiftly achieved. Thus, the Bodhisattva Mahastamaprapta said in the *Surangama Sutra*:

> To gather the six senses together, pure recitation following upon pure recitation without interruption, thus attaining samadhi -- this is uppermost.

Likewise, the Bodhisattva Manjusri taught:

> "Hearing" within, hearing one's Nature -- one's Nature becomes the Supreme Path.

You certainly should not think that oral recitation [Holding the Name] is shallow, and follow other methods, such as Visualization, Contemplation of an Image or Real Mark Buddha Recitation.[12] Of the four Buddha Recitation methods, only oral recitation is well-adapted to the capacities of sentient beings. If one-pointedness of mind is maintained, the sublime truth of Real Mark will be fully revealed and the extraordinary realm of the Western Pure Land will appear clearly.

Therefore, you can achieve Real Mark through Holding the Name; you can see the Western Pure Land without engaging in visualization. This oral recitation method is precisely the wonderful door to the Way, the most expedient path to Buddhahood.

People today generally do not understand the teaching underlying the visualization or Real Mark methods. If they follow these methods, they may at times be subject to demons.[13] Thus, the best approach is to select the easiest practice which still leads to the wonderful fruit of Enlightenment. You should not attempt a shortcut and end up losing the Way, seeking liberation but winding up in perdition. That would be regrettable indeed!

[After summarizing several Pure Land commentaries to reinforce these points, the Master continued.]

Once you have read these books, you will have a complete understanding of the tenets of Pure Land. It does not matter that you have not read the sutras widely. Without fully understanding Pure Land teachings, even if you deeply understand the entire Buddhist canon and have awakened completely to the Self-Mind, it will take you untold eons to fulfill your original vow to escape the cycle of Birth and Death.[14] Buddha Recitation is the panacea for all diseases. To miss knowing about such a wonderful remedy would be a cause for great suffering and regret! To be aware of but not practice it, or to practice it but not in earnest, is to have even greater cause for suffering and regret!

o
oo

As far as receiving the lay precepts is concerned, you can visit this temple if you have the means and the capacity to do so. Otherwise, why get so fixated on travel? All you need is to have an earnest, sincere mind, repent your transgressions before your home altar for seven consecutive days and express the wish to receive the precepts by yourself. On the seventh day, you should kneel before a Buddha image and say aloud:

Your disciple, by the name of so and so, vows to receive the five precepts and fulfill the obligations of a laywoman. I vow that for the rest of my life, I will not take the lives of sentient beings, steal, indulge in sexual misconduct, lie or take intoxicants."

Repeating these vows three times constitutes receiving the precepts. The most important thing is to do so in an utterly sincere frame of mind -- in which case, the benefits and virtues of receiving the precepts are the same whether you do so by yourself or through a monk or nun.

You should not think that receiving the precepts in such a manner is not in accord with the Dharma. You should know that the method described above follows the wise teaching of Sakyamuni Buddha in the *Brahma Net Sutra*.[15]

On P'u T'o Mountain, there are no precept transmission ceremonies in the autumn, but only during a seven-week period following the lunar New Year. However, I sincerely wish that you would stay put at home practicing Buddha Recitation, rather than struggling through fog and snow to reach P'u T'o Mountain.

If you stick to your fixed ideas without changing your mind, you will miss distinguishing the good from the bad, damaging your own pure cultivation and displaying ingratitude toward the sincere, earnest words of this old monk. I want you to attain the goal of your cultivation within this lifetime[16] and certainly do not have the least intention of hindering your development in the Dharma.

If you think it over carefully, you will see so yourself.

o

oo

As for your intention to commit suicide because you cannot become a nun, such determination, however powerful and intense, is deluded and insane.[17] In the midst of this Dharma-Ending Age, how many monks and nuns are worthy of being teachers? ... As a woman, especially, you may be subjected to overbearing masters, insulted or drawn into intrigues.

You only think that to "leave home" and become a nun is liberation, but you do not yet know the many difficulties and obstacles which monks and nuns face.

Do not think, furthermore, that to commit suicide is to free yourself of the cares and worries of this life! Once dead, your soul will be led away by the power of karma to be reborn in another body -- not to mention that, given your angry state of mind, you may well be reborn in the animal realm. Under such circumstances, it will be difficult even to regain a female body. Should you succeed in being reborn as a woman or a man, or even as a ruler in the human or celestial realms,[18] there is still no assurance that you will encounter the Dharma and engage in cultivation! Even if you are so fortunate, who knows if you will be in the good position to discover the Pure Land method -- a method that enables each and every one to escape Birth and Death in one lifetime.

Moreover, even if you were fortunate enough to encounter the Pure Land method then, is it not much better to go on living and cultivating patiently right now, so that when this retribution body[19] comes to an end, you will immediately achieve rebirth in the Land of Ultimate Bliss?

I have exhausted my words in advising and counselling you. Let me ask you: did anyone ever go over these questions with yourself in mind to the extent that I have? If you do not follow the words of this old monk, you have shown ingratitude toward his teaching; moreover, I fear your suffering in the future will be infinitely greater than it is now!

NOTES TO LETTER 7

(1) Letter to the laywoman Hsu Fu-hsien. (Chinese ed. Vol. I, p. 115; VN ed., p. 54)

(2) P'u T'o Mountain: mountain in Chekiang Province, south of Shanghai. It is traditionally believed that the Bodhisattva Avalokitesvara attained Nirvana there.

(3) This letter was written during the lifetime of Master Yin Kuang, which spans a difficult time in Chinese history.

> On the next to last day of 1937, Alexandra was having a pleasant lunch on a terrace with a French doctor in Hankow, a port city up the Yangtse River. It had been nearly a year since she and her son had boarded the trans-Siberian express bound east. Six months earlier, the simmering tension between Japan and China had burst into the flames of war. Forces of the Rising Sun, already in control of Manchuria, advanced rapidly south to the Great Wall ... (Barbara and Michael Foster, *Forbidden City: the Life of Alexandra David-Neel,,* p. 275.)

(4) (a) Lotus grade: see Glossary.

(b) See the following passage on gathering the faculties together:

> The Method of Hearing is in keeping with the fundamental principle that if one sense-organ is intensely concentrated, all the other five sense-organs would be also held still automatically. This is the most fundamental tenet of the reciting method, as said in the *Surangama Sutra*: "when the six sense-organs are simultaneously held in concentration, there will be every pure thought in succession." (Hsu

Heng Chi, *What's Buddhism*, p. 56.)

(5) See Glossary for this important concept. Rebirth in the Pure Land is beyond Birth and Death.

(6) This relates to the Pure Land teaching that the practitioner must develop a dual frame of mind: revulsion toward the Saha World and longing for Enlightenment. Therefore the author has used two diametrically opposed examples. See the Patriarch Chih I, in *Pure Land Buddhism*, p. 31ff.

(7) As Susan Murcott has observed:

> To be born into a woman's body was considered a cause for special suffering on account of menstruation, childbirth and menopause ... (*The First Buddhist Women*, p. 78.)

(8) The ultimate goal of all Buddhist methods and practices is to escape Birth and Death and achieve Buddhahood, as the Buddhas did. This being the case, any other aspirations are mistaken and not in accord with the true intention of the Buddhas. Thus, such aspirations as rebirth as a male or as a king in the realms of gods and men, or even as a high-ranking master known far and wide, are questionable. These goals fall short of the ultimate aim of liberation. They can even be dangerous, given the weak nature of sentient beings, as power and influence provide the opportunity for heavy transgressions. Thus, the merits accrued in this lifetime are potential enemies of the third lifetime. See also Glossary under "Third Lifetime."

(9) Celestial realms in this text refers to the realms of the gods (beings superior to humans in merit and virtue). In Buddhist cosmology, there are two main divisions: realms subject to Birth and Death and realms beyond Birth and Death. Those realms still subject to Birth and Death include hell, animality, human and celestial realms, etc. The Buddha Realms/Lands (of which the Western Pure Land is part) are beyond the cycle of Birth and Death.

The Buddhas' assistance to true seekers of the Way is a process similar to osmosis. It requires utmost faith and sincerity (purity of mind) on the part of the cultivator. Only in this way will he and the Buddhas be on the same wave-length, with no barrier between them.

(10)   Full   benefits   of   the   Pure   Land   method: non-retrogression and ultimate Buddhahood.

Only in the Pure Land and higher realms, such as those of the Buddhas and Bodhisattvas, does the cultivator attain the stage of non-retrogression, at which point he is no longer subject to Birth and Death. Practicing Buddha Recitation with the wrong frame of mind (i.e., without sincerity or the Vow for rebirth in the Pure Land) will not prevent rebirth within samsara.

(11) Bodhi Mind: see Glossary. In this Letter, Master Yin Kuang refers only to developing the Bodhi Mind to rescue sentient beings.   He does not specifically mention saving oneself -- the basis of cultivation. This is because the concept of sentient beings includes the self and others. In the true spirit of Bodhisattvahood/Buddhahood there is no dichotomy between self and others.

(12) Buddha Recitation methods. There are, in general, four methods   of   Buddha   Recitation: Real   Mark   Buddha Recitation; Visualization; Contemplation of an Image; and oral recitation (Holding the Name).

Real Mark Buddha Recitation is, essentially, the Zen practice and entails "entering the Mind's foremost meaning, reciting our   own   Original   Buddha   Nature;"   *Visualization* (Contemplation by Thought) is the method taught in the *Meditation Sutra*, with its Sixteen Contemplations on the features of Amitabha Buddha and His Land of Ultimate Bliss; *Contemplation of an Image* requires the practitioner to face a statue of Amitabha Buddha and impress all the features of that statue in his memory, to the point where he clearly sees Amitabha Buddha all the time, whether his eyes are open or closed.

Oral recitation consists simply of reciting the words "Amitabha Buddha," either silently or aloud. The important point here is to have a truly earnest and reverent mind. In fact, this method is so popular that it is often considered synonymous with Pure Land practice. (For further details, see Master Thích Thiên Tâm, *Buddhism of Wisdom and Faith* sect. 29, p. 117.)

(13) Demons. Evil influences which hinder cultivation. These can take an infinite number of forms, including evil beings or hallucinations. See Glossary.

(14) See the following passage:

> The Ch'an [Zen] meditational practice, relying solely on self-effort, however, is no easy accomplishment, for according to the Dharma, if one is to liberate oneself from rebirth into the sixfold states of transmigration, it is necessary for him to remove subjective views, perceptions and conceptions totally and completely. (Hsu Heng Chi, *What's Buddhism?*, p. 22.)

(15) Receiving the precepts. There are many sets of precepts in Buddhism. All of them, however, can be summarized by three key Bodhisattva injunctions: *avoid all transgressions, perform all good deeds and be of benefit to all sentient beings.* The concept that receiving the precepts is not necessarily dependent upon their being administered by the clergy is a high-level teaching of Mahayana Buddhism, which emphasizes the all-encompassing Mind. Any practitioner who wishes to receive the precepts, and sincerely and earnestly accepts them, has in fact received them. This is in line with the teachings of the *Brahma Net Sutra* (see Glossary), though in the case of the Bodhisattva precepts (the loftiest and most difficult set of precepts), the witnessing of an auspicious sign (light, flowers, the Buddhas coming to rub one's crown, etc.) is additionally necessary:

> The twenty-third minor precept prohibits slighting others and speaking the Dharma in a biased manner ... Whenever a person with wholesome intention sincerely wishes to receive the Bodhisattva precepts, he should first vow, before the Buddha and Bodhisattva images, to accept and uphold the precepts and then cultivate repentance and reform for seven days. If during that period he experiences a vision of auspicious signs, he has received the precepts ... It is essential that he experience an auspicious sign, for only then has he received the precepts before the Buddha and Bodhisattva images. If he has not obtained such auspicious signs, though he may have vowed before the Buddha images to accept

and uphold the precepts, he has not actually received them ... (*The Buddha Speaks the Brahma Net Sutra [Brahma Net Sutra]*, Part II, Commentary by Elder Master Hui Sheng, p. 6.)

Auspicious signs attest to the utter sincerity and earnestness of the practitioner.

(16) All Buddhist methods lead ultimately to liberation. Most of these methods rely on self-effort. However, as human beings are limited in spiritual development and motivation, they can almost never escape Birth and Death in one lifetime, and are in danger of retrogression during transmigration. Pure Land teachings offer an easy method to escape Birth and Death in one lifetime through rebirth in the Pure Land, where practitioners can continue cultivating without fear of retrogression.

(17) The first Buddhist precept, binding upon clergy and laity alike, is not to kill -- and this includes not to kill oneself.

(18) In the Buddhist cosmology, the human and celestial realms are among the many realms subject to Birth and Death. Above these realms are those of the Arhats, Pratyeka Buddhas, Bodhisattvas and Buddhas. The Pure Lands are expedient realms of the Buddhas and as such are beyond Birth and Death.

(19) Our physical body is called the retribution body because we are on this earth, the World of Endurance, as a result of previous evil karma.

*
**

Letter 8.
Let Us Part Ways[1]

(Original letter to Elder Master Yin Kuang)

It took some ten years of Buddha Recitation for me to know something of its wonderful meaning. I venture to think that the Pure Land method, as taught in such writings as your Pure Land letters, is, in general, an expedient for ordinary people of limited capacities. However, if people like ourselves, who are fully literate and accustomed to exercising our minds, follow this method, we certainly cannot be reborn in the Pure Land! According to my limited understanding, those who recite the Buddha's name seeking rebirth in the Pure Land should first understand "who is reciting the Buddha's name," because only when we discover the real Master will Buddha Recitation have meaning and rebirth be assured. This does not apply only to Buddha Recitation. Anyone who recites sutras or chants mantras should also follow this path.

Nowadays, those who teach Buddha Recitation say that we should recite in a mature way with an utterly focussed, "as-if-dead" mind in order to achieve rebirth in the Pure Land. Do they not realize that if we are not clear as to "who is reciting the Buddha's name," we cannot recite in a mature way with an "as if dead" mind? Even if we were to recite one hundred thousand times each day,[2] such recitation would have no relationship to the issue of Birth and Death.

Some people even add that "ancient Masters generally concentrate on oral recitation rather than meditation on the Buddha's name." I, on the contrary, would say: "the ancients practiced oral recitation only after they had achieved success in meditation -- those of limited capacities should not try to emulate them." It is really too bad that, these days, nine out of ten practitioners fail to understand this point. I always do my utmost to caution people about this, but some laymen even think that I have wrong views. The subtle meaning of the Buddha Dharma has sunk to such depths that we can only lament and deplore the situation!

I am baring my heart to you today, and would beg you, Master, to certify my understanding and expand on this truth. This is for the benefit of everyone, and certainly not this writer alone.

o

oo

Answer:

I cannot exhaust my praise nor commend you and your friends enough for the thoughts behind your letter! You have very good intentions, wishing everyone to see his Original Nature[3] so as to achieve rebirth in the upper lotus grades.[4] The *Meditation Sutra* teaches:

Recite the Mahayana sutras, understand the Supreme Meaning, develop the Bodhi Mind, counsel and exhort others to cultivate.

This must certainly be your intention.

Nevertheless, the Dharma should be adapted to the level of the listener. If through failure to examine his level, you administer the wrong remedy, you will be no different from an incompetent physician who kills his patients with the wrong medicine. You should know that although the two Dharma methods, Pure Land and Zen, have the same root, the same source, their methods of cultivation are different.

The main tenet of Zen is to see one's Original Nature, while the teachings of Pure Land are Faith, Vows and Reciting the Buddha's name to achieve rebirth in the Pure Land. *If ordinary people today were of high capacities, your words would indeed be extremely beneficial.* However, on close examination, those of high capacities are few and far between while those of moderate and low capacities form the vast majority. This being the case, failing to teach people to develop Faith and Vows seeking rebirth in the Pure Land, while advising them to meditate on the Buddha's name, is utterly detrimental.[5]

This is because, while awakening to the Way through meditation would be a fortunate development, an utterly sincere Vow for rebirth in the Pure Land would still be necessary.[6]

Meanwhile, if meditation is unsuccessful and the mind constantly grasps at the koan (kung-an)[7] "who is reciting the Buddha's name,"[8] correspondence between the practitioner and the Buddha will be extremely difficult to realize and the benefit of the "welcoming and escorting" Vow will be lost.[9]

Those who really know "who is reciting the Buddha's name" are precisely those who have already awakened and clearly seen their True Nature. Nowadays, how many practitioners can meditate to the point of awakening to the Way ("Great Awakening")?[10]

However, let us not speak about others. Even you and your friends have not reached that level. How do I know? It is because if you had, you would never have dared to make such statements as those in your letter: "the Pure Land method is an expedient for ordinary people of limited capacities ...; not knowing who is reciting the Buddha's name is not reciting in a mature way with an as-if-dead mind ...; reciting a hundred thousand times a day has no relationship to the issue of Birth and Death ...;[11] the ancients practiced oral recitation only after they had achieved success in meditation -- those of limited capacities should not try to emulate them ... "

In truth, while your intention is to benefit yourself and others equally, through your words you have not only erred yourself, you have led others astray as well. From now on, please desist from such talk. Otherwise, you will slam the door on and bury the all-embracing method of the Buddhas to rescue sentient beings everywhere -- preventing this method from being known far and wide. Such a transgression is tantamount to vilifying the Buddhas, the Dharma and the Sangha. You should be careful indeed![12]

Since your understanding of the Dharma is not skillfully adapted to people's capacities, in that you attempt to bring a high-level Dharma to everyone, it is, in the end, a one-sided (biased) attachment -- and a great mistake! Not realizing this, you think that you have correctly understood the subtle meaning of the Dharma and therefore seek my certification. This monk, although lowly and not erudite, would not dare to commend, acquiesce in and support such a request, which would cause all of us to fall into the error of vilifying the Three Treasures!

If you do not believe the words of this old monk, let us part ways once and for all. I would not dare try forcing others to abandon their own ideas and understanding to follow my lowly thoughts. It is only because of your letter that I have reluctantly offered some frank though limited views.

I hope that you will reflect deeply and broadly on this letter.

NOTES TO LETTER 8

(1) Letter to the layman Wang Yu-mu. (Chinese ed. Vol. I, p. 196; VN ed., p. 80)

In this important letter, Master Yin Kuang reiterates the Pure Land view that to teach so rigorous and exacting a method as Zen to those other than the most spiritually advanced is questionable. This is because, being incapable of following it, ordinary practitioners might abandon cultivation altogether or else hop from one method and teacher to another, deriving no real benefit from any of them.

This is clearly shown in a letter to Master Ching Hsiu, in which Master Yin Kuang stated: "There is no shorter or more direct way to reach the fruit of the Sages than Zen. However, in this day and age, it is difficult enough to *achieve Awakening*, much less *attain Enlightenment*, in one lifetime through the practice of Zen."

(2) One hundred thousand recitations a day: this number of recitations is mentioned in several Pure Land commentaries as a goal for the most assiduous cultivators.

(3) Original Nature: see Glossary under "Buddha Nature."

(4) Lotus grades: in Pure Land Buddhism the practitioner can be reborn after death in one of nine grades. These grades depend on his diligence and level of mental concentration during practice. The higher grades are for those who have attained samadhi during their lifetimes. See *Meditation Sutra,* one of the core sutras of Pure Land.

(5) See the following passage:

> In the Dharma-Ending Age, how many cultivators can claim to be awakened to the Way? Awakening to the Way is not easy. There was once a Zen Master who practiced with all his might for forty years before he succeeded. Another Great Master sat for so long that he wore out more than a dozen meditation cushions before he saw his Original Nature. As far as today's Zen practitioners are concerned, with the exception of a few saints who have taken human form to teach sentient beings, the majority only manage to achieve a temporary calming of the mind and body; at most they may witness a few auspicious realms! Even if they have awakened to the Way, they can still encounter dangerous obstacles during transmigration, as described above. The path of birth and death, filled with fearful dangers for those who have not attained the Way, is the same. Therefore, to claim that we should not fear birth and death is merely the viewpoint of shallow and superficial minds. (Master Thích Thiên Tâm, *Buddhism of Wisdom and Faith*, sect. 13, p. 54.)

(6) An awakened person is still within the cycle of Birth and Death. This is because while his greed, anger and delusion may have temporarily settled to the bottom, these evil sediments are not yet entirely eliminated; they can be stirred up at any time. According to Pure Land teaching, to escape the cycle within one lifetime, the cultivator needs to seek rebirth in the Pure Land. For rebirth to be achieved, there must be a correspondence between Amitabha Buddha and the practitioner -- thus the need for an utterly sincere vow on the latter's part.

(7) Koan (kung-an):

> In Zen, a koan is a phrase from a sutra or teaching on Zen realization, an episode from the life of an ancient master ... each pointing to the nature of ultimate reality. Essential to a koan is paradox, i.e., that which is "beyond thinking," which transcends the logical or conceptual. Thus, since it cannot be solved by reason, a koan is not a riddle. Solving a koan requires a leap to another level of comprehension. (*Shambhala Dictionary of Buddhism and Zen*, p. 117.)

(8) In this connection, see the following passage:

> The business of studying Zen is the epitome of the mystic device of transcendence. It is not possible for those who take it easy. You must generate great bravery and great energy. You also must stop thoughts, forget entangling objects and gather in your seeing and hearing and turn them back [onto inherent reality]. You must take your everyday views of

good and evil, your likes and dislikes, and your sentiments of affirmation and denial, and totally sweep them away ... It is like one man battling ten thousand men: there is no time to blink, no time to hesitate in doubt. If you can really generate this kind of adamant, fierce will-power, you have the mettle to study Zen. Once you have the mettle to study Zen, take hold of the phrase "Amitabha Buddha" as if you are resting on the Polar Mountain* and cannot be shaken. Concentrate your mind and unify your attention. Recite the buddha-name a few times, turn the light back and observe yourself, asking: Who is this one reciting the buddha-name? (J.C. Cleary, *Pure Land, Pure Mind.* Unpub. manuscript.)

(*In Buddhist cosmology, a polar mountain is the center of a world system. There are countless world systems and our world is an infinitesimal part of one world system.)

(9) See the following passage:

Nothing prevents people who study Zen and who investigate inherent mind moment to moment from taking vows to be reborn in the Land of Ultimate Bliss when their lives here are over.

Why is this? Though one may have an awakening by studying Zen, if one is as yet unable to abide in the eternal quiescent light like the buddhas, and is still not free of subsequent existence like the arhats, then when this physical body is used up, one is sure to be reborn. (Zen Master Chu Hung in J.C. Cleary, *Pure Land, Pure Mind.*)

(10) Note the essential difference between awakening to the Way and the concept of attaining Enlightenment.

(11) This statement shows that the letter-writer does not yet have a deep understanding of Pure Land teachings. Since everything originates in the mind and is mind-created, any recitation, however distracted, bears some relationship to Birth and Death. (This relationship is, however, very tenuous as long as the mind is not empty and still during recitation.) This is the basis of popular Pure land teaching: recite as much as possible, the rare moments of concentration will add up and in time the wandering, monkey mind will return home!

(12) Everything in Buddhism is expedient and as such should be adapted to the practitioner and his times. According to Pure Land teachings, the present time, some twenty-six centuries after the death of Buddha Sakyamuni, is a time of great spiritual degeneration and perverse, "upside down"

thinking. This is referred to in Buddhist teaching as the Degenerate Age of the Dharma or Dharma-Ending Age. (See Glossary.)

The concept of the Degenerate Age implied in this letter is a general teaching of Buddhism found in Pure Land as well as other schools, such as Zen. See, for example, the *Diamond Sutra* (sect. 6 in the translation by A.F. Price and Wong Mou-lam).

*
**

Letter 9.
Amitabha Buddha -- the
Boundless Self-Nature of Light and Life[1]

Since we parted in mid-spring, time has flown by, and it is now summer. The light of springtime has passed swiftly -- a frightening reminder indeed![2]

Each time I think of the two of you, I recall that despite your true and sincere faith, you lack sufficient understanding of the Dharma, to the point where you have abandoned the lofty ground to follow lowly, dark paths. Not only have you lost correct views and become yourselves a topic of ridicule, even this old monk is embarrassed by the bad reputation he has acquired for being an acquaintance of yours!

In your letter, you mentioned the possibility of having me correct some of your future writings. However, with my weak eyes and bad health, I do not normally take to writing. Even if my advice is needed, whatever I put down is nothing but a heap of empty words. What is there which is worth reading? Still, lest I seem ungrateful for your trust, I am tentatively setting forth some leftover soup and stale rice.[3] If you do not object to the smell, perhaps they can temporarily assuage your hunger until the time when you can taste the exquisite food of the Self-Nature.

o
oo

The verse "Four Options"[4] is very profound and worthy of attention. You should ponder it carefully. By all means do not take it lightly on the basis of the shallow explanations of a few persons, or you will fail to appreciate the great compassionate mind of Master Yung Ming, who has exhausted words and counsel. The treatise *The Benefits of Reciting the Sutras Depend on One's Mind* was written because people today recite the sutras without the least bit of reverence. The true benefit of the Buddha Dharma is found in a reverent mind. Such a state of mind can even lead to swift Supreme Enlightenment -- not to mention the lower levels of sagehood (Arhats and Pratyeka Buddhas)![5]

o
oo

The Pure Land Patriarch Shan Tao, traditionally considered a Transformation Body of Amitabha Buddha,[6] was endowed with great spiritual powers and wisdom. However, in teaching Pure Land, he did not advocate the mystical and sublime but merely emphasized everyday, ordinary realities.[7] His teachings on Exclusive Practice and Sundry Practices are extremely useful.

Exclusive Practice consists of the body bowing exclusively to Amitabha Buddha, the mouth exclusively repeating the Buddha's name, and the mind focussing exclusively on the Buddha's name. Out of ten thousand cultivators who practice in such a manner, ten thousand are assured of rebirth in the Pure Land.

Sundry Practices entail engaging in various methods of cultivation while dedicating the merits accrued toward rebirth in the Western Land. Since the practitioner's mind is not focussed or singleminded, it is difficult to accumulate merits. Thus, only three or four out of hundreds of thousands can hope to achieve rebirth in the Pure Land. These are true, golden words of advice, immutable throughout the ages. Both of you should follow them for your own benefit and in counselling everyone else.

Reciting mantras, too, should be considered an ancillary practice, rather than a principal method along with Buddha Recitation. The merits derived from mantra recitation are indeed inconceivable. However, ordinary people who achieve rebirth in the Pure Land owe it entirely to utterly sincere Faith and Vows, as these correspond to the lofty Vows of Amitabha Buddha. If you are not clear about this truth, thinking that all Dharmas are inconceivable and therefore it does not matter which method you cultivate, you will end up practicing neither Zen nor Pure Land. This will lead to eons of wandering in the wasteland of Birth and Death -- whom, then, could you rely on for help?

You should realize that as a common being full of karmic obstructions, you will certainly find it difficult to escape Birth and Death in this very life unless you rely on the Vows of Amitabha Buddha. Only then will you discover that the Pure Land method surpasses other Dharma methods in power and utility![8]

Reciting mantras and sutras for the purpose of sowing merits and wisdom and eliminating evil karma and transgressions is all to the good. However, to be deluded and seek spiritual powers is to abandon the roots for the branches -- an error in judgement. If, furthermore, your mind is grasping, your understanding of the Dharma nebulous, your precept-keeping lax, your Bodhi Mind undeveloped and your discriminatory, win-lose mind raging unchecked, you will be exposed one day to demons that may drive you insane!

If you want to obtain spiritual powers, you should first attain Enlightenment. Once Enlightenment is attained, you will naturally have full spiritual powers. If you do not strive for the Way but merely seek spiritual powers, let us not even speak about whether anything can be gained. If you should obtain anything, it would become an impediment to the Way.[9] For this reason, the Buddhas and Patriarchs have strictly prohibited this erroneous form of cultivation. Because such ideas are common, I have taken the opportunity to mention them in passing.

o
oo

Both of you still have your parents at home. Therefore, you should keep explaining the Pure Land method and the accounts of rebirth[10] to them, so that they may develop the mind of joy, believe in the accounts and follow the examples therein. If you do not repay your filial debts in this way, even if you are filial in the mundane sense, what good will it do your parents at the end of their lives? ... You should wake up and hasten to ensure that, at death, your parents will participate in the Lotus Assembly. They will then be close to Amitabha Buddha and achieve the boundless Self-Nature of *light and life*.[11]

The sufferings of the Saha World are endless. Even in time of peace, sentient beings are jostling one another in an atmosphere of sorrow and affliction. However, because they have endured it for so long, they have grown accustomed to it and are no longer aware of it.[12] In China recently, insurrection and strife have become daily events; the sufferings of the people are beyond description! Abroad, a great war has been raging for three years. With casualties already legion, the world conflict goes on with no end in sight. This tragic situation is caused by the karma of sentient beings and is the precursor of an extended period of disturbances to come. It is truly frightening to think of the sufferings of the future!

I hope that both of you will develop the Great Mind and seek rebirth in the Pure Land, to achieve the fruits of Enlightenment swiftly before returning to the Saha World to rescue sentient beings. The sutras teach:

> Bodhisattvas fear causes, sentient beings fear effects and results.

Bodhisattvas, being wary of evil results, eliminate evil causes. Sentient beings all too often vie to create evil causes and then have to endure evil results. When enduring suffering, they do not know enough to practice repentance, but create more evil karma in the hope of escaping retribution. Thus, injustice and retribution follow upon one another continuously, without end. It is so pitiful and frightening to think about it![13]

Knowing this truth, those who do not seek rebirth in the Pure Land are not yet truly among the wise![14]

NOTES TO LETTER 9.

(1) Letter to two brothers in Yungchia. (Chinese ed. Vol. I, p. 85; VN ed., p. 29)

(2) Frightening because it reflects impermanence, the evanescence of life. Buddha Sakyamuni became an ascetic after seeing a corpse, among other sad realities of life. In fact, a Pratyeka (Self-Enlightened) Buddha may be defined as one who "awaken[s] ... to the truth of impermanence by observing natural phenomena such as the scattering of blossoms or the falling of leaves." (*A Dictionary of Buddhist Terms and Concepts*, p. 344.)

(3) Stale rice. This is a reference to a well-known story about Buddha Sakyamuni's disciple Visakha, who once said:

> "When a certain Bhikkhu was standing at the door for alms, my father-in-law was eating sweet milk rice-porridge, ignoring him. Thinking to myself that my father-in-law, without performing any good deed in this life, is only consuming the merits of past deeds, I told the Bhikku: 'Pass on Venerable Sir, my father-in-law is eating stale fare ...'"
> (Narada, *The Buddha and His Teachings*, p. 101.)

Most people go through life consuming "stale fare," as they enjoy the results of their past merits without thought of creating new ones. For example, a wealthy person (i.e., one who practiced charity in past lives) spending time and money on himself alone, without thoughts of charity, is eating stale fare.

This concept is also related to the idea that merits accrued in the first lifetime are potential enemies of the third lifetime. In the first lifetime, the practitioner engages in wholesome actions which bring blessings (wealth, power, authority, etc.) in the second lifetime. Since wealth and power tend to corrupt, he is likely to create evil karma, resulting in retribution in the third lifetime.

(4) Four Options: see the following partial translation of these well-known verses:

> "With both dhyana [Zen] and the Pure Land
> One is like a tiger with horns;
> In the present age a teacher of man,
> In the future a Buddhist Patriarch.
>
> With dhyana but without the Pure Land

Nine out of ten will take the wrong road;
Without dhyana and with only the Pure Land,
If ten thousand practice, ten thousand will go [the right way]."
(Hsuan Hua, *Pure Land & Ch'an Dharma Talks*,
p. 23-24.)

(5) Yung Ming (904-975). The eminent Zen Master Yung Ming is the best known advocate of the harmonization of Zen and Pure Land.

Note: in Buddhism, the *sine qua non* for Enlightenment and Buddhahood is a pure mind, that is, a mind free of greed, anger and delusion. In Pure Land Buddhism, the usual terminology is a mind of utmost sincerity, devotion and earnestness or one-pointedness of mind. This is because when the cultivator focusses singlemindly on Amitabha Buddha, he cannot harbor thoughts of greed, anger or delusion.

(6) Shan Tao (613-681) was the third Patriarch of the Pure Land school in China. His teachings particularly influenced Honen, the founder of the Japanese Pure Land school.

Transformation Body: See Glossary under "Three Bodies of the Buddha."

(7) This is an interesting common point between Zen and Pure Land. The Sixth Patriarch, Hui Neng, for instance, taught that when a cultivator splits wood, fetches water, etc. with a pure mind, i.e., a mind free of the three poisons of greed, anger and delusion -- this is Zen. This is also the *ultimate* (transcendental) teaching of Pure Land.

(8) See the following passage:

Han-shan Te-Ch'ing [1546-1623, the best known Zen Master of late Ming times, considered by some to be at the level of a Patriarch] ... on the one hand ... regards the Western Paradise as the most expedient land in the innumerable Hua-yen pure lands. On the other hand, he seems to have considered the Pure Land teaching as a special teaching that lies outside the usual scheme of classification. So far as the exercise of Buddha-recitation as a kung-an is concerned, however, there is no doubt that, for Han-shan, this practice belongs to the "abrupt doctrine" as does Ch'an [Zen]. (Hsu Sung-peng, *A Buddhist Leader in Ming*

China, p. 149.)

(9) Important teaching in Buddhism. During His lifetime, Buddha Sakyamuni discouraged the display of spiritual powers. Once, the story goes, He was waiting at the river's edge for a boat to take him across. An ascetic, passing by, showed off his spiritual powers, crossing the river back and forth by treading over the water. The Buddha then asked him, "How long did it take you to acquire such powers?" "Thirty years," was the reply. The Buddha then said, "Thirty years of effort? Well, I can cross the river for a five-cent fare."

It may be added that for a person still subject to excessive greed, anger and delusion to have access to unusual powers could be harmful to himself and dangerous to society at large.

(10) Accounts of rebirth: see the following passage:

> Pure Land literature offers many stories presented as real life biographical accounts which corroborate the description of the Pure Land paradise drawn from the scriptures. Like most Buddhist biographies, these accounts are very terse, and focus on the subject's religious life. There are stories of men and women, monks and nuns, nobles and high officials and commoners, young and old, all devoted to Pure Land practice ... The climax of a Pure Land biography comes in the subject's death scene, when buddha-name recitation is rewarded and the Pure Land teachings are confirmed. The believer dies peacefully, even joyously, with mind and body composed, in full confidence of rebirth in paradise, reciting the buddha-name. Often the Pure Land devotee is able to predict his own death in advance, and calmly bid farewell to loved ones. Sometimes the believer receives reassuring visits from Amitabha in dreams or visions to prepare him to face the end. (J.C. Cleary, *Pure Land, Pure Mind*, Introduction. Unpub. manuscript.)

(11) Amitabha Buddha is the Buddha of Infinite Light and Life. Our enlightened Self-Nature, intrinsically bright and everlasting, is, therefore, Amitabha Buddha. This is the rationale for Buddha Recitation at the noumenon (transcendental) level.

(12) This paragraph provides a good description of the Saha World, the World of Endurance.

(13) Poverty and want, for example, are the results of miserly

thoughts and actions in past lives. For a destitute person to cheat and steal in order to escape poverty and become wealthy is a classic case of creating more evil karma in the hope of escaping retribution.

(14) This statement is an example of the Buddhist approach to teaching the Dharma. Each method (Pure Land, Zen ...) "has its own area of emphasis. Those who propagate a Dharma door direct all expedient teaching toward that method." (Master Thích Thiền Tâm, *Buddhism of Wisdom and Faith*, 2nd ed., Preface.)

*
**

Letter 10. The Pure Mind is Bodhi[1]

From your letter, I see that you are diligently fighting bad habits but have not yet obtained results. This is because you are not truly concerned about the issue of Birth and Death,[2] nor have you internalized the method that helps people to "transcend the human realm for that of the saints," sever delusive karma and achieve pure thoughts.[3] That is why you have failed to achieve true results.

You should always ponder this truth: "It is difficult to be reborn as a human being, it is difficult to learn of the Buddha Dharma, it is difficult to encounter the Pure Land method. I am fortunate today to have been reborn as a human being and am in the favorable position of having learned about the Pure Land method. How dare I waste this limited lifespan on evanescent form, fragrance, fame and fortune? How can I resign myself to an empty life and useless death, wallowing along the six evil paths -- with no end in sight?"

You should paste the word "death" on your

forehead, so that when you meet with various circumstances unworthy of attachment, you will immediately recognize them as boiling cauldrons and firepits that can only harm you.[4] In this way, you will not be like a moth, freely choosing to fly into the flame and burning to death.

o

oo

You should realize that worthwhile activities are a boat of compassion to rescue you from suffering. Thus, you will no longer shy away from opportunities for charity and justice nor be dilatory on the path of cultivation. In this manner, mundane circumstances can also become conditions for entering the Way, as cultivation is not synonymous with abandoning all worldly activities. If the mind is firm and not swayed by circumstances, "ordinary, everyday activities are precisely liberation."[5] Therefore, the *Diamond Sutra* always teaches "non-attachment to form." Although true cultivators develop the aspiration to rescue all sentient beings, they do not see themselves as the rescuers or sentient beings as the rescued.[6] Even when Supreme Enlightenment is attained, there is no mark of who has attained the fruits of Ultimate Nirvana. This is true cultivation of the Bodhisattva path.

On the other hand, even rescuing sentient beings or cultivating the ten thousand virtues cannot be in accord with the True Mark Supreme Vehicle[7] unless practitioners realize that sentient beings are, *in their nature and essence*, Buddhas.[8] Amid Equal Nature, sentient beings erroneously develop the mind of discrimination, turning "unconditioned" benefits into "conditioned" merits.[9] How, then, can they escape the binding cycle of form, fame and fortune?

o
oo

Living in this world, people all have obligations. However, you should not take on unnecessary activities beyond your normal duties. Instead, use your free time, according to your capacities and circumstances, to recite sutras and the Buddha's name, determined to achieve rebirth in the Pure Land. You can generate merits and virtues by contributing financially to worthwhile activities or by praising those who engage in them. You can also accrue merits by developing a mind of joy and contentment at their accomplishment by others.[10]

All such merits and virtues should be dedicated as additional aids to rebirth in the Pure Land.[11] It is like a boat which not only sails with the wind but also has oarsmen to speed it on its way. How can it fail to return swiftly to the shore?[12]

o
oo

The last day of the twelfth month is the end of the year. If by that day you have not made advance preparations, how can you avoid your creditors? The time of death is precisely the last day of the twelfth month of a life; if you are not ready with the personal provisions of Faith, Vows and Practice, and are still filled with the evil karma of greed, anger and delusion, those whom you have wronged, your creditors from time immemorial, will come pushing and shoving one another for repayment. Those who are unaware of the Pure Land method can do nothing but follow their evil karma, while even Pure Land practitioners who do not cultivate truly and earnestly sink into evil realms, mired in the cycle of Birth and Death for eons and eons.

The key to escaping suffering is to develop, in each and every thought, a fear of death and of perdition along the evil paths after death.[13] Buddha Recitation then naturally grows more earnest, rebirth in the Pure Land is assured and no worldly dusts can "plunder" correct thought.

The *Heart Sutra* states:

> The Bodhisattva Avalokitesvara clearly perceived that the five skandas[14] are all empty and thus overcame all suffering.

The five skandas encompass body and mind as well as the external environment. If we truly realize that they are empty, we are already free of them -- even while remaining part of them. What, then, is not the Great Liberation method, the realm of Great Nirvana?

NOTES TO LETTER 10

(1) Letter to a layman in Ningpo. (Chinese ed. Vol. II, p. 244; VN ed., p. 82)

(2) See the following passage on the thoughts of the eminent Master Han-Shan, one of the "Dragon-Elephants" of Ming Buddhism:

> Students in this age of the decay of the Dharma are superficial in their learning. They do not understand the real truth. Thus, in their study of Buddhist scriptures, they cling to famous sayings and fail to comprehend the ultimate truth. They increase their (relative) knowledge and become boastful of their achievement. They produce increased karmas leading to a continuation of the cycle of life and death precisely by means of Buddhist teachings. This is because they did not start with the question of life and death when they began to search for the Mind. (Han-Shan Te-Ch'ing, in Sung-peng Hsu, *A Buddhist Leader in Ming China*, p. 126.)

See also this famous traditional story, taken from the *Therigatha (Psalms of the Sisters)*:

> Kisagotami was married to a banker's son of considerable wealth. As a young wife, Kisagotami was mistreated by her in-laws ... When she gave birth to a son, she finally received an honorable place among her husband's relatives. But her child died while still a toddler and Kisagotami, who had never seen death before, went mad.
>
> In her state of insanity, Kisagotami took up the dead child and carried him on her hip from house to house, begging for medicine. One kind old man directed her to Buddha Sakyamuni.
>
> The Buddha said, "Go and bring a white mustard seed from a house where no one has died." Hearing his words, she immediately rushed off in the innocent faith that, if she brought a white mustard seed to this enlightened sage, it would be the medicine that could miraculously bring her child back to life.
>
> Kisagotami went from house to house, at each house asking, and at each house learning that there too, someone had died. The truth struck home. Her sanity returned.
>
> "Little son," she said. "I thought that death had happened to you alone; but it is not to you alone. It is common to all people." ... She carried him gently to the forest and left him there. (Susan Murdock, *The First Buddhist Women*, p. 85.)

(3) Pure thoughts: this is the most important criterion on the list. In Pure Land practice, pure thoughts are achieved through singleminded Buddha Recitation.

(4) See the following passage:

> The first principle of Ch'an [Zen] practice is to empty one's mind. One must first paste the two words "life-death" on the forehead, and regard them as seriously as if one owed a debt of a million taels. In day or night, while drinking or eating, traveling or staying at home, sitting or lying, entertaining friends, in a quiet moment or at a noisy hour, you must hold on to the ... [koan]. (Zen Master Han-Shan Te-Ch'ing, in Sung-peng Hsu, *A Buddhist Leader in Ming China*, p. 130.)

(5) This is an expression particularly popular in Zen.

(6) This is a key teaching of the *Prajnaparamita Sutras*, of which the *Diamond* and *Heart Sutras* are summaries. There are no

"rescuers" or "rescued" because the Bodhisattvas have transcended the notion of a separate ego and separate dharmas; Bodhisattvas and sentient beings are like fingers of the same hand. See also the following passage:

> Since that which is real includes nothing worth begrudging, they [Bodhisattvas] give their body, life, and property in charity, without regret, without the vanity of giver, gift or recipient, and without bias or attachment ... And as with charity, they also practice the other virtues. But while practicing the six virtues [paramitas] to eliminate delusion, they practice nothing at all. [Because they have renounced all notions of a separate ego.] This is what's meant by practicing the Dharma. ("Outline of practice" in Red Pine, tr., *The Zen Teaching of Bodhidharma*, p. 7.)

(7) True Mark Supreme Vehicle: the vehicle of Buddhahood, or Supreme, Perfect Enlightenment.

(8) This is a key Mahayana concept, particularly emphasized in Zen.

(9) Conditioned benefits or merits ("merits with outflow") are the blessings of this world, such as wealth, power, longevity, etc. Unconditioned benefits or merits ("merits without outflow") refers to Truth, Nirvana, True Mark, Dharma Realm, etc. ... Turning unconditioned merits into conditioned merits is a common delusion of sentient beings.

Mind of discrimination: the ordinary mind of human beings, constantly making distinctions between right and wrong, the self and others, etc. Such a mind can never fully comprehend the Ultimate Truth -- one and indivisible. The silence of Vimalakirti (see Glossary) illustrates this point.

(10) Important point. In Buddhist teaching, charity, for example, does not necessarily imply an act of actual giving. Thus, anyone, however poor, can practice charity. Buddhist virtues can be achieved by everyone, whatever their means or limitations.

(11) They are additional aids because in Pure Land, the main practice should always be reciting the Buddha's name or meditation on the Buddha.

(12) Returning to the shore: a metaphor for returning to the True Nature, the nature common to sentient beings and Buddhas, the True Mind.

(13) See the following advice to Zen practitioners:

> Dear friends, the murderous demon of impermanence is constantly looking for our lives and will never agree to conclude peace with us! Let us hastily develop a long enduring mind to get out of birth and death. Master Yuan Miao of Kao Feng said: "If one sets a time limit for success in the Ch'an [Zen] training, one should act like a man who has fallen to the bottom of a pit one thousand *chang* [about two miles] deep. His thousand and ten-thousand thoughts are reduced to a single idea on how to escape from the pit. He keeps it up from morning to evening and from evening (to the following morning), and has no other thought. If he trains in this way and does not realize the truth in three, five or seven days, I shall be guilty of a verbal sin for which I shall fall into the hell where tongues are pulled out." ("The Ch'an Training" by Master Hsu Yun, p. 42.)

(14) Five Skandas: represent both body and mind. See Glossary.

*
**

Letter 11.
Awakening is Still within the
Realm of Birth and Death[1]

To receive true benefits in this very life, the practitioner should follow the Pure Land method, reciting the Buddha's name with Faith and Vows, seeking rebirth in the Land of Ultimate Bliss. Escape from the wasteland of Birth and Death will then be assured. Otherwise, not only will those who have not received the true transmission of the Dharma fail to achieve liberation, even those who have received it will have no hope of achieving liberation! This is because to receive the true transmission of the Dharma is to *awaken to the Way* but not to *attain Enlightenment*. Only by attaining Enlightenment will you escape the cycle of Birth and Death. Awakening to the Way is still within that cycle.[2]

Cultivating other methods requires severance of karmic obstructions and attainment of the Truth before you can escape Birth and Death.[3] With the Pure Land method, you need only recite the Buddha's name with deep Faith and earnest Vows, while ceasing transgressions and performing good deeds -- thus engaging simultaneously in the main and subsidiary practices[4] -- in order to be assured of rebirth in the Western Land. In fact, the highest level of rebirth will be achieved.

o
oo

Not only are those who have perfected Pure Land practice assured of rebirth, even those guilty of the five grave offenses and the ten evil acts[5] can also achieve it (as long as, on the verge of death, they awaken, become utterly ashamed of their transgressions, grow frightened and recite the Buddha's name in utmost sincerity a few times).[6] This is because Amitabha Buddha has great, all-embracing compassion and considers it His calling to rescue sentient beings. Anyone who sincerely seeks His assistance will be gathered in and rescued. This is called "taking one's karma along to the Pure Land, through the power of Amitabha Buddha."[7]

In this Dharma-Ending Age, if you cultivate other methods, abandoning the Dharma Door of Pure Land, you can only reap merits and blessings in the celestial and human realms[8] or sow the causes and conditions of liberation in future eons. This is because few in this day and age truly have the strength to sever all karmic obstructions. Therefore the roots of Birth and Death continue to exist. Under these circumstances, how can you prevent the dream-like[9] seeds of Birth and Death from sprouting anew?[10]

NOTES TO LETTER 11

(1) Letter to the layman Yueh Hsien-ch'iao. (Chinese ed. Vol. II, p. 247; VN ed., p. 84)

(2) This distinction between "awakening to the Way" ("Great Awakening") and "attainment of Enlightenment" is very important, because only when a cultivator has attained Enlightenment will he escape Birth and Death. There are many degrees of awakening and Enlightenment, up to Supreme, Perfect Enlightenment, i.e., the Enlightenment of the Buddhas.

In other words, to awaken to the Way means to achieve (through Zen meditation, Buddha Recitation, etc.) a complete and deep understanding of what it means to be a Buddha and how to reach Buddhahood. It is to see one's Nature, comprehend the True Nature of things, the Truth. However, only after becoming a Buddha can one be said to have truly achieved Enlightenment. (See also Master Thích Thiên Tâm, *Buddhism of Wisdom and Faith*, sect. 13, p. 54-5.)

(3) See the following passage:

> We should know, furthermore, that to escape birth and death, we must sever delusions of views and thought. However, according to the ancients, "blocking delusions of views is as difficult as blocking a raging stream coming from forty miles away." Why, then, even mention eliminating all delusions of thought? Thus, if we want to achieve liberation in this Dharma-Ending Age, the most appropriate method is Buddha Recitation. This is because, through this method, the

cultivator, after utilizing his self-power to the utmost, receives additional assistance from other-power. Even though his karma and delusions are not yet extinguished, he can, through Amitabha Buddha's power of welcoming and escorting, "take his residual karma along" to the Pure Land. Once reborn, he will no longer retrogress and will have transcended birth and death forever!

... In the *Great Heap Sutra* and the *Longer Amitabha Sutra*, Sakyamuni Buddha, with his profound wisdom and compassion, predicted the low capacities and evil conditions of people in the Dharma-Ending Age as well as the efficacy and appropriateness of the Pure Land method. Therefore, in this Degenerate Age, when the capacity of Dharma methods to bring people to Enlightenment "in this very life" has declined, only the Pure Land method can prolong the turning of the Dharma wheel and save sentient beings. Other Dharma methods, such as Zen, Sutra Studies, Precept Keeping and Esotericism, while still taught and followed by many, can play only a supporting role. They cannot, by themselves, produce results along the path of liberation. In a letter to a fellow monk, Elder Master Yin Kuang expressed it this way: "Deep into the Dharma-Ending Age, when practicing other methods, we may speak of sowing good seeds and creating favorable conditions for Enlightenment in the future, but we cannot speak of attaining Buddhahood and achieving liberation in this very lifetime." (Master Thích Thiên Tâm, *Buddhism of Wisdom and Faith*, sect. 54, p. 226.)

(4) Main practice: Buddha Recitation, meditation on Amitabha Buddha ...

Subsidiary practices: all wholesome actions and practices other than Buddha Recitation, as long as the merits are dedicated to rebirth in the Pure Land (e.g., precept-keeping, charity, mantra and sutra recitation, etc.).

(5) Five Grave Offenses, Ten Evil Acts. This is a reference to such unthinkable trangressions as killing one's parents, causing disharmony within the Sangha, taking the life of an Arhat or saint, etc. See also Glossary.

(6) See *Meditation Sutra*, Sixteenth Meditation. The two operative phrases here are "on the verge of death" and "utmost sincerity." When a wicked person, on his deathbed, senses evil omens arising from his subconscious and he sees no possible alternative, a mind of utter sincerity and devotion is sometimes possible. Such a frame of mind is practically impossible to develop in the course of everyday life. The

following story provides a good illustration of this point.

There was once a Zen monk meditating on a deserted mountain far away from all human habitation. Because of the rigors of the climate and the isolation of the place, he found it difficult to concentrate. His mind constantly wandered toward life in the village down below. One evening, as he was seated lost in errant thought, he had the sensation that he was being watched. He slowly turned his head, and lo and behold, there was a tiger crouched in the bushes behind him! One false move and the tiger would pounce on him. He had no choice but to remain ramrod straight, in singleminded concentration. When dawn broke, the tiger, fearful of the light of day, gave up this cat-and-mouse game and disappeared. The next two evenings, the monk, faithful to his vows, resumed his meditation at the appointed time and place. The tiger returned and the scene repeated itself each evening. When daylight came on the third day, the monk, after three nights of *singleminded concentration*, experienced a Great Awakening, collapsed and died. At his funeral, it was reported that a tiger was seen watching and wailing in the distance.

(7) See the following passage:

> There is a parable in the *Questions of King Milinda*:
>
> > "A minute grain of sand, dropped on the surface of the water, will sink immediately. On the other hand, a block of stone, however large and heavy, can easily be moved from place to place by boat. The same is true of the Pure Land practitioner. However light his karma may be, if he is not rescued by Amitabha Buddha, he must revolve in the cycle of Birth and Death. With the help of the Buddha, his karma, however heavy, will not prevent his rebirth in the Pure Land."
>
> We can see from this passage that, thanks to "other-power," the Pure Land method can help the practitioner "bring his karma along" to the Pure Land. The huge block of stone represents the weight of heavy karma, the boat symbolizes the power of the Buddha's Vows. Therefore, the cultivator should not think that residual greed, anger and delusion will prevent him from being reborn ... (Master Thích Thiên Tâm, *Buddhism of Wisdom and Faith*, sect. 68 A., p. 284.)

(8) Enjoying merits and blessings in the human and celestial

realms is not a desideratum in Buddhism. These realms are still within the cycle of Birth and Death, while the real goal of Buddhist cultivation is to transcend Birth and Death and achieve Buddhahood.

(9) Dreamlike: cf. *Diamond Sutra*, "All mundane phenomena are like dreams, illusions, bubbles, shadows."

(10) A similar metaphor appearing in the sutras is that of a glass of water containing sediments. As long as the glass is undisturbed, the sediments remain at the bottom and the water is clear. However, as soon as the glass is shaken, the water becomes turbid. Likewise, when a practitioner experiences a "Great Awakening" (awakens to the Way), his afflictions (greed, anger and delusion) are temporarily suppressed but not yet eliminated. To achieve Enlightenment (i.e., to be rid of all afflictions, to discard all the sediments) is the ultimate goal. Only then can he completely trust his mind and actions. Before then, he should adhere to the precepts, keep a close watch on his mind and thoughts, like a cat watching a mouse, ready to pounce on evil thoughts as soon as they arise.

See also Glossary, "Delusions of Views and Thought."

*
**

Letter 12.
Pure Land and Mind-Only[1]

Question One: Are the Self-Nature Amitabha and the Mind-Only Pure Land the same or different from the Pure Land and the Buddha in the Western Pure Land?

Answer: It is because the Mind-Only Pure Land

exists that we are reborn in the Pure Land of the West. If the mind is not pure, it is impossible to achieve rebirth in the Pure Land. Even when those who have committed cardinal transgressions achieve rebirth through ten recitations, such rebirth is due to their reciting the Buddha's name with a *pure mind*, thus eliciting a response.

Ordinary people generally think that if the Pure Land is Mind-Only, then it does not exist.[2] This is the understanding of demons and externalists.[3] Such a deluded view, which appears correct but is in reality wrong, affects more than half of all people and causes practitioners to forfeit true benefits.

It is precisely because of the Self-Nature Amitabha that the practitioner must recite the name of Buddha Amitabha of the West seeking rebirth in the Pure Land -- so as to achieve the Self-Nature Amitabha through gradual cultivation. If he merely grasps at the Self-Nature Amitabha but does not recite the name of Buddha Amitabha of the West, he cannot achieve immediate escape from Birth and Death -- not even if he is truly awakened, much less if (like most people who ask this question) he is pretentious and just indulges in empty talk without engaging in practice.

Thus, the answer to your question [are the Self-Nature Amitabha and the Mind-Only Pure Land the same or different from the Pure Land and the Buddha in the Western Pure Land?] is that they are *one yet two* before Buddhahood is attained, *two yet one* after Buddhahood is attained.

Question Two: What is the meaning of the statement: "birth [in the Pure Land] is certainly birth, but returning [to the Pure Land] is, in fact, not returning?"

Answer: "Birth is certainly birth" is from the viewpoint of phenomena; "Returning is, in fact, not returning" is from the viewpoint of principle or noumenon.[4]

However, those who have not yet penetrated the subtle differences between noumenon and phenomena should just follow phenomena and marks, and recite the Buddha's name in an accomplished manner.[5] In this way, they will achieve results. Otherwise, they will make the mistake, common to externalists and demons, of grasping at noumenon and abandoning phenomena.[6]

Question Three: Some people say: "To see the Buddha is to see the Buddha of the Self-Mind, not the Buddha of the Western Pure Land." This being the case, at the time of death, is it the Buddha of the Self-Mind who appears, or is it Buddha Amitabha who comes to receive and guide us?

Answer: Seeing the Buddha at the time of death is due to our own Self-Mind, which has elicited a response from Amitabha Buddha. You should not revert everything to the Self-Mind and think that there is no Buddha Amitabha arriving to receive and guide you![7]

NOTES TO LETTER 12

(1) Letter to the layman Ch'u. (VN ed., p. 140)

(2) See the words of the eminent Zen Master Chu Hung (16th century):

Some people say that the Pure Land is nothing but mind, that there is no Pure Land of Ultimate Bliss beyond the trillions of worlds of the cosmos. This talk of mind-only has its source in the words of the sutras, and it is true, not false. But those who quote it in this sense are misunderstanding its meaning.

Mind equals object: there are no objects beyond mind. Objects equal mind: there is no mind beyond objects. Since objects are wholly mind, why must we cling to mind and dismiss objects? Those who dismiss objects when they talk of mind have not comprehended mind. (J.C. Cleary, *Pure Land, Pure Mind*.)

(3) Externalists. Literally, followers of external paths. This term is generally used by Buddhists with reference to followers of other religions (e.g., Taoism, Hinduism, etc.).

(4) "Phenomena." Used in plural form to contrast with "noumenon," which is always one and indivisible. (*Phenomena/dharma*: all things and events. *Noumenon*: essence of things in themselves. *Marks*: form and characteristics.)

The noumenon is the doctrine underlying any phenomenal event. For example, in principle a tree has the potential to become a house. Before the house is built, it has that noumenal aspect. Once built, the house itself is the phenomenon, which appears because of the noumenon. In principle, we can all realize Buddhahood, but we have not phenomenally done so. If we have Faith, Vows and Hold the Name, we will arrive at the phenomenon of Buddhahood, just as the tree can be made into a house. (Master Hsuan Hua, *A General Explanation of the Buddha Speaks of Amitabha Sutra*, p. 26.)

Thus, for example, the word "Buddha" can mean the Buddha with His thirty-two auspicious marks (phenomena) or, at a higher level, the True Nature inherent in all sentient beings (noumenon).

(5) Accomplished manner: with utter sincerity, earnestness and, ultimately, one-pointedness of mind.

(6) The concept of "phenomena" vs. "noumenon" is parallel to the concept of existence vs. emptiness. Attachment to either concept is erroneous. However, attachment to noumenon/emptiness is, in Buddhist teaching, the more dangerous.

Of the two types of attachments, to existence and to emptiness, the latter is very dangerous. Both the *Lankavatara* and the *Esoteric Adornment Sutras* state:

"It is better to be attached to existence, though the attachment may be as great as Mount Sumeru, than to be attached to emptiness, though the attachment may be as small as a mustard seed."

Attachment to "existence" leads to mindfulness of cause and effect, wariness of transgressions and fear of breaking the precepts, as well as to Buddha and sutra recitation and performance of good deeds. Although these actions are bound to forms and not free and liberated, they are all conducive to merits, virtues and good roots. On the other hand, if we are attached to emptiness without having *attained* True Emptiness, but refuse to follow forms and cultivate merits and virtues, we will certainly sink in the cycle of birth and death. (Master Thích Thiền Tâm, *Buddhism of Wisdom and Faith*, sect. 20, p. 95.)

(7) That is, Buddha Amitabha is mind-created, but He also appears in concrete form. See Note 2 above and the following passage, which expresses the highest teaching of Buddhism:

...According to the Hua-yen [Avatamsaka school] analysis, every belief represents a vision of the truth, as seen from a particular standpoint. Therefore it cannot contradict, or be contradicted by, any other belief -- for that too is a vision of the truth, only seen from a different standpoint. Nor can a given standpoint be right or wrong in itself, since, on the one hand (from the conventional point of view), being partial and limited by definition, it cannot be the whole truth; while on the other hand (from the ultimate point of view), it simultaneously includes all other standpoints, and so cannot be less than the whole truth. Beliefs are mistaken as long as they are supposed to be absolutely true, in contrast to other beliefs which are then considered false. They actually become absolutely true only when their relative nature is fully realized and there is no longer any question of true vs. false. (A.J. Prince, "The World of Hua-yen Buddhism.")

*
**

Letter 13.
Open Letter to Cultivators[1]

The following lines are simple and unadorned, yet their teachings are based on the sutras. Anyone who acts accordingly will receive truly immense benefits. (Patriarch Yin Kuang.)

o
oo

I) The Pure Land method embraces people of all capacities, gathering in those of high as well as low capacities.[2] It is the great Dharma of the Tathagata, whereby He provides an expedient enabling both sages and ordinary beings to achieve liberation from Birth and Death and reach the stage of non-retrogression in this very lifetime.[3]

Not to believe in and practice this sublime, special Dharma is truly regrettable, a great pity indeed!

o
oo

The main tenets of Pure Land are Faith, Vows and Practice.

Faith: You should believe that the Saha World is filled with the eight sufferings;[4] believe that the Western Pure Land is filled with immense joy; believe that as ordinary beings full of evil karma, you cannot, realistically, rely on your own strength (self-power)

alone to eliminate delusion completely, realize the Truth
and escape Birth and Death in this very lifetime; believe
that Amitabha Buddha has made a profound and lofty
Vow -- any sentient being who recites His name [with
utmost faith and sincerity] seeking rebirth in His land
will, at the time of death, be received and guided to the
Pure Land.[5]

Vows: You should aspire to transcend this world and
achieve rebirth in that blissful Land as soon as possible.

Practice: You should practice Buddha Recitation in
all earnestness and sincerity, without a moment's lapse,
paying respect and reciting morning and evening before
your altar. You can establish an intensive or a leisurely
schedule depending on your own circumstances.

Outside of these sessions, you should constantly
recite the Buddha's name while walking, standing,
sitting, reclining or engaging in other actions that do not
require intense intellectual activity. When resting, you
should recite silently, uttering only the two words
"Amitabha Buddha" to facilitate concentration. You
should also recite silently when not properly dressed or
when doing household chores, bathing, urinating or
defecating, or when walking to and from unclean places.
This silent recitation brings the same benefits as reciting
aloud. In these circumstances, loud recitation is
improper and could reflect disrespect. Whether reciting
loudly or softly or engaging in "diamond recitation"[6] or
silent recitation, you should be attentive and keep each
utterance clearly and distinctly in mind, the mouth
reciting clearly and distinctly and the ears hearing clearly
and distinctly.[7]

When you recite in this way, the mind is no longer
chasing after external realms, deluded thoughts cease

and recitation gradually becomes pure and focussed --
the virtues accrued are thus immense.

II) Buddha Recitation practitioners should dedicate
all virtues toward rebirth in the Pure Land, whether they
are earned through reciting sutras and mantras, paying
respect to the Buddhas, practicing repentance, rescuing
victims of accidents or disasters, or helping the needy.
You should not seek the merits and blessings of the
human and celestial realms either in this lifetime or the
next.[8] If you have such thoughts, you will lose the
benefit of rebirth in the Pure Land and drown in the sea
of Birth and Death.

You should know that the more blessings you enjoy,
the greater the evil karma you are likely to create,
making it exceedingly difficult to avoid the path of hell,
hungry ghosts and animality in the third lifetime.[9] At
that point, it will be more difficult to recover the human
form and hear the Pure Land Dharma of liberation in
one lifetime than to achieve rebirth as a celestial!

Sakyamuni Buddha taught the method of reciting
Amitabha Buddha's name, seeking rebirth in the
Western Pure Land, in order to help sentient beings
resolve the problem of Birth and Death in this very
lifetime. If you aspire to gain the blessings of the
celestial and human realms in the next lifetime, you are
going counter to the teachings of the Buddhas. It is like
exchanging a priceless pearl for a piece of candy -- how
truly regrettable!

III) Pure Land cultivators should not follow Zen
meditation practices. This is because most Zen
followers fail to stress the issue of rebirth in the Pure
Land through Faith and Vows. Even if they practice

Buddha Recitation, they merely stress the koan "who is reciting the Buddha's name?" seeking a Great Awakening. Pure Land practitioners should recite Amitabha Buddha's name seeking only rebirth in the Pure Land. Once having seen Amitabha Buddha, why worry about not having awakened?[10]

In this Saha World, it may be possible to escape Birth and Death through practicing Zen if all delusive karma is eliminated. If, however, all delusive karma is not eliminated, the Zen follower not only cannot rely on his own strength (self-power) to achieve liberation, he cannot -- lacking Faith and Vows -- rely on the Buddha's power (other-power) to escape Birth and Death either. Unable to rely either on self-power or on other-power, how can he escape the sufferings of this world?[11]

You should know that even the Dharma Body Bodhisattvas [highest level Bodhisattvas] must rely on the power of the Buddhas[12] -- not to mention ordinary beings such as ourselves, who are full of karmic obstructions. Who are we to keep weighing the pros and cons of our own strength, while failing to seek the Buddhas' help? Our words may be lofty, but upon reflection, the accompanying actions are low and wanting! The difference between other-power and self-power is as great as the heavens and the abyss![13] I hope fellow-cultivators will carefully examine and forgive my straightforward words.

IV) From the age of twelve or thirteen, until they reach forty-eight or forty-nine, women all have menstrual periods. Some people teach that women should not bow or engage in Buddha and Sutra Recitation during those times. Such advice is certainly not consonant with feelings or reason. The periods may last from a minimum of two or three days to about six or seven. Buddha Recitation practitioners need to cultivate without interruption, so how can they abandon their cultivation over a little bit of natural discomfort? During those times, women should merely shorten the bowing part of the sessions but keep to their regular schedule of Sutra and Buddha Recitation. They should change their protective clothing and wash their hands often, so that they do not finger the rosary, turn the pages of sutras or light incense with dirty hands.

Within the Dharma, each and every method is perfect and unimpeded. Externalists, on the other hand, grasp one-sidedly at theory and noumenon. Ordinary people tend to believe their words, are unclear about the true teachings of Buddhism and thus cannot saturate themselves with the benefits of the Dharma.

o

oo

This ordinary monk has grown old and feeble lately, while his mind and spirit deteriorate with each passing day. He therefore regrets being unable to answer all of the many letters he has received.

It is only because of easy means of communication that people near and far hear of my little bit of empty fame and send me too many letters, seeking the Dharma. If I fail to answer the letters, I have, to some extent, turned my back on the senders. However, in truth, I do not have the energy to reply to each and every one of them. Therefore, I had this letter printed to answer everyone, far and wide.

As time goes by, whenever someone writes to ask about the Dharma, I always reply with this letter. If there are specific points to be addressed, I may add a few lines here and there on the original letter. In this way, we can communicate in thought while I minimize fatigue.

Anyone who wishes to comprehend fully the meaning behind the sutras should direct his inquiries to those Dharma Masters who have raised the Dharma platform high and are thoroughly versed in the various methods and teachings. However, you should realize that even if you have fathomed the sutras and the Dharma, it is not certain that you will be able to escape the cycle of Birth and Death.[14] To escape Birth, Death and transmigration, you should focus on Faith, Vows and reciting Amitabha Buddha's name seeking rebirth in the Pure Land![15]

NOTES TO LETTER 13

(1) Letter to all followers. (VN ed., p. 145)

(2) See the following passage, which expresses the same idea:

> The Pure Land method is not reserved for people with low or moderate capacities alone; it embraces those of the highest capacities as well. Sentient beings of middling and low capacities who recite the Buddha's name will be able to rid themselves of afflictions and karmic obstacles and develop merit, virtue and wisdom, leading in time to the state of concentration. Depending on the amount of effort they exert, they will be reborn within the nine lotus grades of the Land of Ultimate Bliss. Those of high capacities, on the other hand, enter deeply into the sphere of concentration and wisdom as soon as they begin uttering the Buddha's name. Whether walking, standing, lying down or sitting straight up, they are always in the "Buddha Remembrance Samadhi." After death they will be reborn in the highest grade. Some of the sages of old who entered this realm explained it in the following terms:

> > Holding the rosary, I am rid of worldly thoughts,
> > Suddenly, I already became a Buddha a long time ago.

> For this reason, the Buddha Recitation method embraces people of all three levels. For those of high capacities it becomes a sublime method; for those of low capacities it turns into a simple method. (Master Thích Thiên Tâm, *Buddhism of Wisdom and Faith*, sect. 18, p. 73.)

(3) All teachings of the Buddhas are expedients, described in the *Complete Enlightenment Sutra* as "fingers pointing to the moon." One should look at the moon, not the finger.

While we are still treading the path of Practice, not having reached the stage of Perfect Enlightenment, all Dharma methods are expedients; Buddha Recitation is an expedient and so is Zen. According to the three basic Pure Land sutras, Buddha Sakyamuni provided the expedient teaching of the Western Pure Land, and urged sentient beings to recite the Buddha's name seeking rebirth there. With this method, they can escape birth and death, avail themselves of that wonderful, lofty realm to pursue cultivation, and swiftly attain Buddhahood. Diligent Buddha Recitation also leads to awakening, as in Zen; however, the principal goal of the Pure Land School is rebirth in the Land of Ultimate Bliss, while the degree of awakening achieved is a secondary consideration. (Master Thích Thiền Tâm, *Buddhism of Wisdom and Faith*, sect. 29, p. 117.)

(4) Eight sufferings. Although sufferings are countless, Sakyamuni Buddha divided them into eight major categories: birth, old age, disease, death, separation from loved ones, meeting with uncongenial persons, unfulfilled wishes, and the five raging skandas. (For further details, See Glossary and Master Thích Thiền Tâm, *Buddhism of Wisdom and Faith*, 2nd ed., p. 15.)

(5) See *Meditation Sutra*, Sixteenth Meditation and Introduction, sect. D.

(6) Diamond recitation. In this method, neither the lips nor the teeth move, while the tongue does not touch the gums but merely moves slightly within the mouth.

(7) This is a reference to the method of cultivation of the Bodhisattva Avalokitesvara, as described in the *Surangama Sutra*.

(8) Merits and blessings in the celestial and human realms, good as they may be, are necessarily limited in time and scope. Once they are exhausted, the cultivator returns to the cycle of Birth and Death. The Pure Land, a Buddha Land, is beyond the celestial realms. Those reborn there are beyond retrogression.

(9)   Third lifetime.   In the first lifetime, the practitioner engages in mundane good deeds which bring ephemeral worldly blessings (wealth, power, authority, etc.) in the second lifetime.   Since power tends to corrupt, he is likely to create evil karma, resulting in retribution in the third lifetime.   Thus, good deeds in the first lifetime are potential "enemies" of the third lifetime.

To ensure that good deeds do not become "enemies," the practitioner should dedicate all merits to a transcendental goal, i.e., to become Bodhisattvas or Buddhas or, in popular Pure Land teaching, to achieve rebirth in the Pure Land -- a Buddha land beyond Birth and Death.

(10)   Since at the noumenon level, Amitabha Buddha is the cultivator's Self-Nature, to see Him is to see the Self-Nature and awaken to the Way.

(11)   See the following passage:

> We should know, furthermore, that to escape birth and death, we must sever delusions of views and thought. However, according to the ancients, "blocking delusions of views is as difficult as blocking a raging stream coming from forty miles away."   Why, then, even mention eliminating all delusions of thought?   Thus, if we want to achieve liberation in this Dharma-Ending Age, the most appropriate method is Buddha Recitation.   This is because, through this method, the cultivator, after utilizing his self-power to the utmost, receives additional assistance from other-power.   Even though his karma and delusions are not yet extinguished, he can, through Amitabha Buddha's power of welcoming and escorting, "take his residual karma along" to the Pure Land.   Once reborn, he will no longer retrogress and will have transcended birth and death forever!   (Master Thích Thiên Tâm, *Buddhism of Wisdom and Faith*, sect. 54, p. 226.)

(12) Power of the Buddhas/Other-power.   The issue of other-power (the Buddhas' power) is often misunderstood and glossed over by many Buddhists.   However, it must be pointed out that, in Buddhism, other-power is absolutely necessary if a Bodhisattva is to attain Ultimate Enlightenment.   The *Lankavatara Sutra* (the only sutra recommended by Bodhidharma) and the *Avatamsaka Sutra* (described by D.T. Suzuki as the epitome of Buddhist

thought) are emphatically clear on this point:

> As long as [conversion] is an experience and not mere understanding, it is evident that self-discipline plays an important role in the Buddhist life ... but ... we must not forget the fact that the *Lanka [Lankavatara Sutra]* also emphasizes the necessity of the Buddhas' power being added to the Bodhisattvas', in their upward course of spiritual development and in the accomplishment of their great task of world salvation."
> (Daisetz Teitaro Suzuki, tr., *The Lankavatara Sutra*, p. xviii.)

The *Avatamsaka Sutra* states:

> Having purified wisdom and means in the *seventh stage*
> ... The great sages attain acceptance of non-origination ...
>
> On the basis of their previous resolution,
>   the buddhas further exhort them ...:
>
> "Though you have extinguished the burning of
>   the fire of affliction,
> Having seen the world still afflicted, remember
>   your past vows;
> Having thought of the welfare of the world,
>   work in quest
> Of the cause of knowledge, for the liberation
>   of the world."
> (T. Cleary, tr. *The Flower Ornament Sutra*, Vol II, p. 85-86.)

(13) Master Yin Kuang is speaking here at the phenomenal level, the everyday level of our ordinary lives. At the ultimate or noumenon level, self-power is other-power and vice versa. See the *Heart Sutra.*

(14) This is a subtle reminder that practice is the key ingredient in all methods of cultivation -- not verbalization or study. The latter can only increase the discriminating, win-lose nature of the mind, thus negating the very purpose of cultivation -- to calm the wandering "monkey" mind.

(15) Note the ending here. To recite the Buddha's name for the avowed purpose of achieving rebirth in the Pure Land is the hallmark of popular Pure Land practice. See Introduction, sect. B.

*
**

Letter 14.
All Conditioned Dharmas are Like Dreams, Phantoms, Bubbles, Shadows![1]

Many years have passed since we last met but I have thought of you often. Last autumn, when your esteemed brother took the regional civil service examination, he brought your letter to P'u T'o Mountain. Only then did I learn about your cultivation in recent years.

I recall that you had met with great misfortune, having lost your beloved son, and that you were grieving day in and day out, seldom at peace. I wanted to write you in detail about Cause and Effect at that time, but, because of time constraints, I could only send you a short letter.

Today being the last full moon of the year, Master Ch'e Ch'uan visited our mountain. During our conversation, he discussed your plight, as well as the deluded comments of some ignorant people who, on that basis, claim that wholesome deeds bring only misfortune while cultivation brings no benefits. Hearing this, I could not help feeling deeply grieved, lest as a result of your experience, the intelligent grow lax in their cultivation while the dull and ignorant lose all qualms about committing transgressions. I therefore decided to put aside the reservations stemming from my humble background to share some plain, straightforward thoughts with you.

In the sutras, the Buddhas always teach that a) the consequences/ requital of our actions encompass three lifetimes,[2] while b) the birth of a child is generally associated with four causes.

a) The consequences/requital are:

- current requital;
- birth [next lifetime] requital;
- future requital.

"Current requital" refers to the misfortunes and blessings we receive in *this very lifetime* from the transgressions we commit and the wholesome deeds we perform. As an example, we have candidates for the civil service who study hard, pass their examinations and are appointed to high positions. Such occurrences can be seen by our ordinary human eyes.

"Birth requital" means committing transgressions and performing wholesome deeds in this lifetime but only obtaining the results, good or bad, of such actions in the *next lifetime*. Take the case of a family patriarch who stresses education and refinement but who only achieves success through his children and grandchildren.[3] Such occurrences cannot [always] be seen with our human eyes, but those endowed with the Celestial Eye can perceive them.

"Future requital" means committing transgressions or performing wholesome deeds in this lifetime but not obtaining the results until the third, fourth or thousandth lifetime, or, indeed *untold eons in the future*. This is the case of some royal dynasties which only flourish and reach their apogee several generations down the line ...

The Celestial Eye can see events three or four lifetimes away but is powerless with respect to events several hundred thousand lifetimes away. The Eye of the Arhat, however, can see them clearly. As to events occurring untold eons ago or hence, only the perfectly enlightened Tathagata Eye can see them clearly. Such realms are not even in the domain of the Arhat's Eye, much less those of celestial or human beings.[4]

Knowing that requital spans three generations, you should realize that the words of the sages concerning Cause and Effect have never been wrong and that wealth and poverty, honor and disgrace, longevity and early death are all the results of past actions -- where is the discrepancy between cause and effect? A mirror reflects beauty and ugliness as they are. The wise know that it is the object before the mirror that should be changed while the dull and ignorant waste time and effort hating and resenting the image in the mirror! To bear adversity is to know your limitations. Only by not resenting heaven and earth can you succeed in life.

o

oo

b) Children are born from four causes:

- repaying past kindness;
- repaying past wrongs;
- repaying past debts;
- claiming past debts.

"Repaying past kindness" means that the child incurred a debt of gratitude to the parents in a previous lifetime. To repay it, he or she has come to be born in the parents' household and will attend painstakingly to their needs throughout life. He will ensure that they are well provided for while alive and receive decent burials and offerings after death. The child may even perform great public service, helping the country and the people, his name being remembered in history. Thus, when future generations honor him, they will extend their respect and admiration to his parents. Devoted children and virtuous grandchildren, nowadays, generally belong to this category.

"Repaying past wrongs" means that in a past lifetime, the parents committed some wrong toward their present children. Therefore, the children have come to be born in their household seeking retribution. Thus, when still young, the children will be unruly and when grown, they will create misfortune and calamities implicating their parents. In old age the parents will be left in want, while their treatment after death will not only dishonor them, the shame will extend to the ancestors as well. At times, when holding key government positions, the children may even engage in criminal acts, causing the family's assets to be seized, the lineage exterminated and the graves of the ancestors dug up and desecrated. Thus, when future generations abuse and revile them, they will also hate and despise their parents.

"Repaying past debts" means that the child has come to be reborn in his parents' household because, in a previous lifetime, he incurred a debt toward them. If it is a great debt, repayment can take the parents' entire lifetime. If the debt is modest, repayment can cover part of the parents' lifetime before the child dies ... Thus, for example, some children assist their parents in business, only to die suddenly as the enterprise becomes profitable.

"Claiming past debts" means that, in a past lifetime, the parents incurred some obligation toward their child, who has now been born in their household in order to claim payment. If the debt is small, the parents will merely have to spend money to feed and clothe him, attend to his health and education, find him a spouse and train him to establish himself in the community. Once the debt is paid, the child will die suddenly. If the debt is sizeable, the child may sometimes deplete all of the parents' assets before dying.

o

oo

It would seem to me that your son comes under the last category. Fortunately, because your debt is modest, he has passed away suddenly at an early age. You should therefore repent your previous bad karma and strive to cultivate earnestly. Even the great sage Confucius lost his only son when the latter was in mid-life. The great sage Yen Yuan had but a short life. Another ancient sage was destitute, always in want, while yet another died a martyr .... Do you perhaps think that sages and saints are punished by the heavens for cultivating virtues? Or is it because life and death, wealth and honor are determined by past karma?

Thus, you should only deplore the fact that your virtues are still wanting and not waste time pondering misfortunes and blessings! If you are repentant and strive to cultivate earnestly, the god of blessings will come your way while misfortune and calamity will bypass you -- naturally.

During their lives, people are subject to all eight sufferings.[5] Even if they are reborn in the heavens, they cannot escape the five signs of decay.[6] Only the Western Land of Ultimate Bliss is all joy and no suffering. Who knows, perhaps it is precisely thanks to your work in spreading the Pure Land Dharma that the deities used the premature passing of your beloved son as an awakening needle to prick the top of your head. You may thus clearly realize that the Triple Realm knows no peace; it is like a burning house, filled with frightful suffering.[7] The lot of humans is subject to the god of impermanence, as we are born and die in the space of a bolt of lightning. When our time has come, no one can save anyone else.

o

oo

All conditioned dharmas are like dreams, phantoms, bubbles, shadows.[8] If, even now, you have not awakened and do not strive earnestly to practice Pure Land, you are no more alive than wood and stones! How can anyone with grit and determination bear to be a mere mass of flesh running hither and yon, a walking corpse while alive, and once dead, decaying along with the weeds and the trees! How can you have the heart to consign yourself to the world of the ordinary and the deluded while always extolling the realm of the saints? If after encountering such an eye-opening circumstance [as the death of your son], you still do not redouble your efforts, if after hearing the True Dharma you still do not follow it, are the Buddhas turning their backs on sentient beings, or are sentient beings turning their backs on the Buddhas?

As you are someone of intelligence and wisdom, I hope you will think carefully about what I have just said.

NOTES TO LETTER 14

(1) Letter to the layman Lin Chieh-sheng. (Chinese ed. Vol. I, p. 74; VN ed., p. 26)

(2) Master Yin Kuang is referring here to the concept of the "third lifetime" associated with rebirth. In the first lifetime, the practitioner engages in wholesome actions which bring blessings (wealth, power, authority, etc.) in the second lifetime. Since wealth and power tend to corrupt, he is likely to create evil karma, resulting in retribution in the third lifetime. Thus, wholesome deeds in the first lifetime are potential "enemies" of the third lifetime.

(3) "Birth requital spans different generations and lifetimes and is difficult to demonstrate. This is merely a provisional example to aid in understanding. The reader should not grasp at words and betray the ideas underlying them." (Thích Thiên Tâm.)

(4) These Eyes represent different levels of perception.

(5) Eight sufferings: birth, old age, disease, death, separation from loved ones, meeting with enemies, unfulfilled wishes, the five skandas. For details, see Master Thích Thiên Tâm, *Buddhism of Wisdom and Faith*, sect. 5, p. 15ff.

(6) Five signs of decay. Refers to symptoms of imminent death and rebirth in a lower realm, experienced by celestials and deities at the end of their transcendental lives, such as body odor, restlessness, etc. Please note that celestials and deities are still within the realm of Birth and Death. The Pure Land, being a Buddha land, is beyond Birth and Death.

(7) See the following parable of the burning house, found in Ch. 3 of the *Lotus Sutra:*

> A rich man had a very large house. The house had only one entrance, and the timber of which it was made had dried out thoroughly over the years. One day the house caught fire and the rich man's many children, heedless of the fire, continued to play in the house. Their father called to them from outside ... The children, not knowing the meaning of "fire" or "perish," continued to play as before. The man called out once more, "Come out, children, and I will give you ox-drawn carriages, goat-drawn carriages and deer-drawn carriages!" Tempted by the desire for new playthings, the children left the burning house, only to find a single great ox-drawn carriage awaiting them. (Leon Hurvitz, tr., *Scripture of the Lotus Blossom of the Fine Dharma (The Lotus Sutra)*, p. xi.)

The different carriages represent the various vehicles for Enlightenment (those of the Arhats, Pratyeka Buddhas, Bodhisattvas), while the great ox-drawn carriage stands for the ultimate vehicle of Buddhahood.

(8) See the following free translation of the concluding stanza of the *Diamond Sutra*, as quoted by A.F. Price and Wong Mou-Lam (p. 74):

Thus shall ye think of all this fleeting world:
A star at dawn, a bubble in a stream;
A flash of lightning in a summer cloud,
A flickering lamp, a phantom, and a dream.

*
**

Letter 15.
A Little Bit of Knowledge
is Ignorance[1]

Receiving your poetic letter from afar, I cannot but feel embarrassed! From an early age, this old monk has lacked education. My knowledge is uncertain and nebulous. Having drifted here and there for many years, far away from my native village, I am now sojourning on P'u T'o Mountain. Never did I expect that such a remarkable person as yourself, a scholar versed in the Mind-Dharma of Confucianism and Buddhism, who has studied at the feet of masters far and wide and made their outstanding practices his own, would condescend to seek advice from me. Moreover, you have praised me so excessively that my mind is perplexed and uneasy.

I venture to think that with your broad, well-rounded education and your lofty, far-reaching knowledge, you surely cannot have doubts about such ordinary matters as those raised in your letter. It must be that your intention is to act as an example, to show the Way to those who cultivate alongside you.[2]

However, since you have presented knowledge as ignorance, there is nothing to prevent me from presenting ignorance as knowledge and I will try to answer your questions in the order raised. I certainly would never dare imitate the old mandarin who sits as a judge but is in reality an aging student submitting his examination papers.[3] Therefore, if the following explanations contain errors, please revise and amend them.

o
oo

1) Although the mind is what matters most in Buddha Recitation, oral recitation should not be disparaged. This is because body, speech and mind reinforce one another.[4] Although the mind may be focussed on Amitabha Buddha, if the body does not bow respectfully and the mouth does not recite, it is difficult to receive benefits. For example, even when carrying heavy objects, ordinary people assist themselves by shouting aloud; how can you not do at least as much when trying to concentrate the mind and attain samadhi! Thus, the *Great Heap Sutra* teaches:

> To recite loudly is to see a tall Buddha, to recite softly is to see a small Buddha.

The ancients have also said:

> Reciting loudly, we see a large, tall body of the Buddha; reciting softly, we see a small, short body of the Buddha.

Ordinary beings often have lethargic, scattered minds. If they are not "assisted" by their bodies and mouths, it is difficult for them to achieve one-pointedness of mind.

o
oo

2) Only at the level of Ultimate Truth is there no

longer birth and extinction. Except for that, what Buddhist practice is not within the realm of birth and extinction? Even the practices of the highest level Bodhisattvas (who have achieved [virtual] equality with the Buddhas, destroyed the forty-one parts of ignorance and attained the forty-one parts of the Secret Store) are not beyond grasping and rejection, birth and extinction -- not to mention Buddha Recitation as practiced by ordinary beings.

However, while *birth and extinction* are the roots of *Birth and Death*, they are also the very roots of Enlightenment.[5] Birth and extinction depend entirely on the individual. To gather the six senses together in pure, uninterrupted recitation is precisely to convert the birth and extinction which abandons *Enlightenment for worldly dusts* into the birth and extinction which abandons *worldly dusts for Enlightenment*[6] -- as you strive to attain the True Thusness Buddha-Nature free of birth and extinction.

o

oo

3) "Only if thought after thought is on the Pure Land can rebirth be achieved," refers to the condition of those who will be reborn in the *upper lotus grades*. If we hold onto this truth and seek the highest grade of rebirth for ourselves, nothing could be better.[7] However, if we hold onto it to teach those of moderate and low capacities, we will greatly hinder their progress.

Why is this so? It is because they may consider this method too lofty, resign themselves to their lowly condition and refuse to cultivate.

Moreover, although Buddha Recitation centers on the mind-consciousness, it encompasses all other consciousnesses as well.[8] Do the sutras not mention "gathering the six senses together"? If the six senses are gathered together, the six consciousnesses will also be gathered together. Even registering the words "Amitabha Buddha" in the Alaya (Eighth) Consciousness must be achieved through the six consciousnesses[9] [which correspond to the six senses].

o

oo

4) The comment "recite the Buddha's name without a break, so that a knife cannot cut through" should not give rise to any doubts. However, such doubts arise simply because you have not yet clearly delineated the boundaries between Zen and Pure Land and between self-power and other-power.

The Buddha Recitation practitioner relies on the Vow-power of Amitabha Buddha to escape the Triple Realm and achieve rebirth in the Pure Land. If you do not make Vows, you certainly cannot have Faith either. Merely reciting the Buddha's name, without Faith and Vows, falls in the category of self-power. Without Faith and Vows, the practitioner cannot merge with the Vow-power of Amitabha Buddha.

If you can sever all Delusions of View and Delusions of Thought,[10] you may achieve rebirth in the Pure Land. However, if you have not severed them, or you have failed to sever them completely, the roots of evil karma remain and you are still subject to Birth and Death ... You should know that ignoring Faith and Vows while reciting the Buddha's name is no different from Zen meditation practice. If you were to achieve rebirth in the Pure Land under such circumstances, how could Cause and Effect be reconciled?[11] Elder Master Ou I has said:

To achieve rebirth in the Pure Land or not depends entirely upon Faith and Vows; the grade of rebirth (high or low) depends on whether one's practice of Buddha Recitation is deep or shallow.

This is a true statement not subject to change.[12]

o

oo

5) Relying on self-power, you cannot escape Birth and Death as long as you still have even a trace of karmic delusion -- not to mention if you have a great deal.

Reciting the Buddha's name to the level of one-pointedness of mind *without Faith and Vows*, perhaps a few out of countless individuals may achieve rebirth in the Pure Land.[13] Thus, you should by no means teach this approach and squander the good Pure Land roots of future generations. This is because it is difficult to find even a few cultivators in this whole world who can recite to the point of "extinction of karma and emptiness of desire" and attain the Tolerance of Non-Birth, by relying on self-power alone.

Therefore, if everyone followed this approach in cultivation and failed to stress Faith and Vows, countless sentient beings would drown in the sea of suffering -- their escape route blocked.

A single statement can cause so much harm. Not realizing how arrogant they are, those who advocate such doctrines consider themselves very perceptive and profound. Little do they realize that their words are deluded and insane -- severing the "wisdom-life" of the Buddhas and leading sentient beings to err and harbor doubts. What a great pity indeed!

The Pure Land method should be considered a special Dharma method, not to be compared with other general teachings of the Buddhas.[14]

NOTES TO LETTER 15

(1) Letter to the layman P'u Ta-fan. (Chinese ed. Vol. I, p. 31; VN ed., p. 32)

(2) Feigning weakness is a common expedient of leading disciples of Sakyamuni Buddha. For, example, Ananda was allegedly "lured" into the house of the most beautiful courtesan of Vaisali, thus providing the setting for the *Surangama Sutra*. In this key Mahayana text, the Buddha warned cultivators of the various temptations and obstructions to be expected on the way to Enlightenment.

Following this example, some monks and nuns at times expediently confess to certain transgressions they did not actually commit. This is for the express purpose of providing the assembly with an opportunity to learn and grow. These instances, albeit rare, reflect the essence of Bodhisattva practice.

(3) This paragraph, which may strike Westerners as false humility, is a good example of both classical Chinese and traditional Buddhist writing.

(4) As expressed by the Esoteric School, "If there is interpenetration of the three mystic elements (body, speech, mind), the body becomes Buddha."

(5) The expressions "birth and extinction" and "Birth and Death" refer to the same truth of impermanence, which is basic to Buddhism -- everything which is born must decay and disappear. "Birth and Death" refers specifically to human beings, while "birth and extinction" has a more general

meaning and is applied to other dharmas, e.g., the cosmos.

"Birth and Death" (or "birth and extinction") is the root cause of Enlightenment because to attain Enlightenment, one must proceed from "Birth and Death" and transcend it through cultivation. Once "Birth and Death" is transcended, Enlightenment appears.

(6) Worldly dusts. A metaphor for all the mundane things that can cloud our bright Self-Nature. These include form, sound, smell, taste, touch, dharmas (external opinions and views). These dusts correspond to the five senses and the discriminating, everyday mind (referred to as the sixth sense in Buddhism).

(7) Lotus grade/grade of rebirth: see Glossary.

(8) Buddha Recitation begins with the mind and ends with the mind. For "Six consciousnesses," see Glossary, under "Eight consciousnesses."

(9) Alaya consciousness: see Glossary. See also the following passage:

> The Method of Hearing is in keeping with the fundamental principle that if one sense-organ is intensely concentrated, all the other five sense-organs would be also held still automatically. This is the most fundamental tenet of the reciting method, as said in the *Surangama Sutra*: "when the six sense-organs are simultaneously held in concentration, there will be every pure thought in succession." (Hsu Heng Chi, *What's Buddhism*, p. 56.)

(10) Delusions of views and thought: see Glossary. See also the following passage:

> We should know, furthermore, that to escape birth and death, we must sever delusions of views and thought. However, according to the ancients, "blocking delusions of views is as difficult as blocking a raging stream coming from forty miles away." Why, then, even mention eliminating all delusions of thought? Thus, if we want to achieve liberation in this Dharma-Ending Age, the most appropriate method is Buddha Recitation. This is because, through this method, the cultivator, after utilizing his self-power to the utmost, receives additional assistance from other-power. Even though his karma and delusions are

not yet extinguished, he can, through Amitabha Buddha's power of welcoming and escorting, "take his residual karma along" to the Pure Land. Once reborn, he will no longer retrogress and will have transcended birth and death forever! (Master Thích Thiền Tâm, *Buddhism of Wisdom and Faith*, sect. 54, p. 226.)

(11) This is a key distinction, at the *phenomenal* level, between cultivation methods based on existence, such as Pure Land, and those based on emptiness, such as Zen. The Pure Land practitioner uses the expedients of Buddha Amitabha and the Pure Land to focus and purify his mind. Thus, he earnestly wishes to see Amitabha Buddha and His Pure Land. If he then sees these scenes, Cause and Effect coincide and the scenes are considered true and valid.

The Zen practitioner, on the other hand, aspires to empty his mind of all attachment and grasping, including attachment to Amitabha Buddha and the Pure Land. Thus, if a Zen practitioner witnesses these very same scenes, Cause and Effect are not reconciled and the scenes are demons, i.e., hallucinations. To grasp at these scenes, either liking or loathing them, would be a great mistake.

This distinction between Pure Land and Zen, of course, is valid only before the practitioner reaches Enlightenment and Buddhahood, as, at the ultimate level, emptiness is existence, existence is emptiness -- there is no difference between them.

(12) See the following passage:

Elder Master Ou I, a high-ranking Pure Land monk, has said, "To be reborn in the Pure Land or not depends entirely upon Faith and Vows; the grade of rebirth (high or low) depends on whether one's Practice is deep or shallow." He further added, "Without Faith and Vows, you cannot be reborn, even if you recite the Buddha's name to the point where neither the blowing wind nor the falling rain can penetrate and your recitation is as solid as a bronze wall or an iron gate." Those who practice Buddha Recitation assiduously but lack Faith and Vows will merely obtain the merits and blessings of the human and celestial realms, according to their level of cultivation. When their blessings are exhausted they are once again subject to birth and death ... (Master Thích Thiền Tâm, *Buddhism of Wisdom and Faith*, sect. 21, p. 97.)

(13) Since the Pure Land is ultimately Mind-Only, it is theoretically possible to achieve rebirth in the Western Pure Land (or, for that matter, in any one of the innumerable pure lands of the Buddhas) *without* Faith and Vows. However, the cultivator must first attain the level of extinction of all delusions -- an achievement beyond the capacity of virtually all human beings. (Even Buddha Sakyamuni and Buddha Amitabha went through eons of cultivation before attaining Buddhahood.)

(14) See the following passage concerning the famous Ming dynasty Zen Master Han-shan:

Han-shan did not write any commentary on the *Pure Land Sutra*, and it is not clear how he places it in the Hua-yen [Avatamsaka] classification scheme. On the one hand, he regards the Western Paradise as the most expedient land in the innumerable Hua-yen pure lands. On the other hand, he seems to have considered the Pure Land teaching as a special teaching that lies outside the usual scheme of classification. (Sung-peng Hsu, *A Buddhist Leader in Ming China*, p. 149.)

This special teaching is expressed by the metaphor of "vertical" vs. "horizontal" escape:

"Vertically" and "horizontally" are figures of speech, which can readily be understood through the following example. Suppose we have a worm, born inside a stalk of bamboo. To escape, it can take the "hard way" and crawl all the way to the top of the stalk. Alternatively, it can look for or poke a hole near its current location and escape "horizontally" into the big, wide world. The horizontal escape, for sentient beings, is to seek rebirth in the Pure Land. (Master Thích Thiên Tâm, *Buddhism of Wisdom and Faith*, 2nd ed., p. 315.)

*
**

Letter 16.
Bodhisattvas Fear Causes,
Sentient Beings Fear Results[1]

(A layman's house was burned to the ground and everything was lost. His wife, distraught, became seriously ill. The man then lost all sense of right and wrong, as though insane. Master Yin Kuang sent this letter to console and counsel him.)

o
oo

The Lotus Sutra (Ch. 3) states:

There is no peace in the Triple World. It is like a burning house, full of suffering. It is frightening indeed.[2]

Nevertheless, individuals at times achieve awakening through such circumstances as misfortune or blessings, conflict or harmony, suffering or joy, etc. ... The means of achieving awakening are not fixed.[3] To the wise, who know how to adapt flexibly to circumstances and are at peace with their lot, there is no suffering that is not joy, no conflict that is not harmony, no misfortune that is not a blessing.[4]

Therefore, the wise man is at peace with himself and others, knows his destiny, does not resent the heavens or blame his fellow human beings and is always even-tempered, peaceful and calm, regardless of circumstances. The ancients had a saying:

In circumstances of wealth and nobility, he is at peace with wealth and nobility; in circumstances of poverty and deprivation, he is at peace with poverty and deprivation; in circumstances of rudeness and vulgarity, he is at peace with rudeness and vulgarity; in circumstances of adversity and misfortune, he is at peace with adversity and misfortune ...

Although you enjoy performing good deeds, you do not yet understand the essence of Confucianism and Buddhism and are thus confused and frightened after a single instance of adversity. Let me cite a few examples to clarify your understanding.

o
oo

There is nothing in the universe vaster, higher or brighter than Heaven and Earth, the sun and the moon. However, once the sun has reached its zenith, it begins to set; once the moon is full, it wanes. Even the high mountains will in time give way to deep ravines and the vast oceans will be replaced by fields of mulberry. The human condition is the same: the advance and decline of our fortunes, as well as other changes, are merely the norm.

From ancient times to the present, who could surpass Confucius in morality and virtue? Nevertheless, even he was once surrounded by enemies, his life threatened. On another occasion, he was down to his last reserves while at yet another point he was getting nowhere in his efforts to travel and disseminate his teachings throughout the various kingdoms. Worse, his only son died suddenly at the age of fifty.

Confucius and others like him were great sages and saints, yet they could not escape adversity. However, they knew how to live in harmony with their

circumstances and so managed to keep their minds calm
and at peace.

o

oo

During our lives, we make all kinds of plans and
perform all kinds of tasks but, in retrospect, they
essentially revolve around the issues of food, clothing
and the desire to leave some legacy behind for our
children. Yet, as far as food is concerned, a bowl of soup
and some fresh vegetables should suffice; why seek
exquisite seafood and mountain delicacies? As for
clothing, a few simple garments should amply cover our
bodies; what is the use of a wardrobe filled with brocade
and satin? As for our children, they can study, till the
fields or engage in small business; what is the use of
wealth running into the millions?

Besides, who in the history of China can surpass the
Emperor Ch'in Shih Huang[5] in scheming for fame and
fortune for his descendants? This brutal ruler subdued
the six kingdoms, burned books, buried scholars alive
and confiscated all weapons converting them into bells,
all for the purpose of keeping the populace ignorant and
powerless and thus preventing insurrection. However,
with the uprising of Ch'en She, heroes sprang up
everywhere. The Emperor's unification scheme did not
last even thirteen years before collapsing, and all his
direct descendants were put to death. The Emperor
intended that his children be honored, but, in the end,
they were defeated and lost everything.

Think about it: how many can be as exalted as the
Son of Heaven (Emperor), his wealth extending over the
four seas? Yet even he could not ensure lasting wealth
and happiness for his family and clan -- not to mention
ordinary beings who, throughout the eons, have

committed evil karma as thick as the earth's crust and as deep as the oceans! How can they guarantee that their families will flourish forever, always blessed, never encountering setbacks?

o

oo

You should know that all things in life are *intrinsically* false, like dreams, illusions, bubbles, shadows, dew or lightning, the moon reflected in a pond, flowers in the mirror, flickering mirages in the blazing sun, Gandharva cities -- nothing is true or real.[6] Only the Mind-Nature is everlasting and immutable, encompassing all past and present. Although it neither changes nor dies, it always follows causes and conditions.

If conditions are consonant with awakening and purity, we become Arhats, Pratyeka Buddhas, Bodhisattvas or Buddhas -- the level of achievement depending on the depth of our virtues. If conditions are consonant with delusion and impurity, we stray into the realms of gods, humans, asuras, animals, hungry ghosts and hells. The length of our suffering or happiness depends on the weight of our transgressions or merits.

Those who are unaware of the Buddha Dharma cannot be faulted, but as a devout Buddhist, why do you not profit from this painful experience to see life clearly, abandon delusion for awakening and singlemindly recite the Buddha's name seeking rebirth in the Pure Land -- thus escaping Birth and Death and reaching the four levels of sagehood? Would that not be turning a small misfortune into a great blessing?

The way out of your predicament is as described. Why do you remain troubled and confused, daydreaming as though you have lost your mind? If you lose your life through excessive worry, you will not only wallow in Birth and Death for many lifetimes,[7] your sick wife and orphaned children will have no means of support. Thus, all you will do is harm yourself while hurting others at the same time. How can you be so deluded?

o
oo

The sutras teach:

Bodhisattvas fear causes, sentient beings fear results.

To avoid the result of suffering, Bodhisattvas destroy evil causes in advance. Thus, evil karma is eliminated and virtues are accrued in full, up to the time they become Buddhas. Sentient beings constantly create evil causes but wish to escape the suffering that results. They are no different from those who fear their own shadows but continuously run for cover under the glare of the sun. How can they escape their shadows?

Many persons expect huge blessings after performing a few good deeds. When they encounter adversity, they immediately think that "to do good is to meet with misfortune; there is no law of Cause and Effect." From that point on, they regress from their newly awakened state, turn around and vilify the Buddha Dharma. These persons do not understand the truths that "Cause and Effect encompass three lifetimes" and "the mind can change the environment for the better."

How do "Cause and Effect encompass three lifetimes?" As an example, in this lifetime we may perform wholesome or evil deeds, as a result of which we receive benefits or suffer vicissitudes. This is a case of current requital.

If we perform wholesome or evil deeds in this

lifetime and receive benefits or suffer vicissitudes in the next lifetime, it is a case of birth [next lifetime] requital.

If we perform wholesome or evil deeds in this lifetime but only receive benefits or suffer vicissitudes in the third or fourth lifetime, or even the tenth, hundredth, or thousandth lifetime, or countless eons in the future -- it is a case of future requital.

The time frame of future requital is not fixed. However, to create "causes" is to create "effects and consequences." This is a natural occurrence.

In what way can "our minds change the environment for the better"? Take the case of a person who has performed evil deeds and should be condemned to the sufferings of Hell for untold eons. Suppose that individual suddenly becomes extremely frightened and utterly ashamed, develops the Bodhi Mind,[8] changes his ways, recites sutras and the Buddha's name, cultivates personally and enjoins others to do likewise, seeking rebirth in the Pure Land. Thanks to this change of heart, the previous karma of Hell is dissipated and transmuted into a lesser karma in the current lifetime. Thus, for example, he may be subject to contempt by others, suffer a bout of illness, become destitute or meet with unhappy events. After enduring such minor retribution,[9] that person may escape Birth and Death and enter the "stream of the sages," transcending the ordinary world. As the *Diamond Sutra* states:

> If there is anyone who receives and keeps this Sutra but is maligned by others, such a person has created evil karma in previous lifetimes and should have descended upon the evil paths. As a result of this calumny, however, his past karma is instantly extinguished and he will attain Supreme Enlightenment.[10]

This is precisely the meaning of the mind changing

life and the environment for the better.

o

oo

When ordinary beings meet with disaster, if they do not resent the heavens, they blame their fellow-beings. Very few think of repaying their karma and developing a mind of repentance and reform. You should know that "if you plant melons, you reap melons, if you plant beans, you reap beans." This is the natural course of events. Having sown thorns, do not expect, when the harvest comes, to have wheat and rice. If those who create evil still enjoy blessings, it is because in previous lifetimes they amassed great blessings; if not for their transgressions, their blessings would have been much greater.

It is as if the scion of a wealthy family were to lead a dissipated life, lusting and gambling, squandering money like so much dirt, without suffering hunger and cold immediately because of his great fortune. Yet, if he were to continue in this manner day in and day out, even with a family estate in the millions, one day he would surely lose all his property and suffer a premature death.

If those who perform wholesome deeds customarily meet with misfortune, it is because they planted the seeds of transgression deeply in past lifetimes. If not for their good deeds, their misfortunes would have been much worse.

This is similar to the case of a condemned prisoner who manages to perform a small public service while waiting for his sentence to be carried out. Because of the limited impact of his contribution, he cannot yet be pardoned; therefore his sentence is merely commuted to a lighter one. If he continues to contribute to the public good and the sum total of such contributions becomes sizeable, not only will his previous transgressions be wiped away, he may even receive honors, high position and noble rank, with his descendants inheriting honors for generations![11]

o

oo

A superior person should transcend ordinary events and not allow external circumstances to damage his very life. Supposing his storeroom is overflowing with gold and jewelry. When renegade soldiers and outlaws come to steal them, he should abandon his house and escape, rather than risk death in order to hold on to his riches. This is because gold and jewelry may be precious, but they cannot be compared to life. If we cannot safeguard both, property should be abandoned and life preserved.

Now that your wealth and property have been reduced to ashes, it is useless to worry excessively or cry over their loss. You should adapt to conditions, carry on and strive to recite the Buddha's name, seeking rebirth in the Pure Land, so that you may be spared suffering and enjoy only happiness until the end of time. Thus, thanks to this catastrophe, you will ultimately attain Buddhahood. Why continue in delusion -- suffering and grieving?

I hope that you will consider my words carefully. You will then get over your grief, clearing the sky of dark clouds and revealing its brightness, finding happiness in calamity and exchanging intense heat for a cool, joyous breeze. Otherwise, if you continue to dwell on your loss and fail to awaken, you will not escape insanity. Once the Self-Mind is lost, demons will enter.[12] At that time, even if a thousand Buddhas were to appear on earth, they would have no way of saving you![13]

NOTES TO LETTER 16

(1) Letter to the layman Wei Ch'in-chou. (Chinese ed. Vol. I, p. 67; VN ed., p. 36)

(2) Also translated as follows:

> The triple world is not safe,
> Just as a burning house,
> Full of all kinds of sufferings,
> ... Greatly to be feared.
> (Bunno Kato, et. al. *The Threefold Lotus Sutra*, ch. 3, p.98.)

(3) See the following paragraph:

> We usually have to be driven out of our complacency to embark on the spiritual quest. A devastating crisis, much suffering, or growing tiredness of going round and round, repeating the same increasingly meaningless patterns: these are the common precipitating factors. (John Snelling, *The Elements of Buddhism*, p. 117.)

There is a story which illustrates this point. An elderly Zen Master, feeling that his time would soon come, hit upon an expedient to help his chief disciple achieve a Great Awakening. He decided to drive the younger monk out of his complacency by falsely accusing him of being a thief and denouncing him to one and all throughout the land. The accused monk, once the teacher of a huge congregation, now completely debased and with nowhere to turn, his ego totally shattered, mulled over this flagrant injustice and at times even contemplated suicide. After several weeks of utter desperation, he suddenly experienced a Great Awakening: life is a dream, an illusion, a bubble, a shadow. The Master then conferred the succession upon him.

(4) The wise man is at peace with his lot because he understands that everything is subject to the law of Cause and Effect. This, however, does not prevent him from working to improve his condition and environment.

(5) Ch'in Shih Huang (3rd cent. b.c.) This notorious emperor

is remembered for unifying China and for his ruthless ways.

(6) This paragraph summarizes one of the teachings of the *Prajnaparamita Sutras*: life is a dream, an illusion. To internalize this truth is to achieve peace of mind and liberation. A sane person, once awakened from a dream, would never think of asking for the diamonds he accumulated while asleep.

Gandharvas: "spirits on the fragrant mountain so called because they do not eat meat or drink wine, but feed on incense and give off fragrant odours." (Charles Luk.) Gandharvas are also known as the musicians of the god Indra. Gandharva cities represent dream-like, non-existent places, mirages in the desert.

(7) To illustrate the extreme difficulty of rebirth in the human realm, Sakyamuni Buddha compared it to the likelihood that a blind sea turtle, surfacing from the depths of the ocean only once every century, would encounter a tree trunk in which to nest.

(8) Bodhi Mind: see Glossary.

(9) The vicissitudes of life are considered minor compared to Birth and Death -- the single biggest issue for all sentient beings.

(10) For alternate translations, see A.F. Price and Wong Mou-Lam, *The Diamond Sutra and the Sutra of Hui Neng,* p. 50 and Shih Shing-Yun, the *Diamond Sutra (Bilingual Buddhist Series),* p. 122. The latter reads as follows:

> Furthermore, Subhuti, if a virtuous man or woman receives, holds (in mind), reads and recites this sutra and is despised by others, this person who is bound to suffer from evil destinies in retribution for his past sins, and whose karmic sins are now eradicated by the others' contempt, will attain Supreme Enlightenment ...

(11) This apparently innocuous paragraph led to two interesting comments from readers of the draft manuscript: a) Is it fair for a condemned prisoner to receive honors? b) How can the effects of karma be inherited?

In answer to the first question, karma may be likened to a system of "accounting." As an example, a person deeply in debt who labors day and night and succeeds in business will not only be able to repay his obligations, he may even become wealthy.

As for the second issue, the reader is referred to the concept of merit transference, Introduction, Section C.

(12) Demons: generally understood as, though not necessarily limited to, hallucinations. Many kinds of demons are mentioned in the sutras. For an in-depth discussion, see *Buddhism of Wisdom and Faith,*, sect. 52, p. 209ff.

The Self-Mind has been described in Mahayana sutras as a house full of gold and jewelry. To preserve the riches, i.e., to keep the mind calm, empty and still, we should shut the door to the three thieves of greed, anger and delusion. Letting the mind move opens the house to "demons," that is, hallucinations and harm. Thus, Zen practitioners are taught that while in meditation, "Encountering demons, kill the demons, encountering Buddhas, kill the Buddhas." Both demons and Buddhas are mind-made, Mind-Only.

(13) This last sentence touches upon an all-important Buddhist teaching. In the final analysis, the Self-Mind (the Buddha within) determines our future. If we lose our Self-Mind (i.e., are afflicted with greed, anger or delusion), no external Buddha can rescue us. Those who have committed major transgressions but achieve rebirth on their deathbeds have, in effect, recovered the Self-Mind through singleminded recitation of the Buddha's name.

*
**

Letter 17.
The Five Skandas are
All Empty!¹

In Shanghai recently there were many gatherings where revelations and prophecies were proclaimed. Their messages about abandoning evil ways and practicing wholesome deeds, as well as their pronouncements on Birth and Death and Cause and Effect, while superficial and limited, are very useful for everyday morality and the minds of ordinary persons. However the points they made concerning the future and the Buddha Dharma are somewhat vague and not free of error. As disciples of the Buddhas, we should not oppose or reject those pronouncements, because doing so may hinder the good actions of others. At the same time, however, we should not repeat or extol them, lest we be guilty of chimerical statements and conjectures that bring harm and disorder to the Dharma and engender doubts among the people.

This old monk, knowing himself to be beset with many karmic obstructions, would not dare abandon reason for emotion and thus cause others to err. He begs the reader to take both emotion and reason into account when following his advice, in order to avoid harmful actions.²

o
oo

Think this over: the word "samadhi" is translated as correct concentration. It is the state of dissipation of delusion and emergence of the Truth -- tranquil and bright. How can there be any realm or state within it? Therefore, the *Surangama Sutra* states:

Perfect attainment of the fruit of Enlightenment is non-attainment of anything.[3]

The Zen practitioner relies only on his own strength (self-power) without seeking the Buddhas' assistance. Therefore, when he exerts himself to the limit in cultivation, the true and the false assail each other, giving rise to many states and realms that suddenly appear and disappear.

It is as though a heavy rain is abating. The dark clouds disperse, the overcast sky suddenly clears; things change back and forth without warning. These states and realms are difficult for those who do not possess transcendental vision to distinguish. If the cultivator mistakenly considers these manifestations to be true, he is immediately possessed by "demons,"[4] and becomes insane.

On the other hand, when the Pure Land practitioner earnestly recites Buddha Amitabha's name and His ten thousand virtues, it is like the sun shining in the middle of empty space or a walk along a broad, straight path. Not only are demons nowhere in sight, but deluded thoughts disappear as well.

o

oo

Ultimately, when the practitioner recites to the point of pure, unmixed power, the totality of Mind is Buddha, the totality of Buddha is Mind, Mind and Buddha are as one. I am afraid that this principle and practice are not understood by everyone. It has always been my desire to proclaim them and to disseminate the

Original Vows of Amitabha Buddha to rescue all
sentient beings. How would I dare conceal this truth,
transmitting it privately to you alone? If there is any
secret method to be transmitted privately in a hidden
place, it is an externalist teaching, not a [Pure Land]
Buddhist teaching.

Having said so, however, this old monk, in truth,
does have a wonderful method, which only he possesses.
Since you have requested it today, I have no qualms
about revealing it to all Buddhist followers. What is this
wonderful method? It is *utter sincerity and profound
respect*. This secret is known to everyone, yet obscure to
all!⁵

Wishing to eradicate deep-seated karma and repay
the kindness of the Buddhas, I have endeavored, day in
and day out, to probe the shining cultivation of the
ancients. I have thus discovered that utter devotion and
profound respect constitute a wonderful secret method
that lifts human beings to the realms of the saints,
enabling them to escape Birth and Death. Time and
again I have brought these points to the attention of
those who have the right conditions. You should know
that *sincerity* and *respect* are not reserved exclusively to
students of the Dharma, but form the basis of all
activities that you want to complete to perfection.

o

oo

You have planted wholesome roots in previous
lifetimes and belong to a family imbued with Buddhism
for many generations. In your youth, you were well
brought up at home and later on, for some twenty to
thirty years, you attended school and experienced the
ways of the world fully. Why have you decided to
abandon the lofty and sublime to stoop to the common

and ordinary, placing such value on my writings and distributing them to others?

You should know that the most important criteria in dissemination of the Dharma for the benefit of sentient beings are "timing" and "capacities."

Those who are well-versed in Buddhism have failed to point out the most relevant cure for today's illnesses. Instead, all they do is discourse on lofty, sublime methods which, generally speaking, are not the right medicine. Sometimes, this very medicine, however valuable, intensifies the illness. This old monk is like an inexperienced physician -- not only is he unclear about the roots of disease, he does not know the properties of the medication either. He merely prescribes a panacea transmitted "secretly" by ancient sages and saints and dispenses it against each and every symptom, such as falsity or truth, chills or fever. Anyone with faith in the medicine who tries it will recover. Even those afflicted with "incurable" diseases, forsaken by the greatest Immortal physicians,[6] will immediately regain strength and escape death as soon as they take this medicine.

Therefore, I have no hesitation about hanging out my shingle for those who wish to rescue sentient beings and benefit mankind, advertising this medicine to all who are ill. I do realize that the remedies prescribed by those Immortal physicians are miraculous, but I do not advise people to take them -- as illnesses stem from past karma and cannot be cured by physicians, however divine.

o
oo

Heavy karmic obstructions, excessive greed and anger, a weak and ailing body, a fearful, apprehensive mind -- these symptoms will, in time, disappear naturally if you singlemindedly recite the Buddha's name. The "Avalokitesvara [twenty-fifth] Chapter" of the *Lotus Sutra* states:

If ... living beings much given to carnal passion keep in mind and revere the Bodhisattva Regarder of the Cries of the World, they will be set free from their passion. If [those] much given to irascibility [hatred and anger] keep in mind and revere the Bodhisattva Regarder of the Cries of the World, they will be set free from their irascibility. If [those] much given to delusion keep in mind and revere the Bodhisattva Regarder of the Cries of the World, they will be set free from their delusion. (B. Kato, et al, *The Threefold Lotus Sutra*, p. 320.)

The same is true of reciting the Buddha's name. However, you should concentrate your mind to the utmost and put a stop to "sundry [distracting] thoughts," doubts and uncertainties. Whatever you seek will then materialize. As the Bodhisattva Avalokitesvara has great affinities with sentient beings in the Saha World, you should, in addition to your regular Pure Land sessions, recite Her name. Alternatively, you may also recite the Surangama Mantra or the Great Compassion Mantra.[7]

o

oo

If you wish to be a Dharma master, lecturing on the sutras in public, you should first read the original texts, then study the commentaries and subcommentraries. However, should you discover that your intellect is average and your understanding not necessarily above others, you should concentrate on Buddha Recitation rather than wasting time and energy pursuing these non-essential endeavors.

If, on the other hand, you would like to engage in

Sutra Recital[8] in accordance with your limited capacities for the benefits it confers, you should keep the three karmas of body, speech and mind utterly pure, earnest and sincere, bow to the Buddhas and sit erect concentrating your mind for a moment or two, before opening a sutra to read aloud or silently. At that time, you should sit up straight as though you were facing the Buddhas, listening to their perfect voices, without a single lazy, discriminating thought. Then, *without trying to find the meaning of the sutra*, just recite it in one stretch from beginning to end.[9]

By reciting the sutras in such a manner, if you are of superior spirituality, you can awaken to the Non-Dual Truth and reach the Dharma of True Mark. Even if you are dull and of low capacity, you will gain increased merit and wisdom, eradicating karmic obstructions in the process. The Sixth Patriarch once said:

> We can awaken our Mind and see our True Nature just by reciting the *Diamond Sutra*.

This quote refers to the practice of Sutra Recital as explained above. It is therefore called "samatha" (stopping or arresting mental processes).[10] If you follow these steps, reciting any Mahayana sutra can lead to the opening of the Mind, the seeing of your True Nature. This does not apply to the *Diamond Sutra* alone.

You should not use the discriminating mind, trying to understand the meaning of this sentence, the idea behind that paragraph, as all this belongs to the realm of deluded thought, reasoning and comparing.[11] Such a mind cannot be in silent accord with the Buddha Mind, lead to a thorough understanding of the essence of the sutras or provide the causes and conditions for eradicating transgressions and creating blessings.

Practicing Sutra Recital with a discriminating mind, if accompanied by reverential thoughts, may lead to the sowing of a few wholesome karmic seeds. If, on the other hand, it is accompanied by laziness and arrogant thoughts, it cannot fail to generate evil consequences from these very same seeds -- the resulting suffering will be immense!

Once, while reciting a sutra, the Patriarch Chih I[12] [founder of the T'ien T'ai school] suddenly experienced a Great Awakening and silently entered samadhi. If he had had a discriminating mind at that time, how could he possibly have succeeded in such a manner? Another master was copying the *Lotus Sutra*, completely oblivious to the ten thousand conditions (i.e., everything). He was still at his desk writing long after the sun had set, when his disciple walked in and said: "It is so late already, how can you, Master, still be copying the sutra?" The monk was startled to discover that it was so dark he could not even see his hand!

Whether reciting the sutras, meditating, chanting mantras or reciting the Buddha's name, as long as you do it with this level of concentration and persevere for a long time, one day you will understand all and everything and experience a Great Awakening (awaken to the Way).

Thus, during the Ming dynasty, there was a Zen monk by the name of Hsueh Ch'iao Hsin. He had entered the Order in midlife and was completely illiterate. Nevertheless, thanks to his strict observance of austerities, assiduous meditation, extreme forbearance and other difficult practices, before long he suddenly experienced a Great Awakening. Whatever he said after that was in accordance with the Perfect Teaching. From then on, he gradually came to know how to read and write. In a relatively short time, he was transformed into a scholar fully at ease in the exposition of the Dharma. During the Ch'ing period, his writings were incorporated into the Mahayana canon.

Such benefits all stem from a mind completely focussed on meditation, with no discriminating thoughts. Those who practice Sutra Recital should take these examples as models. Thus, when engaging in Sutra Recital, you absolutely must avoid the development of a discriminating mind. In this way deluded thoughts will settle themselves at the bottom, while your transcendental Original Nature will gradually reveal itself.[13]

o

oo

However, if you wish to study the sutras to understand their profound meaning or write commentaries upon them, you should reserve a special period of time to concentrate exclusively on such activity. At that time, it may not be necessary to be as strict and respectful as during Sutra Recital, but you should not adopt an irreverent attitude -- at most, you can be a little more relaxed.

If you have not succeeded in extinguishing evil karma and developing wisdom, you should consider Sutra Recital as your main objective and sutra study as secondary. Otherwise, you will waste months and years pursuing such studies. Even if you were to understand the sutras to the point of pushing away the clouds and revealing the shining moon, sliding open the shutters and admiring the green mountains, it would merely increase your stock of rationalizations and arguments at the "edge of the lips and the tip of the tongue." What relationship does that bear to the issue of Birth and Death? When the last day of the twelfth month has come and death is waiting, you could not use the least bit of such knowledge![14]

If you can follow the Sutra Recital method described above, the various karmas of greed, anger and desire/grasping will gradually disappear and you will develop wisdom. Otherwise, not only will you fail to derive any true benefits, there is the possibility that the power of evil karma accumulated from time immemorial will lead you to develop wrong views and reject Cause and Effect. All the while, the afflictions of lust, killing, stealing and lying will come to the fore one after another like a raging fire. You may even sometimes mistake yourself for a Mahayana luminary, thinking that nothing should be an obstacle, using the Sixth Patriarch's teaching "if the mind is pure, what need is there to keep the precepts," to justify your actions, claiming that "to break the precepts without breaking the precepts is true keeping of the precepts."[15]

There are many such hazards along the path of cultivation, making the True Dharma very difficult to attain! For this reason, the various Patriarchs have generally advocated cultivation of the Pure Land method, relying on the compassionate power of Amitabha Buddha to extinguish evil karmic power, so that it will not flare up.

You should therefore take Buddha Recitation as your principal practice and Sutra Recital as an auxiliary method. You can recite the *Avatamsaka Sutra*, the *Lotus Sutra*, the *Surangama Sutra*, the *Diamond Sutra*, the *Parinirvana Sutra*, the *Sutra of Complete Enlightenment*, etc. one after another or you can limit yourself to one sutra. In either case, you should follow the principles I explained earlier. If you are indifferent and lack restraint and respect, discriminating feelings and views will surely rob you of great benefits. Your evil karma will then know no bounds!

o

oo

I used to think that you and your friend were thorough believers in the Pure Land method. However, when I saw the draft of your letter seeking advice from Hsu Chun, I learned of your intention to recite mantras and investigate the Precept-keeping (Discipline) method. You also said: "I have not seen anything mentioned in Pure Land as lofty and sublime as the blessings and virtues derived from reciting mantras; therefore, my mind is undecided and I do not know whether or not I should follow Pure Land."

Look at yourself and see what your capacities are. Why do you wish to understand and penetrate all Dharma methods in such a manner? I only fear that such confusion and indecisiveness will, in time, unsettle and cloud your mind.

As for Hsu Chun, he has said that "according to the Tantric method, wherever the power of mantras goes, be it on a wisp of air or a grain of dust, sentient beings there will all be liberated. Does the Pure Land method bring such benefits?"

You should know that while reciting mantras brings limitless blessings and virtue, reciting the Buddha's name also has unimaginable power! Do you not recall this passage from the *Meditation Sutra:*

> Even those who have committed the Five Grave Offenses or the Ten Evil Acts, may, on the verge of death, when the marks of hell appear, recite the Buddha's name a few times, and be reborn immediately in the Pure Land.

Do you not also realize that in the Avatamsaka Assembly, even those Bodhisattvas who have "attained [virtual] equality" with the Buddhas must still conceive the Ten Great Vows,[16] dedicating the merits to rebirth in the Pure Land, so as to perfect the fruit of Enlightenment? Moreover, if the Pure Land were not a lofty, transcendental method, why would the Buddhas and Patriarchs, in countless sutras and commentaries, have all carefully and earnestly recommended its cultivation?

In truth, Mahayana methods are all complete, perfect and sublime;[17] it is only because sentient beings differ in conditions and capacities, some high level and mature, others low level and wanting, that the benefits derived from these methods are different. When the Patriarch Shan Tao -- believed to be an incarnation of Amitabha Buddha -- was teaching "uninterrupted practice," he was concerned that cultivators were unsettled in mind and will. He therefore wrote:

> Even if the sages of the Four Fruits, the Bodhisattvas at the stages of the Ten Abodes, Ten Practices, Ten Dedications and Ten Grounds, as well as the Buddhas of the ten directions who fill the empty space of the Dharma Realm, should all appear -- their bodies emitting rays of light -- and request you to abandon the Pure Land method, offering to transmit a loftier method to you, do not dare to follow their words. This is because, having previously resolved with utmost determination to follow the Pure Land method, you cannot go back on your vows.

The Patriarch Shan Tao uttered these words because he anticipated that those of future generations would "stand on one mountain while dreaming of the other," having no true position. These golden words were not followed even by those who venerated him as their direct teacher -- much less by those who have not

heard or understood them! To be exposed to a method
so well adapted to the conditions and capacities of
sentient beings and yet to abandon it for the murky path
of karmic consciousness -- practicing neither Zen nor
Pure Land -- is this not incitement by evil karma
accumulated from time immemorial? What a pity
indeed!

o
oo

The Non-Dual Truth represents No-Self and
No-Dharma.

No-Self (emptiness of self) means true
understanding that the five skandas[18], which together
represent body and mind, are all born of causes and
conditions. When these come apart, body and mind
immediately disappear. There is no real "self" as master.

No-Dharma (emptiness of all phenomena)[19] means
true understanding that the five skandas are empty [not
because they are aggregates] but *by their very nature*.
Thus, the *Heart Sutra* states:

The Bodhisattva Avalokitesvara illumined the five skandas
and saw that they were empty.

The truth of Emptiness of all Dharmas is precisely
the True Mark, attained through eradication of delusion.
Therefore, the *Heart Sutra* continues:

Thus, the Bodhisattva Avalokitesvara overcame all ills and
suffering.

Furthermore, the principle that the Dharma-body --
while being the basis of all marks -- is completely apart
from such marks as birth, extinction, impermanence,
permanence, existence and emptiness, conforms very

much to the Truth, hence the name "True Mark."

This True Mark is common to sentient beings and Buddhas, but ordinary humans, as well as followers of the Two Vehicles, deludedly reject it and therefore cannot take advantage of it. It is as though you had a diamond sewn into the hem of your shirt but, unaware of it, must endure poverty and deprivation.[20]

To awaken to the Way (experience a Great Awakening) is to be in a state of thorough understanding, like the clouds dissipating to expose the moon, the shutters thrown open to reveal the mountain range; it is like someone with clear vision recognizing the way home, or a tramp unexpectedly discovering a treasure trove.

To achieve Enlightenment is like following a well-trodden path home, dusting off your feet and sitting down to rest; it is like taking treasures from the trove to spend as you wish.

Once truly *awakened to the Way*, an ordinary being endowed with the Bodhi Mind achieves a level of insight and understanding equal to that of the Buddhas. As far as achieving *Enlightenment* is concerned, the Bodhisattvas of the first "ground" do not know the comings and goings of those of the next "ground."[21] Understanding the meaning of awakening to the Way and achievement of Enlightenment, you naturally do not become arrogant toward those at a higher level,[22] nor do you develop a mind of retrogression. Rather, your determination to achieve rebirth in the Pure Land cannot be restrained, not even by ten thousand buffaloes![23]

o
oo

Look at the times we are in. The flames of war are now raging. There is fighting between north and south, insurrection and strife are spreading within China and abroad, the number of dead over the last three or four years can be counted in the millions -- we have not heard of such tragedies throughout history. Moroever, disasters such as typhoons, floods, earthquakes and epidemics occur with alarming frequency. Sometimes drought and flooding both create havoc several times within a single year. Because of these events, prices have more than doubled.

At times like these, it is a feat just to remain alive; how dare you fail to redouble your efforts at uninterrupted Buddha Recitation, seeking rebirth in the Pure Land? How can you waste this human body, so difficult to obtain,[24] dreaming of methods which are not suitable for the times?[25] If you do not strive to concentrate on one method now, I fear that in the future, you will no longer have the unique opportunity to encounter this straightforward, sublime shortcut!

NOTES TO LETTER 17

(1) Letter to a layman in Yungchia. (Chinese ed. Vol. I, p. 99; VN ed., p. 40)

(2) These two paragraphs illustrate the Buddhist concept of the Middle Way -- a balance between emotion and reason, phenomena and noumenon, existence and emptiness, neither opposing an idea nor extolling it.

(3) This important concept is also found in the *Diamond Sutra* (translation of A.F. Price & Wong Mou-Lam, sect. VII, p. 32).

See also the following passage:

> Since that which is real includes nothing worth begrudging, they give their body, life, and property in charity, without regret, without the vanity of giver, gift or recipient, and without bias or attachment. And to eliminate impurity they teach others, but without becoming attached to form ... And as with charity, they also practice the other virtues. But while practicing the six virtues [paramitas] to eliminate delusion, they practice nothing at all. This is what's meant by practicing the Dharma. ("Outline of practice" in Red Pine, tr., *The Zen Teaching of Bodhidharma*, p. 7.)

(4) Demons: generally understood as, though not necessarily limited to, hallucinations. Many kinds of demons are mentioned in the sutras. For an in-depth discussion, see *Buddhism of Wisdom and Faith,,* sect. 52, p. 210.

The Self-Mind has been described in Mahayana sutras as a house full of gold and jewelry. To preserve the riches, i.e., to keep the mind calm, empty and still, we should shut the door to the three demons of greed, anger and delusion. Letting the mind move (through anger, desire, etc.) opens the house to "demons," that is, hallucinations and harm. Thus, Zen practitioners are taught that, while in meditation, "Encountering demons, kill the demons, encountering Buddhas, kill the Buddhas." Both demons and Buddhas are mind-made.

(5) This paragraph is ingeniously written to draw attention to a subtle Buddhist teaching, particularly emphasized in Zen: the ordinary mind (i.e., the mind when not swayed by greed, anger and delusion) is the Way, ordinary actions are Bodhi. All Buddhist teachings are to be found within our own mind, in everyday activities. There is no need to travel anywhere in search of gurus, teachers or even Buddhas.

(6) Immortal physicians. The original text referred to two Taoist physicians of quasi-supernatural power.

(7) Surangama Mantra. This mantra is found in the *Surangama Sutra*, which is studied by all Mahayana Buddhists, particularly Zen practitioners. The mantra is recited daily by monks and nuns to free themselves, *inter alia*, of the karma of lust.

The Great Compassion Mantra is very popular among Buddhists, both clergy and laymen. It is associated with the Bodhisattva Avalokitesvara. This mantra is also called the Dharani of the Most Compassionate One. According to Buddhist teachings, anyone reciting this mantra will have his wholesome wishes fulfilled.

(8) Sutra Recital (also translated as "scriptural recital") is a method of mind cultivation widely employed in the East. See the following passage from the biography of the illustrious Zen Master Han-shan (16th century):

> In view of the differences of ability among men, Han-shan mentions two kinds of scriptural studies, one intended for the sharp mind and the other for the dull.

> "Those who have a sharp mind can thoroughly examine the doctrine of the noumenal ... and phenomenal ... and trace the latter to the former as the source. Through the good influence´ ... of great learning, they start from scriptural studies and go on to cultivate the mind. The state of samadhi is then realized ... Those who have dull minds cannot drive the vehicle of scriptural studies but they can practice the method of reciting the scriptures ... In reciting the scriptures, one must concentrate singlemindedly, just as the ancient masters who withdrew into their inner state to meditate on the truth. As soon as words are forgotten in subtle comprehension, the Buddha's doctrine of Mind is grasped." (Sung-peng Hsu, *A Buddhist Leader in Ming China*, p. 126.)

Sutra Recital, as one of the 84,000 methods of calming the monkey mind, is a common practice among Buddhists in Asia. It includes such practices as reciting sutras or commentaries without trying to understand the meaning. Only an attitude of utter sincerity and devotion is required. This method is not always fully understood by Westerners accustomed to an analytic approach. See, for example, the following quote expressing the views of a Western Zen leader:

> And what of chanting? There were many chants, and they were long and often repeated rapidly several times in succession. What was the purpose of this? If the meaning was important, wouldn't speaking the words more slowly avoid the pitfall of speaking them mechanically, by rote? (Lenore Friedman, ed. *Meetings with Remarkable Women*, p. 48.)

(9) See the following passage on discursive thinking within

the Buddhist context:

> Some Zen teachers, particularly from the Rinzai school, see thinking as a dragon guarding the way to Enlightenment, which has to be slain if progress [is] to be made, whereas the Theravadins lull it to sleep and quietly tiptoe round it ... (Guy Claxton, *The Heart of Buddhism*, p. 167.)

(10) All Buddhist schools and traditions teach some form of samatha and vipasyana (see Glossary). Samatha is stopping the monkey mind and vipasyana (contemplation) is reflecting inward. Note, for example, the approach of the Tien T'ai (Lotus Sutra) School:

> The practice of the school consists of meditation based on the methods of Chih-kuan [i.e., stopping and visualization or Samatha and Vipassana]. It contains esoteric elements such as mudras and mandalas. (*Shambala Dictionary of Buddhism and Zen*, p. 226.)

(11) To approach the sutras with a discriminating mind is no different from the Zen allegory of a person attempting to lift a chair while seated on it. If he would only get off the chair, he could raise it easily.

Similarly, the practitioner truly understands the Dharma only to the extent that he "suspends the operation of the discriminating intellect, the faculty of the internal dialogue through which people from moment to moment define and perpetuate their customary world of perception." (J.C. Cleary, *Pure Land, Pure Mind*, Introduction).

(12) Chih I (Patriarch). Also known as T'ien T'ai, Chih K'ai or Chih Che. The Patriarch Chih I (538-597) was one of China's greatest Buddhist thinkers and the founder of the T'ien T'ai or Lotus Sutra School. The Master's name and title are taken from Mount T'ien T'ai (Che Chiang Province), where he lived and preached. His life coincided with the beginning of what is known as the Golden Age of Pure Land doctrinal development (6th to 9th centuries).

In addition to his commentaries on the T'ien T'ai

doctrine, Master Chih I authored at least four treatises on Pure Land, as recorded in the *Tripitaka*, the best known of which is translated under the title "Ten Doubts about the Pure Land" in *Pure Land Buddhism: Dialogues with Ancient Masters.*

(13) A discriminating mind is the ordinary mind subject to thoughts of right/wrong, correct/incorrect, etc. This whole section refers to the core principle of Buddhism. The teachings of the Buddhas have one supreme purpose: to enable people to calm and purify the monkey mind. Once the mind is calm and pure, that is, free from the winds of greed, anger and delusion, it becomes a candle sheltered from the wind, radiating brightly.

(14) The strong language employed by master Yin Kuang is designed to stress practice (reciting the sutra as a Dharma method to calm the mind) versus study and verbalization.

(15) For an explanation of why ordinary persons should not blindly borrow the words of the sages or emulate their extraordinary actions, see the following passage concerning Kumarajiva, the renowned T'ang Dynasty monk/translator of some thirty-five sutras into Chinese:

> When Kumarajiva went to China in the fourth century of this era, the Chinese Emperor thought that such a wise person ought to have descendents, so that his wisdom would carry on. He gave concubines to Kumarajiva, and since they were a royal gift, Kumarajiva had no choice but to accept them. Afterwards, his disciples asked, "Can we have relations with women too?"

> Kumarajiva said, "Sure, but first, let me show you something." He took a handful of needles and ate them as easily as if they were noodles. When he finished, he said, "If you can do that, then you can have relations with women." (Master Sheng-yen, *The Sword of Wisdom*, p. 229.)

16) Ten Great Vows: see the *Avatamsaka Sutra*, Ch. 40 "The Practices and Vows of the Bodhisattva Samantabhadra" (See Appendix.)

(17) See the following passage:

> We may take up any Dharma for practice as long as it is agreeable to our interest and inclination, and since every Dharma is perfect and complete,

therefore in the course of cultivation, we should not think of changing from one Dharma to another, nor should we think that a certain Dharma may be superior or inferior to the others. As no medicine may be called ... bad as long as it can cure, likewise, no Dharma may be said to be ... low as long as it is adaptable to its followers. (Hsu Heng Chi, *What's Buddhism?*, p. 62.)

(18) Five skandas. Also translated as components or aggregates. They represent both body and mind. The five skandas are form, feeling, conception, impulse and consciousness. For example, form is the physical body, consciousness is the faculty of awareness, etc. The best known reference to the five skandas is found in the *Heart Sutra*. By realizing that they are intrinsically empty, the Bodhisattva Avalokitesvara has escaped all suffering, as can all sentient beings. Note the difference between intellectual understanding of this principle and truly internalizing it. (For, example, a good driver slams on the brakes when another car cuts in front of him, without stopping to think about it.) Only by internalizing the truth of emptiness can the cultivator escape suffering.

(19) No-Self, No-Dharma. The concept of No-Dharma technically includes No-Self. The explanation given here illustrates the conceptual difference between the Theravada and Mahayana viewpoints. The Theravada school teaches that everything is a composite -- an aggregate of many other elements. In Mahayana Buddhism, all dharmas (things, events, etc.) are empty not only because they are aggregates, but because they are so in their very nature.

(20) This is a reference to the following parable from the *Lotus Sutra*:

A person sewed a jewel into one corner of his friend's garment. The friend, not aware of this, made no attempt to use the jewel even when in serious straits. Then the man who sewed it into his garment pointed it out to him and thus enabled him to get out of his difficulties. (Leon Hurvitz, *Scripture of the Lotus Blossom of the Fine Dharma*, p. xiii.)

(21) Bodhisattva grounds: see Glossary under "Ten Grounds."

In most schools of Buddhism, Enlightenment is usually

described as a step-by-step process. Only those who have attained a particular stage of cultivation can understand and enjoy the fruits of that stage. Those below that level cannot fully penetrate it. Thus common beings cannot fully understand the thoughts and actions of the sages. What the sutras teach is merely a reflection of the truth, a finger pointing to the moon, not the moon (truth) itself.

(22) "Arrogance toward those above" occurs, for example, when a disciple discovers that his master (whom he has put on a pedestal since joining the Order) is not perfect. There is no longer arrogance once the practitioner has truly understood the false dichotomy between right and wrong, those above and those below, etc.

(23) Retrogression from the Way is the greatest setback for the cultivator. According to Pure Land teaching, this is the core rationale for seeking rebirth in the Pure Land rather than remaining in samsara to pursue cultivation. The possibility of retrogression within the Saha World is a near certainty for all but the most resolute practitioners.

(24) To illustrate the extreme difficulty of rebirth in the human realm, Sakyamuni Buddha compared it to the likelihood that a blind sea turtle, surfacing from the depths of the ocean only once every century, would encounter a tree trunk in which to nest.

(25) There is an important saying in Buddhism: "adapting to conditions but remaining unchanged." The outward manifestations of the Dharma vary continuously, but its essence remains the same. A monk in the West may cover his bare shoulder and wear warm clothing but his first task, all the same, is to "herd the ox," i.e., rein in his mind.

*
**

Letter 18.
Buddha Recitation and Mantras[1]

The Pure Land practitioner may recite mantras as well as the Buddha's name. However, he should make a clear distinction between the main and the subsidiary practice -- in which case the subsidiary practice naturally becomes the main practice. If, on the other hand, he is careless and considers the two practices to be equal, even the main practice is no longer the main practice![2]

The Ten-Thousand-Arm Avalokitesvara Mantra (Cundi Dharani) is neither more nor less efficacious than the Great Compassion Mantra. If the mind is utterly sincere, each and every Dharma method elicits a wonderful response; if the mind is not utterly sincere, no method is effective.[3]

A single recitation of the Buddha's name encompasses all the teachings of the Tripitaka. It includes all methods in full without omitting a single method.[4]

o
oo

Only those who are well-versed in all Buddhist traditions and teachings can be true Buddha Recitation practitioners. On the other hand, the dull, who are ignorant of everything but how to follow instructions sincerely, can also become true practitioners.[5] Outside of these two groups, the correctness of practice depends on the cultivator's diligence and on whether or not he is practicing in accordance with the teachings.

Since you are already determined and have no further doubts about Pure Land practice, why inquire about the results that other practitioners obtain? Even if no one else in the whole world obtains results, you should not develop a single thought of doubt. This is because the true words of Buddha Sakyamuni and the Patriarchs should be proof enough.

If you continually inquire about the results that other practitioners obtain, it means that you lack complete faith in the Buddhas' words -- and thus your practice certainly cannot bring results. The wise must not abandon the words of the Buddhas to follow those of human beings. Those who have no firm position and are only guided by the results of others are greatly to be pitied!

NOTES TO LETTER 18

(1) Letter to another layman in Yungchia. (Chinese ed. Vol. I, p. 134; VN ed., p. 62)

(2) In the Pure Land method, all wholesome practices are valid but the main practice should always be Buddha Recitation to achieve rebirth in the Pure Land. If the practitioner engages *indifferently* in a variety of practices, his cultivation lacks focus and thus cannot lead to one-pointedness of mind and escape from Birth and Death. If, on the other hand, he concentrates on Buddha Recitation, he will eventually reach samadhi and wisdom, at which point all distinctions are moot, the main and subsidiary practices are the same.

(3) See the following question and answer, originally part of the letter to the layman Ch'u:

> What are the differences in effectiveness between reciting the Buddha's name assiduously and chanting mantras?

Answer: The merits and virtues accrued from reciting the Buddha's name or from chanting mantras are identical. However, to obtain a response, the cultivator must be utterly sincere. If in his mind he starts out with even a single thought of disdain toward the Buddha's name, he certainly cannot obtain true benefits. This failure is due to the mind's lacking utter earnestness and harboring doubts.

This paragraph touches on an important Buddhist teaching: all Mahayana methods are perfect and sublime. It is the mind of the cultivator that creates differences in effectiveness.

(4) See the following passage:

High-ranking masters of the Buddhist canon often commented: "The Buddha Recitation method encompasses the Meditation (Zen), Sutra Studies, Discipline (Vinaya) and Esoteric Schools." Why is it that Buddha Recitation encompasses all four methods? It is because when reciting the Buddha's name, we rid ourselves of all delusions and attachments, which is Zen. The sacred words "Amitabha Buddha" contain innumerable sublime meanings, hidden in and springing forth from those words, which is the Sutra Studies School. Reciting the Buddha's name to a deep level purifies and stills the three karma (of mind, mouth and body), which is the Discipline School. The words "Amitabha Buddha" have the same effect as a mantra, eliminating injustices and wrongs, severing evil karma, granting wishes and subduing demons. -- This is the Esoteric School.

For example, during a year of long, severe drought, the Great Master Lien Ch'ih, instead of reciting the "rain mantra," just walked around the countryside hitting his fish gong while reciting the Buddha's name. It was reported that wherever he passed, the rain would begin to fall. There is also the case of the Elder Zen Master Yuan Chao Pen, who, rather than practice meditation, would just recite the sacred words "Amitabha Buddha." In the process, he became enlightened to the Original Nature and attained the Buddha Remembrance Samadhi. Extrapolating from the above, the words "Amitabha Buddha" include the Five Periods and the Eight Teachings and encompass all the paramitas ... (Master Thích Thiên Tâm, *Buddhism of Wisdom and Faith*, sect. 18, p. 73.)

(5) See the following passage:

Ancient masters have said: "Only two types of people can benefit from the Pure Land method. First are those completely deluded but truthful and sincere individuals who, upon hearing the teaching, wholeheartedly believe, accept and begin to practice it. Second are those persons with deep wisdom and good roots in the Pure Land method who clearly understand nature and marks and the virtues achieved through Buddha Recitation and who therefore resolve to believe and practice it. On the other hand, those with mere common intelligence can neither understand profoundly, nor do they have the simple belief of the completely deluded. Therefore, it is difficult for them to receive benefits." (Master Thích Thiền Tâm, *Buddhism of Wisdom and Faith*, sect. 23, p. 104-105.)

*
**

Letter 19.
Mind-Only Pure Land[1]

The main tenets of the Pure Land method are Faith, Vows and Practice. Like a three-legged incense burner, if it lacks one leg, it cannot be stable. You have diligently practiced Buddha Recitation and have no more doubts about the first criterion of Faith. However, you seem to be attached to the idea that there is a dichotomy between Vows and Practice. You therefore cannot have complete understanding and synthesis.[2]

Thus, within the unimpeded, perfect and wonderful Dharma, there suddenly arise numerous impediments and obstacles, causing the bright moon, adorned with ten thousand halos, of Elders Masters Ch'e Wu, Chien Mi and Ou I to pull apart and divide. All this is due simply to a fine silk thread before your eyes.[3] How regrettable!

The true Pure Land practitioner always fully combines the three criteria of Faith, Vows and Practice during recitation. He is like an infant longing for his mother.[4] When, lonely and crying, he searches for her, he certainly never lacks Faith or the desire (Vow) to see her. Therefore, why do you ask whether

"Vows and Practice come separately or together"? Why do you say such things as "with Vows, it is difficult to focus the mind completely," or "in Buddha Recitation, one can neither have Vows and Practice concurrently nor non-concurrently"? This is creating problems where there are none!

From your letter, and from the line of reasoning of the monk [from Hangchou], it would appear that neither of you really knows how to practice Buddha Recitation properly. You are just like someone who has not begun his journey but is already thinking of what it will be like when he returns home.

Therefore, you take the very Dharma pronouncements of ancient masters, which were designed to counteract differentiation and discrimination, to create yet more differentiation![5] Let me ask you this question: Can you really reach the stage of "no Buddha outside Mind, no Mind outside Buddha" without utmost earnestness? Can you really reach that stage without Faith and Vows? While Elder Masters Ch'e Wu and Chien Mi may differ in words, their ideas actually reinforce and complement one another. To reduce them to a question of "whether Vows and Practice are separate or together" is to lack the eye of discernment in the Dharma!

As for the words of Elder Master Ou I,[6] they represent a Dharma medicine intended for those cultivators who, following Zen practice, meditate on the Self-Nature Amitabha and the Mind-Only Pure Land. They are not cultivating in accordance with [traditional] Pure Land tenets, but merely seek an undisturbed mind as the ultimate goal.[7] This aim is something external to the [traditional] Pure Land method; why do you bring it up here and compare it to the criteria of complete Faith and Vows of True Cultivation -- thus creating opportunities for confusion?[8]

o
oo

So far, I have spoken in general, basing myself on principle and noumenon. On the level of practice and phenomena, the Vow for rebirth in the Pure Land should be made early in the morning and again at night after recitation is completed [using one of the available Vow compositions] ... You should realize that reading the text of the Vow is to rely on that text to make your own Vow -- do not think that reading through the text once is equivalent to making the Vow!

Except for morning and evening, when you make your Vow for rebirth in the Pure Land, it is enough merely to recite the Buddha's name with utmost sincerity.

NOTES TO LETTER 19.

(1) Letter to a layman. (Chinese ed. Vol. I, p. 149; VN ed., p. 64)

(2) At the ultimate level, Faith, Vows and Practice form an indivisible whole. One cannot have true "Vows" without Practice and vice versa.

(3) The Masters mentioned in this paragraph are the most eminent traditional Pure Land Masters of China.

The fine silk thread blocking the cultivator's vision is his attachment to the distinction between Vows and

Practice, which are intrinsically one and indivisible.

(4) See *Surangama Sutra* passage in which the Bodhisattva Mahastamaprapta described Her method of achieving Enlightenment. (Dwight Goddard, *A Buddhist Bible*, p. 244-5.)

(5) The mind of discrimination and differentiation is the ordinary human mind which distinguishes between right and wrong, self and others, etc. Since the Truth is one and indivisible, such a mind can never grasp the Truth in its entirety, but only a reflection of it. This is expressed by the silence of Vimalakirti (See Glossary).

(6) See the following passage:

Elder Master Ou I, a high-ranking Pure Land monk, has said, "To be reborn in the Pure Land or not depends entirely upon Faith and Vows; the grade of rebirth (high or low) depends on whether one's Practice is deep or shallow." He further added, "Without Faith and Vows, you cannot be reborn, even if you recite the Buddha's name to the point where neither the blowing wind nor the falling rain can penetrate and your recitation is as solid as a bronze wall or an iron gate." (Master Thích Thiền Tâm, *Buddhism of Wisdom and Faith*, sect. 21, p. 97.)

(7) Please note that Master Yin Kuang is merely saying that such practitioners do not cultivate according to the traditional, popular Pure Land method and therefore are not models for ordinary Pure Land followers -- at least at the beginning stages of practice. At the transcendental level, for cultivators of high capacities, Pure Land and Zen are directed toward the same goal: calming the wandering mind and achieving Buddhahood. See also Introduction, Section B (ii).

(8) The ultimate goal of all Buddhist methods and schools is the same but each approach is different. "All roads lead to Rome," but the city may be approached from the north, south, east or west, depending on the starting point of the individual.

In other words, while Buddhahood is the ultimate goal of both Pure Land and Zen, the two schools approach it from different directions. In Zen, awakening to the Way (Great Awakening) is the first major step. In Pure Land, that first step is one-pointedness of mind, leading to rebirth in the Land of Ultimate Bliss.   In both cases, further cultivation is necessary for the attainment of Ultimate Enlightenment and Buddhahood -- the goal of both Zen and Pure Land:

> I would venture to say here that, while we are still treading the path of Practice, not having reached the stage of Perfect Enlightenment, all Dharma methods are expedients; Buddha Recitation is an expedient and so is Zen. According to the three basic Pure Land sutras, Buddha Sakyamuni provided the expedient teaching of the Western Pure Land, and urged sentient beings to recite the Buddha's name seeking rebirth. With this method, they can escape birth and death, avail themselves of that wonderful, lofty realm to pursue cultivation, and swiftly attain Buddhahood. Diligent Buddha Recitation also leads to awakening, as in Zen; however, the principal goal of the Pure Land School is rebirth, while the degree of awakening achieved is a secondary consideration.
> (Master Thích Thiên Tâm, *Buddhism of Wisdom and Faith*, sect. 29, p. 117-118.)

*
**

Letter 20.
Do Not Mistake a Thief
for Your Son![1]

I am delighted to learn from your letter that you are deeply devoted to the Way.   However, because of numerous commitments, including the need to review a commentary, my answer to you has been somewhat delayed.

Greed, anger and delusion are afflictions common to everyone.   However, if you are aware that they are diseases, their power should not be overwhelming.   They are like thieves who have broken into the house.   If the owner mistakes them for members of the household, all the valuables in the house will be stolen.   If, on the other hand, he recognizes the thieves as such and immediately chases them away, his valuables will be safeguarded and he will be at peace. In this connection, the ancients have said:

> Fear not the early arising of thoughts [greed, anger, delusion, etc.]; fear only the late awareness of them as such.

When greed, anger and delusion arise, as long as you recognize them for what they are, these thoughts will immediately be destroyed.[2] If, however, you take them for the true masters of your household, it is no different from mistaking a thief for your son. How can your riches not be squandered and lost?[3]

o

oo

Your Buddha Recitation is not earnest because you have not learned to recognize the Saha World as a place of suffering and the Western Pure Land as a realm of joy. You should think thus: "It is difficult to obtain a human rebirth, it is difficult to be reborn in a 'central land,' it is difficult to hear the Buddha Dharma and even more difficult to encounter and learn about the Pure Land method.[4] If I do not recite the Buddha's name singlemindedly now, once the ghost of impermanence arrives, I am bound to descend upon the three evil paths, in accordance with the heavy evil karma of this life or of past lives, subject to long periods of suffering, with no liberation in sight."[5] If you keep these thoughts constantly in mind, you will awaken and be earnest.

Moreover, you should think about the sufferings of the various hells and develop the Bodhi Mind.[6] The Bodhi Mind is the Mind striving to benefit oneself and others. Once this Mind develops, it is like a tool which has been electrified; it acquires tremendous power and speed. No ordinary virtues or good roots can compare with it in severing karmic obstructions and increasing merits and wisdom.

o
oo

You are swayed by the environment and external circumstances because your cultivation is still shallow. Therefore, whenever you are affected by feelings of anger or joy, or have evil or wholesome thoughts, such states of mind show clearly on your face.[7] If your mind is filled with correct thoughts, all afflictions will decrease naturally. Therefore, although he may be dwelling in the prison of Birth and Death, the true cultivator always trains himself strenuously. As a result, afflictions and karmic habits are gradually eliminated. This is true cultivation. In this way the mind becomes master of itself, thus escaping the influence and control of external circumstances.

o
oo

Laymen like yourself, residing at home [unlike monks and nuns] can practice as you wish. You may recite the Buddha's name sitting, standing, kneeling or circumambulating the altar, etc. but you should not be attached to any set ways.

If you become attached to a fixed position, your body may tire easily and your mind may find it difficult to merge with the Mind of the Buddhas. To reap benefits, you should make allowances for your health or habits and skillfully select the practice that fits your circumstances.[8]

Traditionally, Pure Land practitioners circumambulate the altar at the beginning of a Buddha Recitation session, then sit down and, finally, kneel. However, if you feel tired when circumambulating or kneeling, you should sit down and recite. If you become drowsy while seated, you can circumambulate the altar or recite standing up, waiting for the drowsiness to go away before sitting down again. When reciting, it is better to determine the length of the session with a clock rather than fingering a rosary, as doing so may make it difficult to focus the mind and keep it empty and pure.[9]

NOTES TO LETTER 20

(1) Letter to Ch'en Hui-ch'ao (Chinese ed. Vol. I, p. 161; VN ed., p. 66)

(2) As an analogy, if you stamp out a smoldering cigaret butt, with very little effort a potential fire is prevented. If, however, nothing is done initially, a forest fire may develop and rage out of control. At that point, the labor expended by thousands of firefighters may be great but the results achieved will be minimal. At best such effort can put out the fire, but it cannot undo the damage which has already occurred. Thus, whenever greed, anger or delusion arises, we should immediately put a stop to it.

(3) This is a classic example taken from the *Surangama Sutra.* For example, when a person says "I'm very short-tempered by nature" he is making the basic mistake of taking a "robber" (anger) for his "son" (inherent nature). According to Buddhist teaching, the mind, in its ideal state, should be empty and still. Afflictions (greed, anger, etc.) deprive the mind of that state of peacefulness -- they "rob" the mind.

To control these "thieves," a Zen Master gave an interesting twist to the classic method of Zen cultivation. All day long he would do nothing but watch his mind, engaging in a dialogue with himself. At regular intervals he would call out loud to himself:

- "True Master, True Master."
- "Yes, yes."

- "Be mindful, do not let yourself be misled."
- "Yes, I am, yes, I am."

In this way, he would keep constant control over his wandering mind, immediately quashing thoughts of greed, anger and delusion.

(4 a) Central land. In Chinese "Chung-kuo." This expression has a double meaning. For any Chinese, it is literally the Middle Kingdom, or China. In Buddhism, it is a place where the Dharma is practiced and the words of the Buddhas are preached.

b) To illustrate the extreme difficulty of rebirth in the human realm, Sakyamuni Buddha compared it to the likelihood that a blind sea turtle, surfacing from the depths of the ocean only once a century, would encounter a tree trunk in which to nest.

(5) See the following parallel advice by a Zen Master:

Dear friends, the murderous demon of impermanence is constantly looking for our lives and will never agree to conclude peace with us! Let us hastily develop a long enduring mind to get out of birth and death. Master Yuan Miao of Kao Feng said: "If one sets a time limit for success in the Ch'an [Zen] training, one should act like a man who has fallen to the bottom of a pit one thousand *chang* [about two miles] deep. His thousand and ten-thousand thoughts are reduced to a single idea on how to escape from the pit. He keeps it up from morning to evening and from evening (to the following morning), and has no other thought. If he trains in this way and does not realize the truth in three, five or seven days, I shall be guilty of a verbal sin for which I shall fall into the hell where tongues are pulled out." ("The Ch'an Training" by Master Hsu Yun, p. 42.)

(6) Bodhi Mind: see Glossary.

(7) All feelings and emotions, whether good or bad, wholesome or evil, disturb the peacefulness of the mind. A person overcome by any kind of emotion is not on an even keel and may not exercise good judgement or do what has to be done. Therefore, all emotions should be avoided equally. As an example, a salesman can take advantage of a customer by bolstering his ego and making him happy through praise ... Thus, joy is an affliction!

(8) This is an example of the simple, pragmatic approach of Pure Land. The accoutrements of practice, while useful as aids, are not essential in themselves and may be adapted to circumstances. There is no absolute need for meditation cushions, mandalas, gurus, etc. Pure Land thus liberates the practitioner, enabling him to concentrate on practice. For an interesting parallel between Pure Land and the "Zen of the Patriarchs," see the following passage:

> While others viewed Zen as purification of the mind ... Bodhidharma equated Zen with Buddhahood -- and Buddhahood with the mind, the everyday mind ... Bodhidharma's Zen was Mahayana Zen, not Hinayana Zen -- the sword of wisdom, not the meditation cushion.
> (Red Pine, *The Zen Teaching of Bodhidharma*, p. xv.)

(9) Another example of the pragmatic approach of Pure Land, as anyone who has fingered a rosary fifty times or more at a stretch can readily testify. This, of course, may not apply to all practitioners, particularly beginners who recite only a few times a day.

*
**

Letter 21.
Buddhism and the Tao[1]

The Taoist Master "Ocean Corpse"[2] recently conveyed your letter to me. From reading it, I learned that you have been practicing Taoism assiduously for a long time and that your achievements are profound. That you are now inquiring into the Pure Land method, which is the foremost practice in Buddhism, demonstrates that in previous lifetimes, you planted deep, wholesome roots in the Buddha Dharma. That is why you have not followed the grasping view of the God of Water,[3] but, out of the ocean of teachings, have learned to seek the shore of Ultimate Liberation.

Since you are acquainted with Master Ocean Corpse, why not seek instruction from him; why leave the lofty, bright ground he represents for a low, dark place? Is it not turning your back on your hopes and aspirations? The Taoist Master Ocean Corpse was originally well-versed in Buddhist teachings and schools, has practiced both Zen and Pure Land and is no less than the boat of Great Vows in the sea of Birth and Death. Because of his modesty, he adopted the name "Corpse." In truth, anyone who encounters such a corpse in the sea of Birth and Death will, without doubt, speedily reach the other shore and peacefully return home.[4] Is it not better [to approach him] than to ask a lowly monk who lacks full understanding of the Dharma?

Nevertheless, since you had the poor judgement to have inquired of me, I shall, for my part, reply to you in accordance with my shallow opinions. Hopefully, my answers may assuage some of your doubts![5]

o
oo

I venture to think that, in their essence, Buddhism and Taoism spring from the same source. However, their various schools differ greatly in their practices today. Buddhism teaches us, first of all, to practice the Four Foundations of Mindfulness, that is, to contemplate the body as impure,[6] all feelings as suffering, the [ordinary] mind as impermanent and all phenomena as lacking self-nature. When we realize that body, feelings, mind and phenomena are impure, the source of suffering, impermanent, without self-nature, false, dream-like and illusory, the True Thusness Nature will manifest itself.

Buddhism encompasses all methods and dharmas. Not only does it clearly explain the issues of body, mind and life, it does not neglect the small issues of human morality,[7] such as "filiality,[8] respect for elders, loyalty, faith, propriety, justice, decency and shame." The exception is the practice of "balancing energy currents," about which not a single word is said in the Buddha Dharma.[9] Not only that, Buddhism forbids the practice entirely. This is because while Taoism regards the preservation of body and mind as an ideal, Buddhism, on the contrary, teaches that body and mind are intrinsically false, born of conditions, disappearing also through conditions.[10] They are not the Self-Nature True Mind.[11]

From your letter, it seems that you already know that "Immortals" have a definite life-span while the Buddha's life is without limit. Therefore, now that you are advanced in age, you should diligently practice the Pure Land method. Keep your investigation of Zen and other teachings to a minimum, as these methods are broad and profound and not easy to study. Even if you were to reach the ultimate source, you would still need to return to the Pure Land method to resolve the problem of Birth and Death in this very lifetime.[12]

You should read the Pure Land sutras and commentaries without delay and practice in accordance with their teachings -- with deep faith in the words of the Buddhas and Patriarchs. Do not develop doubts when you encounter something you cannot yet understand. If you are utterly sincere in your Faith, Vows and Practice, you will naturally be able to rely on the compassionate power of Amitabha Buddha to achieve rebirth in the Pure Land. Once reborn you will be close to the Buddha, in the company of the Ocean-Wide Assembly and gradually attain the fruit of Non-Birth and the rank of a One-Life Bodhisattva.[13] At that time, looking back at your original intention of becoming an Immortal in the assembly of the Lord Brahma, and comparing it to your current status, you will discover that the two are as different as a dark ravine from the blue yonder!

o
oo

"Sarira" is a Sanskrit word translated as "relics," "remains of the body." It also means "miraculous remains," which are the crystallization of the cultivation of precepts, concentration and wisdom and not the result of "balancing energy currents." It is the symbolic mark of the cultivator who has reached the state of union between Mind and Buddha. However, Buddhist relics do not come only from the transformation of flesh, bones and hair during cremation, but also derive from many other circumstances.

For example, once upon a time, an Elder Master, while bathing, suddenly obtained some relics. A Zen Master, having a tonsure, saw his hair turn into a string of relics. There are instances of relics emerging from the mouths of practitioners earnestly reciting the Buddha's name.[14] A printer setting the text of a famous Pure Land commentary saw relics among the wooden typefaces. A laywoman embroidering Buddhist images and sutras found relics under her needle point. In another case, a practitioner who had returned from afar and was wholeheartedly paying respect before his altar, suddenly saw relics emerging from one of the statues. These accounts demonstrate that relics are due to the power of cultivation [not internal energy currents].

o
oo

The Bodhisattva Avalokitesvara (Kuan Yin) has,

since time without beginning, been a Buddha with the name of True Dharma Light. While residing in the Land of Eternal Stillness, because of Her boundless concern and compassion She also appears in all lands and realms. Standing beside Amitabha Buddha, She also manifests Herself everywhere, as Buddha, Bodhisattva, Arhat, Pratyeka Buddha, or takes the form of various beings along the six paths in the Dharma Realm of the ten directions. She accomplishes whatever deeds are of benefit to sentient beings and takes whatever form is necessary to rescue them and teach them the Dharma.[15]

P'u T'o Mountain is the place associated with this Bodhisattva.[16] In order to provide sentient beings with a focal point to express their sincerity, the Bodhisattva manifested Her Parinirvana (earthly demise) on this mountain.

This does not mean that the Bodhisattva resides only on P'u T'o Mountain and not elsewhere. As an analogy, the single moon in the sky appears in ten thousand rivers and lakes. From the oceans to the tiniest dewdrops, wherever there is limpid water, the moon appears. However, if the water is turbid or muddy, the image of the moon will be blurred or hidden. Our Mind-Nature is similar to the water. If sentient beings concentrate singlemindedly on the Bodhisattva Avalokitevara, She employs all kinds of expedients, favorable or unfavorable, hidden or overt, to bring them benefits.[17] If, on the other hand, the cultivator is not utterly sincere and singleminded in his recitation, his "mind water" will be turbid and it will be difficult for him to obtain a response. The meaning of this is very profound. If you read the section on P'u T'o Mountain in my compendium of letters you will understand this yourself.

The Bodhisattva, when in the *causal stage*,[18]

"visualized" (concentrated on) the nature of hearing and thus attained perfect, all-pervading power.[19] When in the *result stage* (as a Bodhisattva), She visualizes the voices of sentient beings calling upon Her and goes to their rescue -- hence the name "Regarder of the Cries of the World."[20] Moreover, the Bodhisattva's Dharma methods are boundless and all-encompassing. She preaches every kind of method to teach and transform sentient beings in accordance with their individual capacities and nature, without insisting on any particular Dharma method. Therefore, Her approach is called "all-sided."

o

oo

What I have just discussed are some superficial issues, which you are not familiar with because you have not examined them. My answers have followed the order of your questions. In fact, these answers do not cover the Pure Land method, a teaching that can bring you full benefits. However, if I were to give a more detailed explanation, I fear it would be lengthy and waste more paper and ink. You should obtain and read the *Longer Amitabha Sutra*, the *Meditation Sutra*, the *Biographies of Pure Land Sages and Saints* ... These books provide a full explanation of the theory and practice of cultivation and attainment.

NOTES TO LETTER 21

(1) Letter to Li Yin-sou (Chinese ed. Vol. I, p. 163; VN ed., p. 68)

(2) Ocean Corpse. This could be an allusion to the "as-if-dead" mind (dead to all concerns) of advanced practitioners. In Mahayana teaching, this state of mind is

attained through rigorous concentration and is a very high stage -- but it is not enough. The cultivator should go beyond this stage as he progresses further toward Buddhahood and the goal of benefitting all sentient beings.

(3)   God of Water: Taoist deity.   The Taoist practitioner traditionally strives for immortality, which, in Buddhist teaching, is a classic example of deluded attachment to the body.

(4)   Other shore; return home: Well-known Buddhist metaphors for returning to the Self-Nature -- the Buddha Mind.   Master Yin Kuang is suggesting here that Master Ocean Corpse could be a Bodhisattva who helps sentient beings return to the other shore of liberation.

(5)   The language of humility employed here is typical of classical Chinese writing.   It should not be construed as false modesty.

(6)   Four Foundations of Mindfulness: basic practices of Buddhism, particularly stressed in the Theravada school.

Contemplation of the body as impure.   According to Buddhist teaching, the body is a skin-bag with nine orifices (eyes, ears, mouth, nostrils, etc.) from which foul-smelling substances ooze out all day long.   See also the following passage on Vimalakirti:

> The sage Vimalakirti discussed the experience of illness at great length ... With many visitors assembled to inquire after his health, the infirm sage took the opportunity to speak out against the human body and its limitations.
>
> "O, virtuous ones, the wise do not rely upon the body. It is like a mass of froth which cannot be grasped, like a bubble which bursts in an instant. The body is like a flame arising from the thirst of love ... like a shadow, appearing as a result of karma. It is like an echo, responding to causes and conditions ... The body does not act of itself; but it is spun around by the force of the winds of passion."
>
> His own face gaunt and creased by illness, vividly impressing upon visitors the transitory nature of earthly existence, Vimalakirti then urged

them to seek the Buddha-body. (Raoul Birnbaum, *The Healing Buddha*, p. 13.)

(7)   These issues are deemed small by comparison with the great matter of Birth and Death.

(8)   See the following anecdote concerning Prince Ajatasattu and the father he murdered, King Bimbisara, which appears at the beginning of the *Meditation Sutra:*

> Immediately he rushed to his beloved mother and questioned, "Mother dear, did my father love me when I was a child?"

> "What, say you, son!   When you were conceived in my womb, I developed a craving to sip some blood from the right hand of your father. This I dared not say. Consequently, I grew pale and thin. I was finally persuaded to disclose my inhuman desire. Joyfully your father fulfilled my wish, and I drank that abhorrent potion. The soothsayers predicted that you would be an enemy of your father. Accordingly you were named Ajatasattu (unborn enemy). I attempted to effect a miscarriage, but your father prevented it. After you were born, again I wanted to kill you. Again your father interfered. On one occasion you were suffering from a boil on your finger, and nobody was able to lull you into sleep. But your father, who was administering justice in his royal court, took you into his lap and caressing you, sucked the boil. Lo, inside his mouth, it burst open. Oh, my dear son, that pus and blood! Yes, your affectionate father swallowed it out of love for you."

> Instantly, he cried, "Run and release my beloved father quickly!"

> His father had closed his eyes forever. (Narada, *The Buddha and His Teachings*, p. 108-109.)

This vivid and poignant story serves a reminder of the need for filial devotion and provides the setting for the *Meditation Sutra*, one of the three core sutras of the Pure Land School.

(9)   On the question of "balancing energy currents," see the following passage:

> There are some who appear to be monks and nuns, residing in temples and pagodas; however they neither study nor understand Buddhism and only follow the practices of other religions. These people are peddling a panoply of other beliefs under the label of Buddhism. They and their followers secretly transmit their beliefs to one another. Many of them, while claiming to practice meditation, in fact specialize in exercises to

balance energy currents with little knowledge of what meditation is all about. As far as the Pure Land method is concerned, they teach that one should visualize the Buddha's name "shooting" from the navel to the back of the body and up the spinal column, and then returning to the navel. This, they say, is "turning the Dharma wheel." This is the practice of "releasing blockages in the energy system," [i.e., balancing energy currents] according to externalist schools. Such teaching is not consonant with Buddhism. (Master Thích Thiên Tâm, *Buddhism of Wisdom and Faith*, sect. 16, p. 64-65.)

These heterodox practices are referred to nowadays under a variety of names, such as polarity therapy, Dr. Randolph Stone's method, life energy healing arts, spiritual/energy healing, healing ministry, laying on hands ministry ...

(10)   Basic teaching in Buddhism: body and mind are intrinsically empty of true nature, the five skandas are empty.

(11)   See Introduction and Glossary under "Mind."   All Buddhist teachings revert the everyday mind to the Self-Nature True Mind.

(12)   This letter is presumably directed to an elderly Confucian scholar. To escape Birth and Death through most Buddhist methods, it is imperative to extinguish all delusions to the last iota -- a feat beyond the capacity of all but a very few, let alone someone already advanced in age. This being the case, rebirth in the Pure Land is the most expedient approach.

(13) Non-Birth; One-life Bodhisattva: see Glossary.

(14) A parallel image of Buddhas emerging from the mouths of Great Masters appears frequently in Japanese Pure Land paintings, particularly in the depiction of the Patriarch Shan Tao. (cf. Joji Okazaki, *Pure Land Buddhist Painting*, p. 17, 173. This book is an excellent treatment of Pure Land thought, as seen through Japanese paintings.)

(15)   The Bodhisattva Kuan Yin is one of the Three Pure Land Sages, the others being Buddha Amitabha and the Bodhisattva Mahastamaprapta (Ta Shih Chih). The *Meditation*

Sutra teaches, *inter alia*, visualization of their features. In many texts, these two Bodhisattvas are referred to in the masculine form. However, we have chosen the feminine pronouns to reflect popular East Asian imagery.

(16) P'u T'o Mountain. Mountain in Chekiang Province, south of Shanghai. It is traditionally believed that the Bodhisattva Avalokitesvara manifested Parinirvana there.

(17) This is a manifestation of expedient means (skill-in-means or upaya). See, for example, this passage from a basic Zen text, the *Vimalakirti Sutra:*

> They [Bodhisattvas] play with illusory manifestations/In order to develop living beings,/Showing themselves to be old or sick,/And even manifesting their own deaths.

> They demonstrate the burning of the earth/In the consuming flames of the world's end,/In order to demonstrate impermanence/To living beings with the notion of permanence." (Robert Thurman, *The Holy Teaching of Vimalakirti,* p. 69).

(18) Causal stage(s): All the stages before a given level of attainment (Arhatship, Bodhisattvahood, Buddhahood) is reached. The Jakata stories provide good illustrations of Sakyamuni Buddha in the causal stages, that is, as a Bodhisattva, Arhat, human being, even as an animal.

(19) See the *Surangama Sutra* for a description of the Bodhisattva Avalokitesvara's method of Enlightenment, based on the nature of hearing.

(20) See the *Lotus Sutra*, Ch. 25, in which Sakyamuni Buddha explained to the Assembly the efficacy of invoking the Bodhisattva Avalokitesvara. See also the following:

> Kuan-yin's widespread popularity in Chinese Buddhism continues to the present day. In part, this popularity is based on what is perceived as practical experience by Chinese Buddhists, attested by many stories of miraculous events written in classical and popular styles. Even Hsuan-tsang, the intrepid T'ang traveller to India in search of the Law, who was steeped in highly abstruse philosophical studies of Buddhist doctrine, continually invoked the aid of Kuan-yin at times of danger, and thus was enabled to pass safely through desert wastes and bandit-infested mountain passes. In this way, according to traditional

accounts, he often was saved from death ... (Raoul Birnbaum, *The Healing Buddha*, p. 243.)

*
**

Letter 22.
Cultivate, Do Not Verbalize![1]

The tenets of the Pure Land method are Faith, Vows and Practice. Only with true Faith and earnest Vows can Practice be assiduous and pure. The common disease of sentient beings is to be diligent and earnest when catastrophe strikes but lax and remiss in normal times.

However, living in this current period [of strife and war] is no different from lying peacefully on a huge pile of dried wood under which a fire has already started. Though it has not yet reached the body, in no time flames and smoke will cover everything, leaving no possibility of escape. If you are indifferent or careless, remiss in seeking help through reciting the Buddha's name, your understanding and perception are shallow indeed![2]

o
oo

When cultivating various Dharma methods, you must reach the level of "development of true practice, cessation of analysis" before you can receive true benefits.[3] This is not unique to the Visualization Method of Pure Land.[4] In Zen, a meaningless koan (kung an) becomes the "very life and mind" of the cultivator;[5] he puts his entire mind and thought into it, constantly meditating on it, oblivious to the passage of time, be it days or months, until he reaches the point of extinguishing all discriminating, delusive views with respect to internal and external realms. Only then does he achieve Great Awakening.[6] Is this not "development of true practice, cessation of analysis"?

The Sixth Patriarch has said:

Simply by reading the *Diamond Sutra*, we can illumine our Mind and see our True Nature.

Is this not also "development of true practice, cessation of analysis"?

The word "development" should be understood here as "[developing to] the utmost." Only by striving to the utmost can the cultivator forget altogether about body, mind and the world around him, remaining completely still and tranquil, as though of one hue.[7]

If your cultivation has not reached the highest level, you may practice Visualization and Recitation, but you will still be making the distinction between subject and object (yourself and the Buddhas). You will be engaged in an entirely mundane, ordinary activity, entirely within the realm of discriminatory views and understanding. How can you, then, achieve true benefits? That is why, when the ancients were in meditation, their mind and thoughts were like withered trees.[8] Thus, their lofty conduct was known far and wide and later generations continue to admire and esteem them. These benefits are all due to the single word "utmost."

People today prefer empty talk; few care to cultivate. Pure Land should include both theory and practice, with a definite emphasis on practice.[9] Why? It is because for the person who thoroughly comprehends theory, all of practice is theory -- practicing all day at the phenomenal level is practicing at the noumenon level.

When those who lack clear understanding of noumenon and phenomena hear the words "practice at the noumenal level," they consider the meaning to be profound and sublime. They also find it consonant with their lazy, lethargic minds, which loathe the effort and difficulties of Buddha Recitation. Thus, they immediately grasp at noumenon and abandon the phenomenal.[10] Little do they realize that when the phenomenal aspect is abandoned, noumenon becomes hollow and meaningless as well! I hope that you will explain cultivation at both the phenomenal and noumenal levels to everyone, counselling them accordingly. The benefits will be great indeed!

NOTES TO LETTER 22

(1) Letter to the layman Fan Ku-nung (Chinese ed. Vol. I, p. 174; VN ed., p. 72)

(2) Note the words of Bodhidharma:

> To dwell in the three realms is to dwell in a burning house. To have a body is to suffer. Does anyone with a body know peace? Those who understand this ... stop imagining or seeking anything. The sutras say, "to seek is to suffer." ("Outline of Practice," in Red Pine, tr., *The Zen Teaching of Bodhidharma*, p. 5.)

(3) "Development of true practice." The Chinese word is "ch'i," which encompasses a range of meaning from "begin" to "arise" and "rise." The Master is describing here the true spirit of practice arising in the cultivator.

"True benefits" refers to escape from Birth and Death and, ultimately, Buddhahood. See also the following words of Bodhidharma:

> Greedy for the small mercies of this world, they remain blind to the great suffering to come. Such disciples wear themselves out in vain. Turning

from the true to the false, they talk about nothing but future blessings. ("Breakthrough Sermon" in Red Pine, tr., *The Zen Teaching of Bodhidharma*, p. 113.)

(4)   The Visualization method in Pure Land is akin to the meditation methods of other Buddhist schools. It is described in the *Meditation Sutra*.

(5)   A koan (kung an, also called hua t'ou) is "meaningless" because it cannot be solved by the discriminating mind. A leap to another level of understanding is required.

(6)   Note the difference between the concept of Great Awakening and the concept of achieving Enlightenment.

(7)   On a related question, see the following passage concerning the practice of reciting the sutras without trying to comprehend the passages, so as to avoid the mind of differentiation.

> To get out of the circle of habit, a reflection of what the scripture calls the "mundane whirl," Buddhist practice proposes a dual process of arresting involutionary patterns and incorporating evolutionary patterns. In the practice of scriptural recital, the focus of concentration works to halt the wandering mind and take the attention off habitual trains of thought, while the structure and imagery of the scripture that then flow into the mind, bypassing the conditioned intellect, are able to set up new patterns of perception. (Thomas Cleary, *The Flower Adornment Sutra*, Vol. III, p. 6).

(8)   "Withered tree," like "Ocean Corpse," could be an allusion to the "as if dead mind" of the meditator (dead to all concerns). Please note, however, that while this is a very high level of cultivation achieved by few persons, it is still a preliminary stage along the path to Enlightenment. The practitioner should transcend this stage as he pursues his cultivation. There is a famous Zen koan regarding a disciple who burned down her teacher's meditation hut and chased him away because after years of cultivation, he had stopped at that level:

> Once there was a devoted old woman who built a place of retreat for a monk, arranging that he would not lack for anything, so that he could concentrate upon his meditation and practice. One day, after twenty years,

she instructed her daughter: "Today, after serving the Master his meal, take advantage of the situation to embrace him tightly, asking him at the same time, 'how does it feel to be hugged these days?' Come back and let me know his answer as faithfully as you can."

The daughter dutifully did as she was told, putting her arms around the Master and asking the question. The Master replied, "I am not moved in the very least by sexual desire, no different from a dried up tree leaning against a cold mass of rocks in the middle of winter, when not even a drop of warmth can be found." The young girl repeated the answer to her mother, who said unhappily, "I have really wasted my time and effort during the last twenty years. Little did I know that I was only supporting a common mortal!" Having said this, she went out, evicted the monk, lit a fire and burned the meditation hut to the ground.

In truth, it is rare enough these days for anyone to cultivate to the level of that monk. As far as the old woman is concerned, she is said to be a Bodhisattva in disguise. Her action of burning down the hut was to "enlighten" the Master. Why is this so? It is because, while not moved by sexual desire, he still saw himself as pure and was still attached to the empty and still aspects of meditation. Thus, he had not attained True Enlightenment. (Master Thích Thiền Tâm, *Buddhism of Wisdom and Faith*, sect. 36, p. 148.)

(9) Pure Land as a method is first and foremost practice/praxis.

(10) Note the danger of grasping at noumenon, abandoning phenomena and overreaching oneself.

For an explanation of why ordinary persons should not blindly borrow the words of the sages or emulate their extraordinary actions, see the following passage concerning Kumarajiva, the renowned T'ang Dynasty monk (who translated some thirty-five sutras into Chinese):

When Kumarajiva went to China in the fourth century of this era, the Chinese Emperor thought that such a wise person ought to have descendents, so that his wisdom would carry on. He gave concubines to Kumarajiva, and since they were a royal gift, Kumarajiva had no choice but to accept them. Afterwards, his disciples asked, "Can we have relations with women too?"

Kumarajiva said, "Sure, but first, let me show you something." He took a handful of needles and ate them as easily as if they were noodles. When he finished, he said, "If you can do that, then you can have relations with women." (Sheng-yen, *The Sword of Wisdom*, p. 229.)

*
**

Letter 23.
This Mind is the Buddha[1]

There are, in general, four methods of Pure Land practice: oral recitation (Holding the Name), contemplation of a Buddha image, Visualization (contemplation by thought) and True Mark Recitation.[2]

Among the four methods, oral recitation has the broadest appeal. It is not only easy to practice, it does not lead to "demonic events."

If you wish to practice the Visualization method, you should carefully read the *Meditation Sutra* and clearly understand such principles as "This Mind is the Buddha,"[3] "If the mind is pure, the Buddha appears," "All realms and states are Mind-Only, there should be no attachment to them." Once you understand that realms and states do not come from the outside and avoid developing attachments to them, these states then become more sublime and the mind grows purer and more focussed.[4] If you reach that point, the benefits of Visualization are significant.

On the other hand, if you are unfamiliar with the realms visualized and have not comprehended the essence of the Dharma, but are over-eager to see [auspicious] realms, everything is delusion. Not only are you not in communion with the Buddhas, you even begin to create the causes of demonic events (hallucinate). This is because the more eager you are to see realms, the more agitated and deluded your mind becomes.[5]

Since from the outset, you have failed to apply your mind correctly, you will not be able to realize that these realms are demonic apparitions. Therefore, you are overcome with joy; your thoughts and feelings are not peaceful and calm. Taking advantage of this, demons will cloud your mind and plunder your Self-Nature.[6] At that point, even if a living Buddha were to appear, He would have no way of rescuing you!

o

oo

You should, therefore, take your capacities and circumstances into consideration and not aim for what is too lofty and beyond your reach -- seeking benefits only to receive harm. The Patriarch Shan Tao has said:[7]

"Sentient beings in the Dharma-Ending Age have agitated, inverted minds. Visualizing lofty realms with such coarse minds is certainly difficult to accomplish!"

Therefore, the Great Sage took pity and specifically recommended oral recitation because He feared that those who are not skillful in using their minds would be lost in demonic realms.[8]

Cultivation through oral recitation is very easy. To achieve rebirth in the Pure Land, you need only ensure that singleminded thought follows singleminded thought.[9] Moreover, utmost sincerity and earnestness are also wonderful methods to treat the deluded mind and demonic realms.

You should think this over carefully and strive with all your mental strength to cultivate.

NOTES TO LETTER 23

(1) Letter to the layman Wu Hsi-chen (Chinese ed. Vol. I, p.

177; VN ed., p. 73)

(2)   The Pure Land School as presented here is currently practiced in China, Vietnam and Korea, among other nations. In the case of Japan, the Pure Land School is mainly divided into two branches, the Jodo (Pure Land) School and the Jodo Shinshu (True Pure Land) School. The teachings of the Jodo School (founded by Honen, 1133-1212) are substantially the same as the teachings presented here. In the case of Jodo Shinshu (founded by Honen's best known disciple, Shinran Shonin, 1173-1262, and represented in the United States by the Buddhist Church of America), overwhelming emphasis is placed on faith in "other-power," sometimes defined as the all-encompassing Mind.

> The nembutsu [recitation of the Buddha's name] then becomes an expression of gratitude to Amida for the gift of faith that leads to birth in the Pure Land, rather than a meritorious act that effects rebirth. (Joji Okazaki, *Pure Land Buddhist Painting, p. 23.*)

(3) See the following:

> This mind is the buddha. This is Mahayana Buddhism in a nutshell. Once a monk asked Big Plum what Matsu taught him. Big Plum said, "This mind is the buddha." The monk replied, "Nowadays Matsu teaches That which isn't the mind isn't the buddha." To this Big Plum responded, "Let him have That which isn't the mind isn't the buddha. I'll stick with This mind is the buddha." When he heard this story, Matsu said, "The plum is ripe." (from *Transmission of the Lamp*, Ch. 7, as quoted in Red Pine, *The Zen Teaching of Bodhidharma*, p. 116.)

(4) For the true cultivator, attachment to any state, good or bad, blissful or sorrowful, should be avoided. A cage is still a cage, gilded or not. In the words of Bodhidharma:

> As mortals, we're ruled by conditions, not by ourselves. All the suffering and joy we experience depend on conditions. If we should be blessed by some great reward, such as fame or fortune, it's the fruit of a seed planted by us in the past. When conditions change, it ends. Why delight in its existence? But while success and failure depend on conditions, *the mind neither waxes nor wanes.* Those who remain unmoved by the wind of joy silently follow the Path. ("Outline of Practice" in Red Pine, tr., *The Zen Teaching of Bodhidharma*, p. 5.)

(5) The Zen Patriarch Bodhidharma expressed the same idea

in the following words:

> Even if a buddha or bodhisattva should suddenly appear before you, there's no need for reverence. This mind of ours is empty and contains no such form. Those who hold onto appearances are devils. They fall from the path. Why worship illusions born of the mind? Those who worship don't know, and those who know don't worship. By worshipping you come under the spell of devils ... At the appearance of spirits, demons, or divine beings, conceive neither respect nor fear. Your mind is basically empty. All appearances are illusions. Don't hold on to appearances. ("The Bloodstream Sermon" in Red Pine, tr. *The Zen Teaching of Bodhidharma, p. 25.*)

For a related discussion on demons, see the following passage:

> Thus, when you are practicing Zen, all thoughts other than the method [koan] should be considered as demons, even if it feels like you have entered a 'heavenly' state. Some people, as they are sitting, may suddenly enter a completely new world which is very beautiful and comfortable. Afterwards, they want to return to it in each meditation. They may be able to get into that state again, but nonetheless it is an attachment. There are also other states that are terrifying. Such visions, good and bad, are generally manifestations of our own mental realms. (Master Sheng-Yen, *Faith in Mind*, p. 66.)

(6) The immediate purpose of all Buddhist cultivation is to rein in the monkey mind, that is, to master the three karmas of greed, anger and delusion, thus returning to the True Nature. In this connection, see also the following passage, by the late founder of the Buddhist Lodge and Buddhist Society (London), on the true goal of all Buddhist practice:

> In the West, the need for some guidance in mind-development was made acute ... by a sudden spate of books which were, whatever the motive of their authors, dangerous in the extreme. No word was said in them of the sole right motive for mind-development, the enlightenment of the meditator for the benefit of all mankind, and the reader was led to believe that it was quite legitimate to study and practice mindfulness, and the higher stages which ensue, for the benefit of business efficiency and the advancement of personal prestige. In these circumstances, *Concentration and Meditation* ... was compiled and published by the [British] Buddhist Society, with constant stress on the importance of right motive, and ample warning of the dangers, from a headache to insanity, which lie in wait for those who trifle with the greatest force on earth, the human mind. (Christmas Humphreys, *The Buddhist Way of Life*, p. 100.)

(7)   Shan Tao (613-681): one of the major Pure Land Patriarchs, well-known both in China and Japan. See also Introduction.

(8)   See the following passage:

In his *Treatise on the Awakening of the Faith*, the Patriarch Asvaghosha admonished:

"There may be some disciples whose root of merit is not yet mature, whose control of mind is weak and whose power of application is limited -- and yet who are sincere in their purpose to seek Enlightenment -- these for a time may be beset and bewildered by maras [demons] and evil influences who are seeking to break down their good purpose.

"Such disciples, seeing seductive sights, attractive girls, strong young men, must constantly remind themselves that all such tempting and alluring things are mind-made, and, if they do this, their tempting power will disappear and they will no longer be annoyed.   Or, if they have visions of heavenly gods and Bodhisattvas ånd Buddhas surrounded by celestial glories, they should remind themselves that these, too, are mind-made and unreal.   Or, if they should be uplifted and excited by listening to mysterious Dharanis, to lectures upon the paramitas, to elucidations of the great principles of the Mahayana, they must remind themselves that these also are emptiness and mind-made, that in their essence they are Nirvana itself.   Or, if they should have intimations within that they have attained transcendental powers, recalling past lives, or foreseeing future lives, or, reading others' thoughts, or freedom to visit other Buddha-lands, or great powers of eloquence, all of these may tempt them to become covetous for worldly power and riches and fame. Or, they may be tempted by extremes of emotion, at times angry, at other times joyous, or at times very kind-hearted and compassionate, at other times the very opposite, or at times alert and purposeful, at other times indolent and stupid, at times full of faith and zealous in their practice, at other times engrossed in other affairs and negligent.

"All of [these] will keep them vacillating, at times experiencing a kind of fictitious samadhi, such as the heretics boast of, but not the true samadhi.   Or later, when they are quite advanced [they] become absorbed in trances for a day, or two, or even seven, not partaking of any food but upheld by inward food of their spirit, being admired by their friends and feeling very comfortable and proud and complacent, and then later becoming very erratic, sometimes eating little, sometimes greedily, and the expression of their face constantly changing.

"Because of all such strange manifestations and developments in the course of their practices, disciples should be on their guard to keep the mind under constant control.   They should neither grasp after nor become attached to the passing and unsubstantial things of the senses or concepts and moods of the mind. If they do this they will be able to keep far away from the hindrances of karma." (translation by Wei-tao, in *A Buddhist Bible*, p. 402-3.)

(9) See the following passage:

In the *Treatise on the Awakening of the Faith*, after summarizing the essential points of Mahayana doctrine and explaining the path of cultivation, the Patriarch Asvaghosha added:

"Next, suppose there is a man who learns this teaching for the first time and wishes to seek the correct faith but lacks courage and strength. Because he lives in this world of suffering, he fears that he will not always be able to meet the Buddhas and honor them personally, and that, faith being difficult to perfect, he will be inclined to fall back.

"He should know that the Tathagathas have an excellent expedient means by which they can protect his faith: that is, through the strength of wholehearted meditation-recitation on the Buddha, he will in fulfillment of his wishes be able to be born in the Buddha-land beyond, to see the Buddha always, and to be forever separated from the evil states of existence.

"It is as the sutra says: 'If a man meditates wholly on Amitabha Buddha in the world of the Western Paradise and wishes to be born in that world, directing all the goodness he has cultivated toward that goal, then he will be born there.' Because he will see the Buddha at all times, he will never fall back ... [If a cultivator follows this path], he will be able to be born there in the end because he abides in the correct samadhi." (Asvaghosha, *The Awakening of the Faith*, tr. by Yoshito S. Hakeda, p. 102.)

*
**

Letter 24.
The Bodhi Mind[1]

I just received your letter and am glad to learn that you have finally recovered from your long illness! The great issue of Birth and Death,[2] the swiftness with which the ghost of impermanence can strike -- these are things which we have all heard of and fear, but only when we have actually had a near-death experience, do these realities truly hit home.[3]

You should, therefore, develop the great Bodhi Mind[4] and refer to your own circumstances to counsel your family, your friends and all who have the right conditions. Only in this manner can the benefits spread far and wide.

o

oo

You wrote that you suffered from overexertion as a result of reciting the Buddha's name too rapidly and hurriedly. This is, of course, because you were not skillful. Buddha Recitation should be practiced according to one's strength; it can be done silently or audibly, softly or loudly. Why did you insist on reciting in such a loud voice that you became exhausted and fell ill?

Although the immediate cause of your grave illness was shortness of breath, if you look deeper, the underlying cause must really have been the force of evil karma accumulated from time immemorial. Your diligent Buddha Recitation must have transformed future karma into current karma, heavy karma into light karma.[5] You should not grow discouraged or develop doubts. Who knows how many eons of transgressions along the Three Evil Paths have been erased by this single illness! The Buddhas' power is difficult to imagine, their kindness is difficult to repay! You should rejoice, feel great remorse and develop stronger faith.

From now on, you should cultivate diligently and counsel others to practice Buddha Recitation, so that those near and far may achieve rebirth in the Western Pure Land. This is precisely the way to avoid ingratitude toward the Buddhas, who, through your illness, have awakened you.[6]

o

oo

There is no need to come to P'u T'o Mountain, considering the travel expenses involved. Reciting the Buddha's name at home will bring progress and results just as easily, while saving money and preserving your health. Is it not better that way?[7]

NOTES TO LETTER 24

(1) Letter to the layman Liu Chih-k'ung (Chinese ed. Vol. I, p. 181; VN ed., p. 74)

(2) On the issue of Birth and Death, see the following passage:

> Students in this age of the decay of the Dharma are superficial in their learning. They do not understand the real truth. Thus, in their study of Buddhist scriptures, they cling to famous sayings and fail to comprehend the ultimate truth. They increase their (relative) knowledge and become boastful of their achievement. They produce increased karmas leading to a continuation of the cycle of life and death precisely by means of Buddhist teachings. This is because they did not start with the question of life and death when they began to search for the Mind. (Han-Shan Te-Ch'ing, in Sung-peng Hsu, *A Buddhist Leader in Ming China*, p. 126.)

(3) See this beautiful account of the meeting between the Pure Land Patriarch T'an Luan and the famed translator/monk Bodhiruci:

> T'an Luan (488-554), seeking immortality, travelled about China obtaining teachings from various noted sages, including the Taoist master T'ao Hung-ching. Eventually (ca. 530) he met with the Indian Buddhist teacher Bodhiruci: "T'an Luan opened the conversation by saying 'Is there anything in the Teaching of the Buddha which is superior to the methods for obtaining immortality found in this country's

scriptures on the immortals?'

"Bodhiruci spat on the ground and said, 'What are you saying? There is no comparison! Where on this earth can you find a method for immortality? Suppose that you can obtain youth in your old age, and never die: even having done that, you would still be rolling around in the triple world!'

"So he gave him the *Meditation Sutra* and said, 'These are the recipes of Amitabha Buddha: if you rely on his practices, you will be liberated from samsara.'" (Raoul Birnbaum, *The Healing Buddha*, p. 241.)

(4) Bodhi Mind: see Glossary.

(5) For an example a heavy karma being transmuted into a lighter one, see the following passage from the *Diamond Sutra:*

Furthermore, Subhuti, if a virtuous man or woman receives, holds (in mind), reads and recites this Sutra and is despised by others, this person who is bound to suffer from evil destinies in retribution for his past sins, and whose karmic sins are now eradicated by the others' contempt, will attain Supreme Enlightenment. (Shih Shing-yun, ed. *Bilingual Buddhist Series*, p. 122.)

(6) See the following passage:

Similar to Vimalakirti's concept and to Sakyamuni's fundamental teachings, an illness when properly dealt with can serve as a major event that propels one onwards towards higher spiritual attainment. (Raoul Birnbaum, *The Healing Buddha*, p. 69.)

(7) Pure Land does not stress visits to temples and other places of worship to meet with gurus or mentors. Rather, the emphasis is on recitation of the Buddha's name and the sutras as well as direct communion with Buddha Amitabha. See also the following passage:

Since one reaches salvation by realizing the Mind that is hidden in oneself, Han-Shan teaches that one does not have to and cannot seek salvation outside of oneself. Enlightenment is not to be found in faraway mountains, by traveling to various monasteries, or visiting famous masters. These activities are helpful but they are not the source of salvation ... Han-Shan criticizes those monks who seek salvation by wandering here and there without this basic understanding. They merely waste their money on traveling sandals. According to him, P'u T'o or Patola, the special mountain of Kuan-Yin, is ultimately in the mind and not located in the East Sea in Chekiang. One does not have to go to the East Sea in order to "see" Kuan Yin. (Sung-peng Hsu, *A Buddhist Leader in Ming China*, p. 122.)

*
**

Letter 25.
Self-power/Other-power[1]

I see from your letter that you have developed faith and wish to take refuge in the Buddhas and their teachings. When taking refuge in the Triple Jewel, however, you should cease all evil actions, perform wholesome deeds, fulfill your moral obligations, develop Faith and Vows and practice Buddha Recitation, seeking rebirth in the Pure Land.[2] You should also refrain from killing, protect sentient beings and be vegetarian several days a month.[3] If you cannot yet eat frugally all the time, at least do not be too demanding in your diet. In this way, you will not go counter to the compassionate Mind of the Buddhas.

Since your name is "Precious Wood," I shall give you the Dharma name "Verdant Wisdom." This is because the Mind-Nature is like a tree; when consumed by the fire of afflictions, it withers and dries up. Once you have wisdom, afflictions will not arise and the tree of the Mind-Nature grows naturally healthy and verdant.

If you wish to receive the five lay precepts,[4] you should, first of all, examine your mind. If you believe that you can keep the precepts without transgressing, you may ask the layman Hua San about self-administration of the precepts before your altar; he will be glad to instruct you.[5]

Having now returned to the Dharma, you should read my compendium of letters carefully and follow closely the teachings described therein. Only then will you avoid being deceived by misguided persons into seeking merits and blessings in future lives[6] or trying to become an Immortal through the practice of balancing energy currents.[7] If you truly understand the teachings set out in my compendium, no externalist can cause you to vacillate. Do not doubt the words in the compendium. You should realize that they are based on the essence of the sutras or the enlightened words of the Patriarchs and other Dharma teachers. I did not invent these teachings. If you reflect carefully upon what I have just said, you will receive great benefits.

o
oo

Your aspirations are as lofty as the heavens, while your will is as low as the ground. Although you claim to follow my teachings, you are, in fact, merely pursuing your own biased views. Faith constitutes the very basis of Pure Land teaching.[8] With solid Faith, even those guilty of the Five Transgressions and the Ten Evil Deeds can achieve rebirth in the Pure Land.[9] Without solid Faith, even those fully versed in the various schools and teachings have no conditions or hope of escaping Birth and Death unless they have severed all delusive karma.[10]

You are not yet versed in the various schools and teachings. Therefore, you cannot rely on your own strength (self-power) to eradicate karmic delusion and transcend Birth and Death. Now, if you do not believe that the power of the Buddhas and the virtues of the Self-Nature are boundless, how can you achieve liberation?

You should know that no one who seeks rebirth in the Pure Land with deep and earnest Faith and Vows will fail to achieve it. Buddha Recitation is the perfect shortcut to escape from the wasteland of Birth and Death.[11] You do not even realize the loftiness of this method, yet harbor the ambition to study the *Treatise on the Awakening of the Faith*.[12] Although this treatise presents the essence of the Dharma, it is not too helpful for those of limited capacities and shallow roots. Even if you study and understand it thoroughly, severing all doubts, once you begin practicing, you must still follow the method of reciting the Buddha's name seeking rebirth in the Pure Land. This is the only prudent, safe course.[13] As for the Consciousness, Zen and Sutra Studies schools, how can you expect to grasp their subtlety and profundity?

o

oo

Your mind has such high aspirations but you do not know how to adjust their loftiness to your capacities! Yet you also think that "with humble, limited capacities, it is difficult to achieve rebirth in the Pure Land; to avoid sinking into the Three Evil Realms is enough cause for rejoicing."[14] Little do you realize that without rebirth in the Pure Land, you will, in the future, descend upon the Three Evil Paths. Ideas such as yours fail to conform to the teachings of the Buddhas and are contrary to my own advice. How can you then say that you are "following my words and singlemindedly reciting the Buddha's name"?

You are currently engaged in an ordinary profession and do not yet have a lofty, magnanimous character. Thus, such high determination will only make others sigh and laugh. You should completely abandon your ambition to become a great scholar,[15] concentrating instead on studying the Pure Land sutras. Reread the letters I sent to Kao Shao-lin and Miss Hsu and practice accordingly. You should not look at your humble, limited capacities and consider rebirth in the Western Pure Land as too lofty and beyond your reach. You should cling to the Buddha's name as to your life and mind, holding fast at all times without letting go.[16] Moreover, you should keep your thoughts and actions in conformity with the tenets of Buddhism, that is, put a stop to all evil actions and practice all wholesome deeds. In addition, if you still have spare time, you may recite sutras and mantras, but always keep in mind the need for utter sincerity. Do not rush to fathom meaning and substance.[17] If you rush to understand everything at the outset and do not concentrate on utterly sincere recitation of the Buddha's name and the sutras, even thorough understanding will bring no true benefits -- not to mention that, to begin with, understanding is difficult.[18]

As far as the Consciousness, Zen and Sutra Studies methods are concerned, even if you pursue them all your life, you will find it difficult to grasp their profound essence. Even if you do, you will still have to sever delusive karma completely to escape Birth and Death.[19] When speaking of this, I fear that your dream will not come true and will remain just that -- a dream!

You have not read my compendium carefully enough and, therefore, your words rise as high as the Milky Way and then descend to the depths of the ocean. In the compendium, I frequently refer to the sutras and commentaries that should be read, how to go about reading them and the difficulty of benefitting from the Consciousness, Zen and Sutra Studies methods. This is because the Pure Land method calls upon the compassionate power of Amitabha Buddha (other-power), while other methods rely on self-power, self-cultivation alone.

Dharma doors other than Pure Land are ordinary methods. They resemble the approach of a scholar in everyday life who, through his own talents and virtues, becomes an official of high or low rank. The Pure Land method is a special teaching[20] -- just like a prince who, right at birth, is more honored than courtiers or ministers. Thus, methods based on self- power and those based on other-power cannot be compared. Should not ordinary beings, full of karmic afflictions, exercise caution in the selection of a method of cultivation?

You admit that human beings have a limited life-span and that your own real strength is limited. Why, then, continue to pursue such lofty ambitions? If you can become a great scholar, it will be a great honor for Buddhism. My only fear is that if you do not succeed and do not have firm faith in the Pure Land method either, you will fail on both accounts. Furthermore, if you do accrue some limited virtues in this life, in the next life you will certainly be reborn within the cycle of worldly blessings and merits. Think this over: among the wealthy and noble, how many can avoid creating evil karma?

Today the fate of the nation is in great peril and the people are in misery. This is all due to the influence of the merits and blessings of those who, in previous lifetimes, cultivated without wisdom.[21] Once having gone astray and having been reborn in the Triple Realm, how can you ensure that you will not be deluded and descend upon the evil paths? If you do not achieve rebirth in the Pure Land, it may be possible to escape perdition for one lifetime, but to do so for two lifetimes is rare indeed![22]

o
oo

Sakyamuni Buddha taught a great many sutras and mantras. No one can recite and uphold them all. Therefore, the ancients selected only a few important ones for use in daily recitation. [Among these important sutras and mantras are the *Heart Sutra*, the *Amitabha Sutra*, the *Longer Repentance Liturgy*, the Surangama Mantra, the Great Compassion Mantra, the Ten Mantras.] Regardless of which sutra or mantra is recited, to be in accord with the tenets of Pure Land you should include recitation of the Buddha's name and dedicate the merits to rebirth in the Pure Land ... You should know that the very words "Amitabha Buddha," if recited to the level of one-pointedness of mind,[23] have ample power to lead sentient beings to Buddhahood. Do you really think that reciting the *Amitabha Sutra* and the Buddha's name cannot eliminate "fixed karma"?[24]

The Dharma is like money. It is up to the individual to use it wisely. To those with money, many courses of action are open. If you can concentrate on cultivating one method, whatever you wish will be fulfilled.[25] Why insist upon reciting this mantra or that sutra to accrue this or that merit, but not other merits?[26] If you follow my instructions in a flexible way, you will naturally "understand one thing and penetrate one hundred things." If not, even if I speak at length, your mind will not be focussed and you will not obtain any benefits!

o
oo

It is taught in the sutras:

There are two types of heroes in this world: those who do

not commit transgressions and those who, having done so, are capable of repentance.

The word "repentance" should spring from the depth of the mind. If you do not truly repent and change your ways, whatever you say is useless. It is like reading the label on a medicine bottle but refusing to take the medicine. How can your illness be cured? If you take the medicine according to instructions, the disease will certainly be cured -- with body and mind calm and at peace. I only fear for those who, lacking strong and determined will, put things out in the sun to warm for one day and then let them freeze for ten days. All they get is empty fame and no true benefits!

NOTES TO LETTER 25

(1) Letter to the layman Chou Chih-mao (Chinese ed. Vol. I, p. 182; VN ed., p. 75)

(2) This an elaboration of the basic Buddhist teaching, common to all traditions, i.e., "Do not what is evil, do what is good, keep your mind pure."

(3) Vegetarianism several times a month: this is an example of expedience and flexibility in Pure Land. The ideal is to be vegetarian at all times, in accordance with the precept not to kill. Master Yin Kuang is leading the cultivator gradually along this path.

(4) Five lay precepts: not to kill, steal, lie, engage in illicit sex or take intoxicants. Please note that these basic precepts are all negative injunctions. The corresponding positive injunctions are found in the Bodhisattva precepts, i.e., do not kill, but release life.

(5) Receiving the precepts. There are many sets of precepts in Buddhism. All of them, however, can be summarized by three key Bodhisattva injunctions: *avoid all transgressions,*

perform all good deeds and be of benefit to all sentient beings. The concept that receiving the precepts is not necessarily dependent upon their being administered by the clergy is a high-level teaching of Mahayana Buddhism, which emphasizes the all-encompassing Mind. Any practitioner who wishes to receive the precepts, and sincerely and earnestly accepts them, has in fact received them. This is in line with the teaching of the *Brahma Net Sutra*, though in the case of the Bodhisattva precepts (the loftiest and most difficult set of precepts), the witnessing of an auspicious sign (light, flowers, the Buddhas coming to rub one's crown, etc.) is additionally necessary:

> The twenty-third minor precept prohibits slighting others and speaking the Dharma in a biased manner ... Whenever a person with wholesome intention sincerely wishes to receive the Bodhisattva precepts, he should first vow, before the Buddha and Bodhisattva images, to accept and uphold the Precepts and then cultivate repentance and reform for seven days. If during that period he experiences a vision of auspicious signs, he has received the precepts ... It is essential that he experience an auspicious sign, for only then has he received the precepts before the Buddha and Bodhisattva images. If he has not obtained such auspicious signs, though he may have vowed before the Buddha images to accept and uphold the precepts, he has not actually received them ... *(The Buddha Speaks the Brahma Net Sutra [Brahma Net Sutra]*, Part II, Commentary by Elder Master Hui Sheng, p. 6.)

(6) The ultimate goal of all Buddhist methods and practices is for sentient beings to escape Birth and Death and achieve Buddhahood, as the Buddhas did. This being the case, any other aspirations are mistaken and not in accord with the true intention of the Buddhas. Thus, such aspirations as rebirth as as a male or as a king in the realms of gods and men, becoming a high-ranking master known far and wide, etc. are questionable. These aspirations fall short of the ultimate aim of liberation and can be dangerous, given the weak nature of sentient beings, as power and influence provide the opportunity for further and worse transgressions. Thus, the sutras teach that the merits accrued in this lifetime are potential enemies of the third lifetime.

7) Balancing energy currents:

> There are some who appear to be monks and nuns, residing in temples and pagodas; however they neither study nor understand Buddhism and

only follow the practices of other religions. These people are peddling a panoply of other beliefs under the label of Buddhism. They and their followers secretly transmit their beliefs to one another. Many of them, while claiming to practice meditation, in fact specialize in exercises to balance energy currents with little knowledge of what meditation is all about. As far as the Pure Land method is concerned, they teach that one should visualize the Buddha's name "shooting" from the navel to the back of the body and up the spinal column, and then returning to the navel. This, they say, is "turning the Dharma wheel." This is the practice of "releasing blockages in the energy system," according to externalist schools. Such teaching is not consonant with Buddhism. (Master Thích Thiền Tâm, *Buddhism of Wisdom and Faith*, sect. 16, p. 64-65.)

(8) Faith is one of the three pillars of Pure Land, or, to use a Chinese metaphor, one of the three legs of an incense burner. However, each of the three (Faith, Vows, Practice) encompasses the other two, when carried to the utmost level. See *Buddhism of Wisdom and Faith*, sect. 15, p. 60ff.

(9) See the *Meditation Sutra*, Sixteenth Meditation. See also Introduction, sect. D.

(10) Severing all delusive karma. This is the aim of all Buddhist teachings. Those who achieve this will attain liberation and rebirth in the Pure Land -- in their pure mind. This is so regardless of school, or even whether they are Buddhist or not. However, this severance of karma must be accomplished to the utmost level, without a trace of delusion remaining. The key question is: how many in this Saha World can accomplish this?

(11) See the following passage, concerning the "horizontal escape" from Birth and Death:

Suppose we have a worm, born inside a stalk of bamboo. To escape, it can take the "hard way" and crawl all the way to the top of the stalk. Alternatively, it can look for or poke a hole near its current location and escape "horizontally" into the big, wide world. The "horizontal escape," for sentient beings, is to seek rebirth in the Pure Land. (Master Thích Thiền Tâm, *Buddhism of Wisdom and Faith*, 2nd ed., p. 315, Note 4B.)

(12) *Awakening of the Faith* (treatise): see Glossary.

(13) See the following passage from Zen Master Chu Hung, one of the dragon/elephants of Ming Buddhism:

> Nothing prevents people who study Zen and who investigate inherent mind moment to moment from taking vows to be reborn in the Land of Ultimate Bliss when their lives here are over.
>
> Why is this? Though one may have an awakening by studying Zen, if one is as yet unable to abide in the eternal quiescent light like the buddhas, and is still not free of subsequent existence like the arhats, then when this physical body is used up, one is sure to be reborn [within samsara]. (Zen Master Chu Hung in J.C. Cleary, *Pure Land, Pure Mind*.)

(14) This is another example of one-sided grasping: thinking that the Pure Land is beyond one's reach because it is too lofty compared to one's limited achievements.

(15) Buddhism is first and foremost practice, not scholarship. A scholar who only studies sutras and commentaries but does not engage in practice may actually betray the true spirit of Buddhism. The more he employs the discriminating mind, the more likely he is to err and miss the unifying spirit of the Truth -- one and indivisible.

(16) The following anecdote expresses the idea of singleminded concentration:

There is a story of a Zen Master who was practicing on Châu Thơi Mountain, in a remote mountainous area of central Vietnam famous for supernatural occurrences. One evening, as he sat in meditation, he suddenly became aware of something watching him. It was a tiger, ready to pounce on him at the slightest movement, just like a cat stalking a mouse. The monk, petrified, marshalled all his concentration so as to remain ramrod straight and perfectly still in body and mind. Hours passed until, at dawn, the tiger left. The next night, this scene repeated itself, and again the night after that. After three nights of utmost concentration, the monk achieved a Great Awakening. He then passed away. At his burial, so the story goes, a tiger was seen watching the event, after which it disappeared, never to be seen again.

(17) See the following passage:

> To get out of the circle of habit, a reflection of what the scripture calls the "mundane whirl," Buddhist practice proposes a dual process of arresting involutionary patterns and incorporating evolutionary patterns. In the practice of scriptural recital, the focus of concentration works to halt the wandering mind and take the attention off habitual trains of thought, while the structure and imagery of the scripture that then flow into the mind, bypassing the conditioned intellect, are able to set up new patterns of perception. (Thomas Cleary, *The Flower Adornment Sutra*, Vol. III, p. 6).

(18) Master Yin Kuang once again underscores the importance of practice over purely intellectual understanding, as true understanding is practice and vice versa. A contemporary analogy is the person who keeps reading the drivers' manual but refuses to get behind the wheel.

(19) See the following passage:

> We should know ... that to escape birth and death, we must sever delusions of views and thought. However, according to the ancients, "blocking delusions of views is as difficult as blocking a raging stream coming from forty miles away." Why, then, even mention eliminating all delusions of thought? Thus, if we want to achieve liberation in this Dharma-Ending Age, the most appropriate method is Buddha Recitation. This is because, through this method, the cultivator, after utilizing his self-power to the utmost, receives additional assistance from other-power. Even though his karma and delusions are not yet extinguished, he can, through Amitabha Buddha's power of welcoming and escorting, "take his residual karma along" to the Pure Land. Once reborn, he will no longer retrogress and will have transcended birth and death forever! (Master Thích Thiên Tâm, *Buddhism of Wisdom and Faith*, sect. 54, p. 226.)

(20) See the following passage concerning the views of the eminent Ming dynasty Zen Master Han-shan:

> Han-shan did not write any commentary on the *Pure Land Sutra*, and it is not clear how he places it in the Hua-yen [Avatamsaka] classification scheme. On the one hand, he regards the Western Paradise as the most expedient land in the innumerable Hua-yen pure lands. On the other hand, he seems to have considered the Pure Land teaching as a special teaching that lies outside the usual scheme of classification. (Sung-peng Hsu, *A Buddhist Leader in Ming China*, p. 149.)

(21) There are two main aspects of cultivation: a) samadhi

and wisdom and b) merits and blessings. For example, today's business and political leaders are rich and powerful because of past good karma. Human nature being what it is, however, many become corrupted by fame and fortune. This chain of events was initiated because in past lifetimes they cultivated without *wisdom*, i.e., they did not cultivate samadhi, which leads to wisdom. Instead, they cultivated merits and blessings (e.g., practicing charity) hoping for wealth and fame.

(22) This is a major difference *at the phenomenal level* between the expedient approaches of Zen and Pure Land. The true Zen Master, being of the highest caliber, is not afraid of rebirth within samsara, as he expects to continue his cultivation life after life. According to Pure Land teaching, however, the vast majority of people are nowhere near that level and cannot be sure that they will continue to improve in future lifetimes. As a matter of fact, in all probability, many will not. It is, therefore, imperative for them to escape Birth and Death in this very lifetime through rebirth in the Pure Land.

(23) One-pointedness of mind (singleminded concentration) leads to rebirth in the Pure Land and, ultimately, Buddhahood.

(24) Fixed karma. In principle, all karma is subject to change. Fixed karma, however, is karma which can only be changed in extraordinary circumstances, because it derives from an evil act committed simultaneously with mind, speech and body. An example of fixed karma would be a premeditated crime, versus a crime of passion.

(25) See the following passage:

> We may take up any Dharma for practice as long as it is agreeable to our interest and inclination, and since every Dharma is perfect and complete, therefore in the course of cultivation, we should not think of changing from one Dharma to another, nor should we think that a certain Dharma may be superior or inferior to the others. As no medicine may be called ... bad as long as it can cure, likewise, no Dharma may be said to be ... low as long as it is adaptable to its followers. (Hsu Heng Chi, *What's Buddhism?*, p. 62.)

(26) In popular Buddhism, individual mantras and sutras are associated with the resolution of particular kinds of problems. For example, the *Amitabha Sutra* is recited at the time of death and at funerals (for the benefit of both the dead and the living) while the name of the Bodhisattva Avalokitesvara (Kuan Yin) is uttered in times of danger and distress. However, to the true cultivator, all mantras and sutras have equal efficacy in any circumstances -- as long as the mind is utterly sincere and pure.

I vow that when my life approaches its end,
All obstructions will be swept away;
I will see Amitabha Buddha,
And be born in his Land of Ultimate Bliss and Peace.

When reborn in the Western Land,
I will perfect and completely fulfill
Without exception these Great Vows,
To delight and benefit all beings.

The Vows of Samantabhadra

Appendix:

The Practices and Vows of the Bodhisattva Samantabhadra

(Avatamsaka Sutra, ch. 40)

Buddhist Text Translation Society

Note to the Reader

The *Avatamsaka Sutra*, which is described by D.T. Suzuki as the "epitome of Buddhist thought, Buddhist sentiment and Buddhist experience," consists of eighty-one fascicles, divided into forty chapters. The chapter on "The Practices and Vows of the Bodhisattva Samantabhadra," the last and best-known chapter, represents the essence of Bodhisattva practice.

The Great Vows of Samantabhadra are the right *causes* of Buddhahood and the pure *conditions* for rebirth in the Pure Land. For precisely this reason, the ancients, down through the centuries, have copied, printed and disseminated this chapter separately, so that everyone may recite it and put its teachings into practice.

Precisely because these practices and vows contain the right causes of Buddhahood as well as the pure conditions for rebirth in the Pure Land, the ancients have also excerpted several passages and incorporated them in the daily liturgy of the faithful.

During his lifetime, Elder Master Yin Kuang frequently lectured on this chapter to encourage Pure Land practice and to demonstrate that rebirth in the Western Land is the common vow of the Bodhisattvas in the Ocean-Wide Avatamsaka Assembly. *(From the preface of Master Thích Trí Tịnh.)*

The following passages are excerpted from the translation prepared by the Buddhist Text Translation Society, Talmadge, California. We have made a number of changes to correspond to the main part of this book -- for which we beg the indulgence of the original translators.

Avatamsaka Sutra, ch. 40:

On Entering the Inconceivable State of Liberation through the Practices and Vows of the Bodhisattva Samantabhadra[1]

At that time, having praised the exalted merits and virtues of the Thus Come One,[2] the Bodhisattva Samantabhadra addressed the Bodhisattvas, along with Sudhana,[3] as follows:

"Good men, even if all the Buddhas of the ten directions were to speak continuously, for as many eons[4] as there are fine motes of dust in an ineffably ineffable number of Buddha lands, the virtues and merits of the Thus Come One could never be fully described.

"Those wishing to achieve these merits and virtues should cultivate ten vast and great practices and vows. What are these ten?

First, Pay homage and respect to all Buddhas.
Second, Praise the Thus Come Ones.
Third, Make abundant offerings.
Fourth, Repent misdeeds and evil karma.
Fifth, Rejoice at others' merits and virtues.
Sixth, Request the Buddhas to turn the Dharma wheel.
Seventh, Request the Buddhas to remain in the world.
Eigth, Follow the teachings of the Buddhas at all times.
Ninth, Accommodate and benefit all living beings.
Tenth, Transfer all merits and virtues universally."

[The explanation of the first to eighth vows is omitted here. What follows is the Bodhisattva Samantabhadra's exposition of the ninth and tenth vows.]

"Sudhana, *to accommodate and benefit all living beings* is explained like this: throughout the oceans of worlds in the ten directions exhausting the Dharma Realm and the realm of empty space, there are many different kinds of living beings. That is to say, there are those born from eggs, the womb-born, the transformationally born, as well as those who live and rely on earth, water, fire, and air for their existence. There are beings dwelling in space, and those who are born in and live in plants and trees. This includes all the many species and races with their diverse bodies, shapes, appearances, lifespans, families, names, and natures. This includes their many varieties of knowledge and views, their various desires and pleasures, their thoughts and deeds, and their many different deportments, clothing and diets.

"It includes beings who dwell in different villages, towns, cities and palaces, as well as gods, dragons, and others of the eight divisions, humans and non-humans alike. Also there are footless beings, beings with two feet, four feet, and many feet, with form and without form, with thought and without thought, and not entirely with thought and not entirely without thought. I will accord with and take care of all these many kinds of beings, providing all manner of services and offerings for them. I will treat them with the same respect I show my own parents, teachers, elders, Arhats, and even the Thus Come Ones. I will serve them all equally without difference.

"I will be a good doctor for the sick and suffering. I will lead those who have lost their way to the right road. I will be a bright light for those in the dark night, and cause the poor and destitute to uncover hidden treasures. The Bodhisattva impartially benefits all living beings in this manner.

"Why is this? If a Bodhisattva accords with living beings, then he accords with and makes offerings to all Buddhas. If he can honor and serve living beings, then he honors and serves the Thus Come Ones. If he makes living beings happy, he is making all Thus Come Ones happy. Why is this? It is because all Buddhas, Thus Come Ones, take the Mind of Great Compassion as their substance. Because of living beings, they develop Great Compassion. From Great Compassion the Bodhi Mind is born; and because of the Bodhi Mind, they accomplish Supreme, Perfect Enlightenment.

"It is like a great regal tree growing in the rocks and sand of barren wilderness. When the roots get water, the branches, leaves, flowers, and fruits will all flourish. The regal bodhi-tree growing in the wilderness of Birth and Death is the same. All living beings are its roots; all Buddhas and Bodhisattvas are its flowers and fruits. By benefitting all beings with the water of Great Compassion, one can realize the flowers and fruits of the Buddhas' and Bodhisattvas' wisdom.

"Why is this? It is because by benefitting living beings with the water of Great Compassion, the Bodhisattvas can attain Supreme, Perfect Enlightenment. Therefore, Bodhi belongs to living beings. Without living beings, no Bodhisattva could achieve Supreme, Perfect Enlightenment.

"Good man, you should understand these principles in this way: When the mind is impartial towards all living beings, one can accomplish full and perfect Great Compassion. By using the Mind of Great Compassion to accord with living beings, one perfects the making of offerings to the Thus Come Ones. In this way the Bodhisattva constantly accords with living beings.

"Even when the realm of empty space is exhausted,

the realms of living beings are exhausted, the karma of living beings is exhausted, and the afflictions of living beings are exhausted, I will still accord endlessly, continuously in thought after thought without cease. My body, mouth, and mind never weary of these deeds.

"Moreover, good man, *to transfer all merits and virtues universally* is explained like this: all the merits and virtues, from the first vow, to pay homage and respect, up to and including the vow to accommodate and benefit all living beings, I universally transfer to all living beings throughout the Dharma Realm and to the limits of empty space. I vow that all living beings will be constantly peaceful and happy without sickness or suffering. I vow that no one will succeed in doing any evil, but that all will quickly perfect their cultivation of good karma. I vow to shut the door to evil destinies and open the right paths of humans, gods and that of Nirvana. I will stand in for beings and receive all the extremely severe fruits of suffering which they bring about with their evil karma. I will liberate all these beings and ultimately bring them to accomplish unsurpassed Bodhi. The Bodhisattva cultivates transference in this way.

"Even when the realm of empty space is exhausted, the realms of living beings are exhausted, the karma of living beings is exhausted, and the afflictions of living beings are exhausted, I will still transfer all merits and virtues endlessly, continuously, in thought after thought without cease. My body, mouth and mind never weary of these deeds.

"Good man, these are the Bodhisattva-Mahasattvas' Ten Great Vows in their entirety. If all Bodhisattvas can follow and abide by these Great Vows, then they will be able to bring all living beings to maturity. They will be able to accord with the path of Supreme, Perfect Enlightenment and complete Samantabhadra's ocean of conduct and vows. Therefore, good man, you should know the meaning of this" ....

"Further, when a person is on the verge of death, at the last instant of life, when all his faculties scatter and he departs from his relatives, when all power and status are lost and nothing survives, when his prime minister, great officials, his inner court and outer cities, his elephants, horses, carts, and treasuries of precious jewels can no longer accompany him, these Great Vows alone will stay with him. At all times they will guide him forward, and in a single instant he will be reborn in the Land of Ultimate Bliss. Arriving there, he will see Amitabha Buddha, the Bodhisattva Manjusri, the Bodhisattva Samantabhadra, the Bodhisattva who contemplates at Ease [Avalokitesvara], the Bodhisattva Maitreya, and others. The appearance of these Bodhisattvas will be magnificent and their merits and virtues complete. Together they will surround him.

"This person will see himself born from a lotus flower and will receive a prediction of Buddhahood. Thereafter, he will pass through an immeasurable, incalculable number of eons and, with his power of wisdom, he will accord with the minds of living beings in order to benefit them everywhere throughout the ineffably ineffable worlds in the ten directions.

"Before long he will sit in a Bodhimandala,[5] subdue the demonic armies, accomplish Supreme, Perfect Enlightenment, and turn the wonderful Dharma wheel. He will cause living beings in worlds as numerous as the fine motes of dust in Buddha lands to develop the Bodhi Mind.[6] According with their inclinations and basic

natures, he will teach, transform, and bring them to
maturity. To the exhaustion of the oceans of future
eons, he will greatly benefit all living beings" ....

o
oo

At that time, the Bodhisattva Mahasattva
Samantabhadra, wishing to restate his meaning,
contemplated everywhere in the ten directions and
spoke in verse.

1 - Before the Lions Among Men[7] throughout the
  worlds of the ten directions,
In the past, in the present, and also in the future,
With body, mouth, and mind entirely pure,
I bow before them all, omitting none.

With the awesome spiritual power of Samantabhadra's vows,
I appear at the same time before every Thus Come One,
And in transformed bodies as numerous as motes of dust in all lands,
Bow to Buddhas as numerous as motes of dust in all lands.

In every mote of dust are Buddhas as numerous as motes of dust,
Each dwelling amid a host of Bodhisattvas.
Throughout motes of dust in endless Dharma Realms it is the same:
I deeply believe they all are filled with Buddhas.

2 - With oceans of sound I everywhere let fall
Words and phrases, wonderful and endless,
Which now and through all the eons of the future,
Praise the wide, deep sea of the Buddhas' merits and virtues.

3 - Flower garlands supreme and wonderful,
Music, perfumes, parasols, and canopies,
And other decorations rich and rare,
I offer up to every Thus Come One.

Fine clothing, superior incense,
Powdered and burning incense, lamps and candles,
Each one heaped as high as mount Sumeru,
I offer completely to all Tathagatas.

With a vast, great, supremely liberated mind,
I believe in all Buddhas of the three periods of time;
With the strength of Samantabhadra's conduct and vows,
I make offerings to all Thus Come Ones everywhere.

4 - For all the evil deeds I have done in the past,
Created by my body, mouth, and mind,
From beginningless greed, anger, and delusion,
I now know shame and repent them all.

5 - I rejoice in the merits and virtues
Of all beings in the ten directions,
The Learners and Those-Past-Study in the Two Vehicles,[8]
And all Thus Come Ones and Bodhisattvas.

6 - Before the Lamps of the Worlds[9] *of the ten directions,*
Who have just accomplished Supreme Bodhi,
I now request and beseech them all
To turn the foremost, wondrous Dharma wheel.

7 - If there are Buddhas who wish for Nirvana,
I request with deep sincerity
That they dwell in the world for a long time
To bring benefits and bliss to every being.

I worship those with blessings, praise them and make offerings;
I request that the Buddhas remain in the world and turn the
  Dharma wheel;
The good roots gained from following and rejoicing in merit and
  virtue and from repentance and reform,
I transfer to living beings and the Buddha Way.

8 - I study with the Buddhas and practice
The perfect conduct of Samantabhadra;
I make offerings to all the Thus Come Ones of the past
And to all present Buddhas throughout the ten directions.

All future Teachers of Gods and Men
Whose aspirations and vows have been completed,
I will follow in study throughout the three periods of time
And quickly attain Great Bodhi.

In all lands of the ten directions,
Vast, great, pure, and wonderfully adorned,
All Tathagatas sit beneath regal Bodhi trees,

While assemblies circumambulate them.

I vow that every being in all directions
Will be peaceful, happy, and without worry.
May they obtain the proper Dharma's profound aid,
And may all their afflictions be wiped away, without exception.

While striving to attain Bodhi,
I will gain the knowledge of past lives in all destinies.
I will always leave the home-life and cultivate pure precepts,
Without outflows,[10] never broken, and without stain.

Be they gods, dragons, yakshas, or kumbhandas,
Humans, non-humans, and the rest,
In the many languages of all such living beings,
With every sound I will speak the Dharma.

I will cultivate the pure paramitas with vigor,
And never abandon the Bodhi Mind.
I will banish all obstructions and defilements,
And fulfill all wondrous practices.

From all delusions, karma, and demon-states,
Amid all worldly paths, I will be freed,
As the lotus does not touch the water,
As sun and moon do not stop in space.

9 - Ending the sufferings of the paths of evil,
And to everyone equally bringing joy,
May I for eons like the motes of dust in all lands
Ever benefit all in the ten directions.

Always in accord with living beings,
Cultivating through all future eons
The vast conduct of Samantabhadra,
The unsurpassed Great Bodhi will I perfect.

May all who cultivate with me
Assemble with me in one place,
Our karmas of body, mouth, and mind the same,
As we cultivate and study all practices and vows.

With all advisors good and wise who aid me
By explaining Samantabhadra's deeds,
I vow always to congregate together:

May they never be displeased with me.

*I vow always to meet Thus Come Ones face to face
And the hosts of disciples who gather around them.
I will raise offerings which are vast and great,
Untiring to the end of future eons.*

*I will hold high the subtly wondrous Buddhadharma
And illuminate all the practices of Bodhi;
I will be ultimately pure in Samantabhadra's way,
Practicing until the end of time.*

*Inexhaustible blessings and wisdom
I cultivate throughout all worlds;
By concentration, wisdom, skillful means, and liberation,
I will gain an endless store of merits and virtues.*

*In one mote of dust are lands as numerous as motes of dust;
In each land are incalculable numbers of Buddhas.
In every place where Buddhas dwell I see the host assembled,
Endlessly proclaiming all the practices of Bodhi.*

*In ten directions everywhere, throughout the sea of lands,
Every hair-tip encompasses oceans of past, present and future.*[11]
*So, too, there is a sea of Buddhas, a sea of Buddha lands;
Pervading them all I cultivate for seas of endless time.*

*The speech of all Tathagatas is pure;
Each word contains an ocean of sounds.
According with what beings like to hear,
The Buddhas' sea of eloquence flows forth.*

*All Tathagatas of the three periods of time
Forever turn the wonderful Dharma wheel,
With these inexhaustible seas of words and languages.
I understand all with my deep wisdom.*

*I can penetrate the future
And exhaust all eons in a single thought.
In a single thought I completely enter
All eons of the three periods of time.*[12]

*In one thought I see all Lions of Men
Of the past, present, and future;*[13]
*I constantly fathom the Buddhas' states,
Their magical liberations and their awesome strength.*

On the tip of an extremely fine hair,
Appear jewelled lands of past, present and future;
Lands on hair-tips as numerous as dust motes in all
   lands of the ten directions,
I deeply enter, adorn, and purify.

All Lamps of the Future that light the world,
Complete the Way, turn the Dharma wheel, and rescue living beings,
As they perfect the Buddhas' work and manifest Nirvana,
I draw near and attend to each one and obtain:

The spiritual power to go everywhere swiftly;
The power to enter the Mahayana universally through the Universal
   Door;
The power of wisdom and conduct to cultivate merits and virtues
   universally;
The subtle spiritual power to shield all with Great Compassion;

The power to purify and adorn [all] with supreme blessings everywhere;
The power of wisdom which is unattached and independent;
The awesome spiritual powers and the powers of concentration,
   wisdom, and skill-in-means;
The power of universally accumulating Bodhi;

The power of good karma which purifies all things;
The power to eradicate all afflictions;
The power to subdue all demons;
The power to perfect Samantabhadra's conduct.

The sea of lands I everywhere adorn and purify,
And I liberate all living beings, without exception.
With skill I make selections from among the sea of Dharmas[14]
And enter deeply into the wisdom sea.

I cultivate the ocean of practices to purity,
Perfect and complete a sea of vows.
I draw near to a sea of Buddhas and make offerings,
And cultivate without fatigue for a sea of time.

To all Tathagatas of the three periods of time,
With Bodhi, conduct, and vows most supreme,
I completely offer up my perfect cultivation;
With Samantabhadra's practices, I awaken to Bodhi.

Each Tathagata has an elder disciple
Named Samantabhadra, Honored One.
I now transfer all good roots, and I vow
To perform deeds of wisdom identical to his.

I vow that my body, mouth, and mind will be forever pure
And that all practices and lands will be also.
I vow in every way to be identical
To the wisdom of Samantabhadra.

I will wholly purify Samantabhadra's conduct,
And the great vows of Manjusri as well.
All their deeds I will fulfill, leaving nothing undone.
Till the end of the future I will never tire.

Infinite and measureless is my cultivation;
Boundless merit and virtue I obtain.
Amid limitless practices I will dwell in peace,
And penetrate the strength of spiritual powers.

10 - Manjusri has wisdom, courage and bravery;
Samantabhadra's conduct and wisdom are the same.
I now transfer all good roots
In order to follow them in practice and in study.

In the three periods of time, all Buddhas praise
Such vows as these, lofty and great.
I now transfer all good roots, wishing to perfect
The supreme practices of Samantabhadra.

I vow that when my life approaches its end,
All obstructions will be swept away;
I will see Amitabha Buddha,
And be born in his Land of Ultimate Bliss and Peace.[15]

When reborn in the Western Land,
I will perfect and completely fulfill,
Without exception, these Great Vows,
To delight and benefit all beings.

The Assembly of Amitabha Buddha is completely pure;
When from a matchless lotus I am born,
I will behold the Tathagata's Measureless Light as He appears
  before me
To bestow a prediction of Bodhi.

Receiving a prediction from the Thus Come One,
I will take countless appearances and forms,
And with wisdom power vast and great, pervade ten directions
To benefit all the realms of living beings.

Realms of worlds in empty space might reach an end,
And living beings, karma and afflictions be extinguished;
But they will never be exhausted,
And neither will my vows.

With myriad jewels in boundless lands in all directions,
I make decorations and offerings to the Thus Come Ones.
For eons as numerous as the motes of dust in all lands, I bring
The foremost peace and joy to gods and humans.

Yet, if anyone believes in these Great Vows,
As they pass by the ear but a single time,
And in search of Bodhi thirstily craves these vows,
The merits and virtues gained will surpass these offerings.

With bad advisors forever left behind,
From paths of evil he departs for eternity,
Soon to see the Buddha of Limitless Light
And perfect Samantabhadra's Supreme Vows.

Easily obtaining the blessings of long life,
Assured of a noble rebirth in the human realm,
Before long he will perfect and complete
The practices of Samantabhadra.

In the past, owing to a lack of wisdom power,
The five offenses of extreme evil he has committed;
In one thought they can all be wiped away by reciting
The Great Vows of Samantabhadra.

His clan, race, and color, marks and characteristics
With his wisdom are all perfected and complete;
Demons and externalists will have no way to harm him,
And he will be a field of merits in the Three Realms.[16]

To the regal Bodhi tree he will quickly go,
And seated there subdue hordes of demons.
Supremely and perfectly enlightened, he will turn the Dharma wheel,
To benefit the host of living beings.

*If anyone can read, recite, receive, and hold high
Samantabhadra's Vows and proclaim them,
His reward only the Buddhas will know,
And he will obtain Bodhi's highest path.*

*If anyone recites Samantabhadra's Vows,
I will speak of a portion of his good roots:
In one single thought he can fulfill
The pure vows of sentient beings.*

*The supreme and endless blessings from Samantabhadra's conduct
I now universally transfer.
May every living being, drowning and adrift,
Soon return to the Land of Limitless Light!* .

When the Bodhisattva Mahasattva Samantabhadra finished speaking these pure verses on the Great Vows of Samantabhadra before the Thus Come One, the youth Sudhana was overwhelmed with boundless joy. All the Bodhisattvas were extremely happy as well, and the Thus Come One applauded saying, "Good indeed, good indeed!" ....

NOTES TO APPENDIX

(1) Sometimes translated as "Universal Worthy."

(2) In Sanskrit, "Tathagata," i.e., Buddha Sakyamuni or the Buddhas in general.

(3) See Glossary. Sometimes translated as "Good Wealth."

(4) May also be translated as "era." In Sanskrit, "kalpa."

(5) Bodhimandala: literally, seat or site of Enlightenment. By extension, a temple or place of retreat.

(6) Bodhi Mind: see Glossary for this important concept.

(7) Lions Among Men: i.e., Buddhas.

(8) Learners and Those-Past-Study in the Two Vehicles. This is a reference to those who have attained Arhatship and the three levels of sagehood immediately preceding it.

(9) Lamps of the Worlds, Lamps of the Future: metaphors for the Buddhas.

(10) Without outflows: i.e., unconditioned. See Glossary, "Unconditioned."

(11) This stanza expresses a key concept of the Avatamsaka Sutra school: the complete interpenetration of time and space.

(12) In Buddhism, time is a relative concept; it can be long or short, depending on the state of mind.

(13) All the Buddhas are present in one thought. As the Sixth Patriarch said, "An enlightened thought makes one a Buddha" (*Platform Sutra*, ch. 2).

(14) Dharma(s): see Glossary. When capitalized, it refers to the teachings of the Buddha.

(15) This stanza and the following one are well-known in Pure Land. They are incorporated into the daily liturgy and recited over and over.

(16) Fields of merits: Buddhas, Bodhisattvas, Arhats and all sentient beings, whether friends or foes, are fields of merits for the cultivator because they provide him with an opportunity to cultivate merits and virtues. For example, needy people provide the opportunity for the cultivator to practice charity. Thus, they are a field of merits for him. As this text states, "Bodhi belongs to living beings. Without living beings, no Bodhisattva could achieve Supreme, Perfect Enlightenment."

Editors' Glossary

Alaya consciousness. Also called "store consciousness," "eighth consciousness," or "karma repository." See also "Eight consciousnesses."

All karma created in the present and previous lifetimes is stored here. The alaya consciousness is regarded as that which undergoes the cycle of birth and death ... All the actions and experiences of life that take place through the first seven consciousnesses are accumulated as karma in this alaya consciousness, which at the same time exerts an influence on the workings of the seven consciousnesses. (*A Dictionary of Buddhist Terms and Concepts.*)

Amitabha (Amida, Amita, Amitayus). Amitabha is the most commonly used name for the Buddha of Infinite Light and Infinite Life. A transhistorical Buddha venerated by all Mahayana schools (T'ien T'ai, Esoteric, Zen ...) and, particularly, Pure Land. Presides over the Western Pure Land (Land of Ultimate Bliss), where anyone can be reborn with ten utterly sincere recitations of His name at the time of death.

Amitabha Buddha at the highest or noumenon level represents the Mind of the Buddhas and sentient beings, all-encompassing and all-inclusive. This deeper understanding provides the rationale for the harmonization of Zen and Pure Land, two popular schools of Mahayana Buddhism.

Arhat. Buddhist saint who has attained liberation from the cycle of Birth and Death, generally through living a monastic life in accordance with the Buddhas' teachings. Arhatship is the goal of Theravadin practice, as contrasted with Bodhisattvahood in Mahayana practice. (*A Dictionary of Buddhism.*)

Avatamsaka Sutra. The basic text of the Avatamsaka School. It is one of the longest sutras in the Buddhist Canon and records the highest teaching of Buddha Sakyamuni, immediately after Enlightenment. It is traditionally believed that the Sutra was taught to the Bodhisattvas and other high spiritual beings while the Buddha was in samadhi. The Sutra has been described as the epitome of Buddhist thought, Buddhist sentiment and Buddhist experience and is quoted by all schools of Mahayana Buddhism, in particular, Pure Land and Zen.

Awakening vs. Enlightenment. A clear distinction should be made between *awakening to the Way* (Great Awakening) and *attainment of Supreme Enlightenment* (attaining the Way). To experience a Great Awakening is to achieve (through Zen meditation, Buddha Recitation, etc.) a complete and deep understanding of what it means to be a Buddha and how to reach Buddhahood. It is to see one's Nature, comprehend the True Nature of things, the Truth. However, only after becoming a Buddha can one be said to have truly attained Supreme Enlightenment (attained the Way). Caveat: there are many degrees of awakening and enlightenment ... A Great Awakening is like peeling away the many layers of an onion, one after another, and finally reaching its core.

A metaphor appearing in the sutras is that of a glass of water containing sediments. As long as the glass is undisturbed, the sediments remain at the bottom and the water is clear. However, as soon as the glass is shaken, the water becomes turbid. Likewise, when a practitioner experiences a Great Awakening (awakens to the Way), his afflictions (greed, anger and delusion) are temporarily suppressed but not yet eliminated. To achieve Supreme Enlightenment (i.e., to be rid of all afflictions, to discard all sediments) is the ultimate goal. Only then can he completely trust his mind and actions. Before then, he should adhere to the precepts, keep a close watch on his mind and thoughts, like a cat watching a mouse, ready to pounce on evil thoughts as soon as they arise.

A Zen story illustrates the distinction between awakening to the Way (Great Awakening) and attaining Supreme Enlightenment:

To make sure that his disciple would reach the great ocean and not be misled by smaller bodies of water, a Master explained the difference between rivers, lakes and seas, the characteristics of fresh water, salt water, etc. Finally, he took the disciple to the highest mountain peak in the area and pointed to the ocean in the distance. For the first time, glimpsing the ocean with his own eyes, the disciple experienced a Great Awakening. However, only after he followed the long, arduous path and actually reached the ocean, tasting its waters, did he achieve Enlightenment.

Awakening of the Faith (Treatise). A major commentary by the Patriarch Asvaghosha (1st/2nd cent.), which presents the fundamental principles of Mahayana Buddhism. Several translations exist in English.

The text deals with the doctrine of One Mind ... and the idea of the two aspects of One Mind: the absolute, or noumenal, and the relative, or phenomenal. (Sung-peng Hsu.)

Bardo stage. The intermediate stage between death and rebirth.

Bodhi. Sanskrit for Enlightenment.

Bodhi Mind, (Bodhicitta, Great Mind). The spirit of Enlightenment, the aspiration to achieve it, the Mind set on Enlightenment. It involves two parallel aspects: i) the determination to achieve Buddhahood and ii) the aspiration to rescue all sentient beings.

Bodies of the Buddha. See "Three Bodies of the Buddha."

Bodhisattva Grounds. See "Ten Grounds."

Brahma Net Sutra (Brahmajala Sutra). This is a sutra of major significance in Mahayana Buddhism. In addition to containing the ten major precepts of Mahayana (not to kill, steal, lie, etc.) the Sutra also contains forty-eight less important injunctions. These fifty-eight major and minor rules constitute the Bodhisattva Precepts, taken by most Mahayana monks and nuns and certain advanced lay practitioners. A major characteristic of the *Brahma Net Sutra* is that the Bodhisattva Precepts stress the positive as well as negative aspects of the injunctions: do not kill but release sentient beings; do not steal but practice charity, etc.

Buddha Nature. The following terms refer to the same thing: Self-Nature, True Mind, True Nature,

Dharma Nature, True Mark, Nirvana, Dharma Body,
Original Face, Original Nature, Prajna, True Emptiness,
True Thusness, etc.:

According to the Mahayana view, [buddha-nature] is the
true, immutable, and eternal nature of all beings. Since all
beings possess buddha-nature, it is possible for them to
attain enlightenment and become a buddha, regardless of
what level of existence they occupy ... The answer to the
question whether buddha-nature is immanent in beings is
an essential determining factor for the association of a
given school with Theravada or Mahayana, the two great
currents within Buddhism. In Theravada this notion is
unknown; here the potential to become a buddha is not
ascribed to every being. By contrast the Mahayana sees
the attainment of buddhahood as the highest goal; it can
be attained through the inherent buddha-nature of every
being through appropriate spiritual practice. (*The Shambhala
Dictionary of Buddhism and Zen.*)

See also "Dharma Nature," "True Thusness."

Buddha Recitation. General term for a number of
practices, such as oral recitation of Amitabha Buddha's
name and visualization or contemplation of His
auspicious marks and those of the Pure Land. When
used in a broad sense, it also includes such sundry
practices as cultivating the Ten Great Vows of
Samantabhadra, building temples and reciting sutras.

Reciting the buddha-name proceeds from the mind. The
mind remembers Buddha and does not forget. That's why
it is called buddha remembrance, or reciting the
buddha-name mindfully. (Cited in J.C. Cleary, *Pure Land,
Pure Mind.*)

Conditioned (compounded). Describes all the
various phenomena in the world -- made up of separate,
discrete elements, with no intrinsic nature of their own.

Conditioned merits and virtues, for example, are subject to Birth and Death, whereas unconditioned merits and virtues are beyond Birth and Death. See also "Unconditioned."

Consciousness. See "Alaya consciousness" and "Eight consciousnesses."

Definitive Meaning. See "Ultimate Meaning."

Delusion (Ignorance). "Delusion refers to belief in something that contradicts reality. In Buddhism, delusion is ... a lack of awareness of the true nature or Buddha nature of things, or of the true meaning of existence.

"According to the Buddhist outlook, we are deluded by our senses -- among which intellect (discriminating, discursive thought) is included as a sixth sense. Consciousness, attached to the senses, leads us into error by causing us to take the world of appearances for the world of reality, whereas in fact it is only a limited and fleeting aspect of reality." (*Shambhala Dictionary of Buddhism and Zen.*)

Delusions of Views and Thought. Delusion of views refers to greed and lust for externals (clothing, food, sleep, etc.) which are viewed as real rather than empty in their true nature.

> The delusion of thought consists in being confused about principles and giving rise to discrimination ... Thought delusions are unclear, muddled thoughts, taking what is wrong as right, and what is right as wrong. (Master Hsuan Hua, *A General Explanation of the Buddha Speaks of Amitabha Sutra.*)

Demons. Evil influences which hinder cultivation. These can take an infinite number of forms, including evil beings or hallucinations. The three poisons of greed, anger and delusion are also equated to demons, as they disturb the mind. See the following passage:

> T..us, when you are practicing Zen, all thoughts other than the method [koan] should be considered as demons, even if it feels like you have entered a 'heavenly' state. Some people, as they are sitting, may suddenly enter a completely new world which is very beautiful and comfortable. Afterwards, they want to return to it in each meditation. They may be able to get into that state again, but nonetheless it is an attachment. There are also other states that are terrifying. Such visions, good and bad, are generally manifestations of our own mental realms. (Master Sheng-Yen.)

The Self-Nature has been described in Mahayana sutras as a house full of gold and jewelry. To preserve the riches, i.e., to keep the mind calm, empty and still, we should shut the doors to the three thieves of greed, anger and delusion. Letting the mind move opens the house to "demons," that is, hallucinations and harm. Thus, Zen practitioners are taught that, while in meditation, "Encountering demons, kill the demons, encountering Buddhas, kill the Buddhas." Both demons and Buddhas are mind-made, Mind-Only.

> Even if a buddha or bodhisattva should suddenly appear before you, there's no need for reverence. This mind of ours is empty and contains no such form. Those who hold onto appearances are devils. They fall from the path. Why worship illusions born of the mind? Those who worship don't know, and those who know don't worship. By worshipping you come under the spell of devils ... At the appearance of spirits, demons, or divine beings, conceive neither respect nor fear. Your mind is basically empty. All appearances are illusions. Don't hold on to appearances. (The Patriarch Bodhidharma.)

For a detailed discussion of demons, see Master Thích Thiền Tâm, *Buddhism of Wisdom and Faith*, sect. 51, p.204ff.

Dharma. a) Duty, law, doctrine. b) Things, events, phenomena, everything. c) The teachings of the Buddha (generally capitalized in English).

Dharma Body. See "Three Bodies of the Buddha."

Dharma-Ending Age, Degenerate Age. The present spiritually degenerate era.

The concept of decline, dissension and schism within the Dharma after the passing of the Buddha is a general teaching of Buddhism and a corollary to the Truth of impermanence. See, for example, the *Diamond Sutra* (sect. 6 in the translation by A.F. Price and Wong Mou-lam).

The modern reader, unfamiliar with the concept of the Dharma-Ending Age may wish to recall the famous story of Hui K'o, the second Chinese Patriarch of Zen, who, according to tradition, knelt in the snow behind Bodhidharma for a whole night before being accepted as a disciple. Contrast this with the contemporary situation when even the holiest of all Buddhist holidays, Vesak (Birthday of Sakyamuni Buddha), must be held on the week-end to ensure adequate attendance.

Dharma Nature. The intrinsic nature of all things. Used interchangeably with "emptiness," "reality." See also "Buddha Nature," "True Thusness."

Dharma Realm (Cosmos, Dharmadhatu, realm of reality, realm of truth). The term has several meanings in the sutras: i) the nature or essence of all things; ii) the infinite universe, consisting of worlds upon worlds *ad infinitum*; iii) the Mind.

Dharmakara. The Bodhisattva who later became Amitabha Buddha, as related in the *Longer Amitabha Sutra*. The Bodhisattva Dharmakara is famous for forty-eight vows, particularly the eighteenth, which promises rebirth in the Pure Land to anyone who recites His name with utmost sincerity at the time of death.

Diamond Sutra. "An independent part of the *Prajnaparamita Sutra*, which attained great importance, particularly in East Asia. It shows that all phenomenal appearances are not ultimate reality but rather illusions, projections of one's own mind ... The work is called *Diamond Sutra* because it is 'sharp like a diamond that cuts away all unnecessary conceptualizations and brings one to the further shore of enlightenment.'" (*Shambhala Dictionary of Buddhism and Zen.*) See also "Prajnaparamita Sutras."

Difficult Path of Practice (Path of the Sages, Self-Power Path). According to Pure Land teaching, all conventional Buddhist ways of practice and cultivation (Zen, Theravada, the Vinaya School ...), which emphasize self-power and self-reliance. This is contrasted to the Easy Path of Practice, that is, the Pure Land method.

Dusts (Worldly Dusts). A metaphor for all the mundane things that can cloud our bright Self-Nature. These include form, sound, smell, taste, touch, dharmas (external opinions and views). These dusts correspond to the five senses and the discriminating, everyday mind.

Easy Path of Practice). Refers to Pure Land practice. The Easy Path involves reliance on the power of the Buddhas and Bodhisattvas, in particular Buddha Amitabha ("other-power") in addition to one's own cultivation ("self-power"). Usually contrasted with primary reliance on self-power (Difficult Path of Practice), taught in other Buddhist schools.

Equal reliance on self-power and other-power distinguishes the Pure Land School from other schools of Buddhism, which stress self-power. The distinction is, however, a matter of emphasis, as all schools of Buddhism rely on both self-power and other-power. Ultimately, self-power is other-power, and vice-versa.

Eight Adversities. The eight conditions under which it is difficult to meet Buddhas and Bodhisattvas or hear the Dharma: 1. rebirth in hell; 2. rebirth as a hungry ghost; 3. rebirth as an animal; 4. rebirth in Uttarakuru (a world where life is so pleasant that people have no motivation to practice the Dharma); 5. rebirth in any long-life heaven (where one is also not motivated to seek the Dharma); 6. rebirth with impaired faculties; 7. rebirth as an intelligent, educated person in the mundane sense (as such an individual often looks down on religion and on the Dharma); and 8. rebirth in the intermediate period between a Buddha and his successor (e.g., our current period). Thus, even rebirth under "favorable" circumstances (fourth and seventh conditions, for example) may constitute adversity with respect to the Buddha Dharma.

Eight consciousnesses. The term "consciousnesses" refers to the perception or discernment which occurs when our sense organs make contact with their respective objects. They are: 1) sight consciouness; 2) hearing consciousness; 3) smell consciousness; 4) taste consciousness; 5) touch consciousness; 6) mind consciousness; 7) Mano consciousness (defiled mind); 8) Alaya consciousness. The first five consciousnesses correspond to the five senses. The sixth consciousness (i.e., our ordinary mind) "integrates the perceptions of the five senses into coherent images and makes judgments about the external world ..." (*A Dictionary of Buddhist Terms and Concepts*.) "The seventh consciousness [afflicted or defiled mind] is the active center of reasoning, calculation, and construction or fabrication of individual objects. It is the source of clinging and craving, and thus the origin of the sense of self or ego and the cause of all illusion that arises from assuming the apparent to be real ..." (Sung-peng Hsu.) For the eighth or Alaya consciousness, see "Alaya consciousness."

Eight Sufferings. Birth, old age, disease, death, separation from loved ones, meeting with the uncongenial, unfulfilled wishes and the suffering associated with the five raging skandas. (For a detailed exposition of the eight sufferings, see Thích Thiền Tâm, *Buddhism of Wisdom and Faith*, sect. 5, p. 15.)

Emptiness (Void, Sunyata). Connotes "first, Void in the sense of antithesis of being; second, the state of being 'devoid' of specific character; third, Void in the highest sense, or Transcendental Void, i.e., all oppositions synthesized ...; and fourth, the Absolute Void or the Unconditioned." (Vergilius Ferm, ed. *An Encyclopedia of Religion*).

Contrasted with "hollow emptiness," or "stubborn emptiness," which is one-sided and leads to nihilism (the belief that nothing exists after death). Thus, we have the Mahayana expression, "True Emptiness, Wonderful Existence." True Emptiness is not empty!

Enlightenment. See "Awakening vs. Enlightenment."

Evil Paths. Hells, hungry ghosts, animality.

Expedient means (Skillful means, Skill-in-means). Refers to strategies, methods, devices, targetted to the capacities, circumstances, likes and dislikes of each sentient being, so as to rescue him and lead him to enlightenment. "Thus, all particular formulations of the Teaching are just provisional expedients to communicate the Truth (Dharma) in specific contexts." (J.C. Cleary). "The Buddha's words were medicines for a given sickness at a given time," always infinitely adaptable to the conditions of the audience.

Externalists. Literally, followers of external paths. This term is generally used by Buddhists with reference to followers of other religions (e.g., Taoism, Hinduism, etc.).

Five Grave Offenses (Five Deadly Sins). Offenses which cause rebirth in the Uninterrupted Hell. They are: killing one's father, one's mother, or an Arhat, causing dissension within the Sangha, causing the Buddhas to bleed.

Five Precepts. See "Ten Virtues."

Five Skandas. Also translated as "components" or "aggregates." They represent both body and mind. The five skandas are form, feeling, conception, impulse and consciousness. For example, form is the physical body, consciousness is the faculty of awareness, etc. The best known reference to the five skandas is found in the *Heart*

Sutra. By realizing that they are intrinsically empty, the Bodhisattva Avalokitesvara has escaped all suffering. Note the difference between intellectual understanding of this principle and truly internalizing it (a good driver slams on the brakes when another car cuts in front of him, without stopping to think about it). Only by internalizing the Truth of emptiness can the cultivator escape suffering.

> The Buddha is known to have taught the doctrine of five skandas (heaps or aggregates) as an account of man. Man is regarded as simply a bundle or conglomeration of form, feelings, perceptions, impulses and consciousness. There is no "I" over and above the five skandas. (Sung-peng Hsu.)

Five Turbidities (Corruptions, Defilements, Depravities, Filths, Impurities).

They are: 1. the defilement of views, when incorrect, perverse thoughts and ideas are predominant; 2. the defilement of passions, when all kinds of transgressions are exalted; 3. the defilement of the human condition, when people are usually dissatisfied and unhappy; 4. the defilement of the life-span, when the human life-span as a whole decreases; 5. the defilement of the world-age, when war and natural disasters are rife. These conditions, viewed from a Buddhist angle, however, can constitute aids to Enlightenment, as they may spur practitioners to more earnest cultivation.

Flower Store World.

The entire cosmos, as described in the *Avatamsaka Sutra.* It is the land of Vairocana Buddha, the transcendental aspect of Buddha Sakyamuni and of all Buddhas. The Saha World, the Western Pure Land and, for that matter, all lands, are realms within the Flower Store World.

Four Fruits.

These are the four stages of

Enlightenment in Theravada Buddhism, culminating in Arhatship.

Four Great Debts. Debts to 1) one's parents, 2) the Three Treasures (Buddha, Dharma, Sangha), 3) the founders of the nation/enlightened temporal leaders and 4) all sentient beings ("all men were my fathers, all women my mothers" in past lives).

Good Spiritual Advisor. Guru, virtuous friend, wise person, Bodhisattva, Buddha -- anyone who can help the practitioner progress along the path to Enlightenment. This notwithstanding, *wisdom* should be the primary factor in the selection of such an advisor: the advisor must have wisdom, and both advisor and practitioner must exercise wisdom in selecting one another.

Great Awakening. See "Awakening vs. Enlightenment."

Insight into Non-arising of the Dharmas. See "Tolerance of Non-Birth."

Ksana. "The shortest measure of time; sixty ksana equal one finger-snap, ninety a thought, 4,500 a minute." (Charles Luk.)

Lankavatara Sutra. The only sutra recommended by Bodhidharma, the First Zen Patriarch in China. It is a key Zen text, along with the *Diamond Sutra* (recommended by the Sixth Patriarch), the *Surangama Sutra*, the *Vimalakirti Sutra*, the *Avatamsaka Sutra* ...

Lotus Grades. Refer allegorically to nine possible degrees of rebirth in the Pure Land. The more merits and virtues the practitioner accumulates, the higher the grade. The highest grade is achieved by cultivators who have attained samadhi.

Lotus Sutra. A major Buddhist text and one of the most widely read sutras in the present day.

One of the earliest and most richly descriptive of the Mahayana sutras of Indian origin. It became important for the shaping of the Buddhist tradition in East Asia, in particular because of its teaching of the One Vehicle under which is subsumed the usual Hinayana [Theravada] and Mahayana divisions. It is the main text of the Tendai [T'ien T'ai] school. (Joji Okazaki).

This School has a historically close relationship with the Pure Land School, so much so that Elder Master T'ai Hsu taught that the *Lotus Sutra* is the *Longer Amitabha Sutra* in expanded form, while the *Longer Amitabha Sutra* is a summary of the *Lotus Sutra*.

Maitreya. The future Buddha of this Saha World. One of the few transhistorical Buddhas (i.e., Buddhas with no basis in human history) recognized by the Theravada School.

Manjusri. The Bodhisattva who represents the Ultimate Wisdom of the Buddhas. (The Elder Sariputra exemplifies the wisdom of the Arhats.) See also "Sariputra."

Marks. See "Noumenon/Phenomena."

Meditation Sutra. See "Three Pure Land Sutras" and "Vaidehi."

Middle Way (Madhyamika). The way between and above all extremes, such as hedonism or ascetism, existence or emptiness, eternalism or nihilism, samsara or Nirvana, etc. The Middle Way is a basic tenet of Buddhism. See also "Nagarjuna."

Mind. Key concept in all Buddhist teaching.

> Frequent term in Zen, used in two senses: (1) the mind-ground, the One Mind ... the buddha-mind, the mind of thusness ... (2) false mind, the ordinary mind dominated by conditioning, desire, aversion, ignorance, and false sense of self, the mind of delusion ... (J.C. Cleary, *A Buddha from Korea.*)

The ordinary, deluded mind (thought) includes feelings, impressions, conceptions, consciousness, etc. The Self-Nature True Mind is the fundamental nature, the Original Face, reality, etc. As an example, the Self-Nature True Mind is to mind what water is to waves -- the two cannot be dissociated. They are the same but they are also different.

Nagarjuna. (2nd/3rd cent.) "One of the most important philosophers of Buddhism and the founder of the Madhyamika school. Nagarjuna's major accomplishment was his systematization ... of the teaching presented in the *Prajnaparamita Sutras.* Nagarjuna's methodological approach of rejecting all opposites is the basis of the Middle Way ..." (*Shambhala Dictionary of Buddhism and Zen.*) See also "Middle Way."

Nature and Marks. See "Noumenon/Phenomena."

Non-Birth (No-Birth). "A term used to describe the nature of Nirvana. In Mahayana Buddhism generally,

No-Birth signifies the 'extinction' of the discursive thinking by which we conceive of things as arising and perishing, forming attachments to them." (Ryukoku University). See also "Tolerance of Non-Birth."

Non-Dual. Key Buddhist truth. Can be understood as not two and not one -- transcending two and one. Equivalent to reality, emptiness.

Noumenon/Phenomena. *Noumenon*: principle, essence of things, always one and indivisible. *Phenomena*: All things and events. Used in plural form to contrast with noumenon.

"Noumenon" (principle) is reason, the realm of enlightenment, and belongs to the sphere of "nature." "Phenomena" are expedients, practices, deeds, "form," and fall under the heading of "marks." However, in the end, phenomena are noumenon, nature is mark, and both belong to the same truth-like Nature, all-illuminating, all-pervading. In cultivation, noumenon and phenomena are the two sides of a coin, interacting with one another and helping one another. With noumenon, we have a basis, a direction, a goal to develop into action. With phenomena, we are able to actualize what we think, demonstrate our understanding, arrive at an objective goal and, ultimately, achieve results. (Thích Thiền Tâm.)

Ocean Seal Samadhi. A state of concentration of the highest level, mentioned, *inter alia*, in the *Avatamsaka Sutra*. ... The mind is likened to the ocean, which, when calm and without a single wave, can reflect everything throughout the cosmos, past, present and future.

Ocean-Wide Assembly. Term used in the *Avatamsaka Sutra* to denote a transcendental gathering of Buddhas, Bodhisattvas, Arhats and other sentient beings, as immense as the ocean.

One-Life Bodhisattva. A Bodhisattva who is one lifetime away from Buddhahood. The best known example is the Bodhisattva Maitreya.

One-pointedness of mind. Singlemindedness or singleminded concentration. This is a *sine qua non* for rebirth in the Pure Land.

Original Nature. See "Buddha Nature."

Other-Power. See "Easy Path of Practice."

Paramita. Means "the perfection of" or "reaching the other shore" (Enlightenment) as contrasted with this shore of suffering and mortality. The paramitas are usually six in number (charity, discipline, forbearance, energy, concentration, wisdom) or expanded to ten (adding the four paramitas of expedients, vows, power and knowledge). The Mahayana tradition emphasizes the paramita of expedients, or skill-in-means.

Path of Sages. See "Difficult Path of Practice."

Perfect Teaching (Round Teaching). Supreme teaching of the Buddhas, as expressed in the *Avatamsaka* and *Lotus Sutras*.

Prajnaparamita Sutras. "Term for a series of about forty Mahayana sutras gathered together under this name because they all deal with the realization of prajna [intuitive wisdom] ... Best known in the West are the *Diamond Sutra* and the *Heart Sutra*. Their most important interpreter was Nagarjuna." (*Shambhala Dictionary*.) The truth of sunyata, or emptiness, is central to these sutras, which teach non-attachment to self or dharmas. See also "Diamond Sutra."

Pure Land. Generic term for the realms of the Buddhas. In this text it denotes the Land of Ultimate Bliss or Western Land of Amitabha Buddha. It is "a paradise realm of the spirit world" (Raoul Birnbaum), an *ideal place of cultivation*, beyond the Triple Realm and samsara, where those who are reborn are no longer subject to retrogression. This is the key distinction between the Western Pure Land and such realms as the Tusita Heaven. There are two conceptions of the Pure Land: as different and apart from the Saha World *and* as one with and the same as the Saha World. When the mind is pure and undefiled, any land or environment becomes a pure land (*Vimalakirti, Lotus, Avatamsaka Sutras* ...). At the noumenal level, everything, the Pure Land included, is Mind-Only, a product of the mind. See also "Triple Realm."

Pure Land Sutras. See "Three Pure Land Sutras."

Reward Body. See "Three Bodies of the Buddha."

Saha World. World of Endurance. Refers to this world of ours, filled with suffering and afflictions, yet gladly endured by its inhabitants.

Samadhi. Meditative absorption. "Usually denotes the particular final stage of pure concentration." There are many degrees and types of samadhi (Buddha Remembrance, Ocean Seal ...)

Samantabhadra. Also called Universal Worthy or, in Japanese, Fugen. A major Bodhisattva, who personifies the transcendental practices and vows of the Buddhas (as compared to the Bodhisattva Manjusri, who represents transcendental wisdom). Usually depicted seated on an elephant with six tusks (six paramitas). Best known for his "Ten Great Vows." See Appendix.

Samatha-Vipasyana. Samatha is "silencing the active mind and [vipasyana] is developing an insight into the still mind. The chief object is the concentration of the mind ... for the purpose of clear insight into the truth and to be rid of illusion." (Charles Luk.)

Samsara. Cycle of rebirths, realms of Birth and Death.

Sariputra. Major disciple of Sakyamuni Buddha, foremost in wisdom among Arhats. See also "Manjusri."

Self-Power. See "Difficult Path of Practice."

Seven Treasures. Gold, silver, lapis lazuli, crystal, agate, red pearl and carnelian. They represent the seven powers of faith, perseverance, "shame," avoidance of wrongdoing, mindfulness, concentration and wisdom.

Six Directions. North, South, East, West, above and below, i.e., all directions. In the *Avatamsaka Sutra*, they are expanded to include points of the compass in-between and are referred to as the Ten Directions.

Six Dusts. See "Dusts."

Skandas. See "Five Skandas."

Skillful Means. See "Expedient Means."

Spiritual power. Also called miraculous power. Includes, *inter alia*, the ability to see all forms (deva eye), to hear all sounds (deva ear), to know the thoughts of others, to be anywhere and do anything at will, etc.

Subhuti. One of Buddha Sakyamuni's major disciples. Foremost among Arhats in understanding the doctrine of the Void (Emptiness). However, the Buddha predicted in the *Lotus Sutra*, Ch. 6 that he would achieve Buddhahood with the title Name-and-Form Buddha, thus demonstrating that Emptiness is Form and Form is Emptiness -- the two are not different (*Heart Sutra*).

Sudhana. The main protagonist in the next-to-last and longest chapter of the *Avatamsaka Sutra*. Seeking Enlightenment, he visited and studied with fifty-three spiritual advisors and became the equal of the Buddhas in one lifetime. When he was born, myriad treasures suddenly appeared in his father's home. Thus the name "Sudhana" or "Good Wealth."

Suffering. See "Eight Sufferings."

Surangama Sutra. Also called *Heroic Gate Sutra*.

> The "Sutra of the Heroic One" exercised a great influence on the development of Mahayana Buddhism in China [and neighboring countries]. It emphasizes the power of samadhi, through which enlightenment can be attained, and explains the various methods of emptiness meditation through the practice of which everyone ... can realize ... enlightenment ... The Sutra is particularly popular in Zen.

(*Shambhala Dictionary of Buddhism and Zen.*)

Ten Evil Deeds (Ten Evil Acts, Ten Sins).

1. Killing; 2. stealing; 3. sexual misconduct; 4. lying; 5. slander; 6. coarse language; 7. empty chatter; 8. covetousness; 9. angry speech; 10. wrong views. Opposite of the Ten Virtues. See also "Ten Virtues."

Ten Great Vows.

The famous vows of the Bodhisattva Samantabhadra in the *Avatamsaka Sutra*. These vows represent the quintessence of this Sutra and are the basis of all Mahayana practice. Studying the Vows and putting them into practice is tantamount to studying the *Avatamsaka Sutra* and practicing its teachings. See also "Samantabhadra."

Ten Grounds (Bodhisattva Grounds).

Also known as "Ten Stages." According to the Mahayana sutras, there are 52 levels of attainment before a cultivator can achieve Buddhahood. These levels are in ascending order of complexity and importance. The Ten Grounds constitute the 41st to 50th levels.

Ten Mysterious Gates (Ten Esoteric Doors, Ten Mysteries, Ten Profound Propositions).

Ten aspects of the interrelationship of all phenomena, as seen from the enlightened point of view. To explain such relationship and harmony,

> The [Avatamsaka] School advances the Ten Profound Propositions: 1) All things are co-existent, corresponding to one another. 2) The intension and extension of one thing involve those of others without any obstacle. 3) The One and the Many are mutually inclusive. 4) All things are identical with one another. 5) The hidden and the manifested mutually perfect each other. 6) All minute and abstruse things mutually penetrate one another. 7) All

things reflect one another. 8) Truth is manifested in facts and facts are the source of Enlightenment. 9) The past, present and future are inter-penetrating. 10) All things are manifestations and transformations of the mind." (Vergilius Ferm.)

Ten Precepts. See "Ten Virtues."

Ten Recitations. "Ten recitations" refers to the Ten Recitations method, based on the lowest grade of rebirth described in the *Meditation Sutra*. It is taught to persons busy with mundane activities, so that they, too, can practice Buddha Recitation and achieve rebirth in the Pure Land. The method consists of uttering the Buddha's name up to ten times with each inhalation or exhalation. The real intent behind this practice is to use the breath to concentrate the mind. Depending on the cultivator's breath span, he can recite ten times, or only seven or eight. After ten such inhalations and exhalations (or some seventy to one hundred utterances) the cultivator should proceed to transfer the merits toward rebirth in the Pure Land.

Ten Stages. See "Ten Grounds."

Ten Thousand Conducts. All the countless activities and cultivation practices of the Bodhisattvas.

Ten Virtues (Ten Precepts). Virtues of the body, mouth and mind, leading to rebirth in the celestial realms (not Buddha realms). Cultivating the Ten Virtues leads the practitioner to rebirth in, for example, the Tusita Heaven, though not yet in the Western Pure Land. The Ten Virtues include an expanded version of the Five Precepts of body and mouth (not to kill, steal, engage in illicit sex, take intoxicants, or lie) with the addition of the virtues of the mind (elimination of greed, anger and delusion). See also "Ten Evil Deeds."

Third Lifetime. In the first lifetime, the practitioner engages in mundane good deeds which bring ephemeral worldly blessings (wealth, power, authority, etc.) in the second lifetime. Since power tends to corrupt, he is likely to create evil karma, resulting in retribution in the third lifetime. Thus, good deeds in the first lifetime are potential "enemies" of the third lifetime.

To ensure that mundane good deeds do not become "enemies," the practitioner should dedicate all merits to a transcendental goal, i.e., to become Bodhisattvas or Buddhas or, in popular Pure Land teaching, to achieve rebirth in the Pure Land -- a Buddha land beyond Birth and Death.

Three Bodies of the Buddha (Trikaya). According to Mahayana teachings, these are:

1) Dharma Body (Dharmakaya, Body of Reality) -- the Buddha as the personification of Suchness, Emptiness, the Truth;

2) Reward Body (Sambhogakaya, Noumenal Body, Body of Enjoyment, Bliss Body, Celestial Body of the Buddha) -- "the body which is obtained as a reward of completing Bodhisattva practice and having understood the Buddha-wisdom ... transcendent and imperceptible to common mortals" (*A Dictionary of Buddhist Terms and Concepts*);

3) Transformation Body (Nirmanakaya, Phenomenal Body, Manifested Body, Incarnate Body) -- The Buddha as manifested in the ordinary world of samsara. For example, Sakyamuni is the Transformation Body of Vairocana Buddha.

Three Pure Land Sutras. Pure Land Buddhism is based on three basic texts:

a) *Amitabha Sutra* (or *Shorter Amitabha Sutra*, or *Smaller Sukhavati-Vyuha*, or the *Sutra of Amida*);

b) *Longer Amitabha Sutra* (or *Larger Sukhavati-Vyuha*, or the *Teaching of Infinite Life*);

c) *Meditation Sutra* (or the *Meditation on the Buddha of Infinite Life*, or the *Amitayur Dyana Sutra*).

Sometimes the last chapter of the *Avatamsaka Sutra* ("The Practices and Vows of the Bodhisattva Samantabhadra") is considered the fourth basic sutra of the Pure Land tradition.

Tolerance of Non-Birth. "Tolerance" (insight) that comes from the knowledge that all phenomena are unborn. Sometimes translated as "insight into the non-origination of all existence/non-origination of the dharmas."

A Mahayana Buddhist term for the insight into emptiness, the non-origination or birthlessness of things or beings realized by Bodhisattvas who have attained the eighth Stage [Ground] of the path to Buddhahood. When a Bodhisattva realizes this insight he has attained the stage of non-retrogression. (Ryukoku University.) See also "Ten Grounds."

The Pure Land School teaches that anyone reborn in the Pure Land attains the Tolerance of Non-Birth and reaches the stage of non-retrogression, never to fall back into samsara.

Three Realms. See "Triple Realm."

Transference of Merit. The concept of merit transference is reflected in the following passage:

> Some of us may ask whether the effect of [evil] karma can be ... [changed] by repeating the name of Kuan-Yin. This question is tied up with that of rebirth in Sukhavati [the Pure Land] and it may be answered by saying that invocation of Kuan-Yin's name forms another cause which will right away offset the previous karma. We know, for example, that if there is a dark, heavy cloud above, the chances are that it will rain. But we also know that if a strong wind should blow, the cloud will be carried away somewhere else and we will not feel the rain. Similarly, the addition of one big factor can alter the whole course of karma ...
>
> It is only by accepting the idea of life as one whole that both Theravadins and Mahayanists can advocate the practice of transference of merit to others. With the case of Kuan-Yin then, by calling on Her name we identify ourselves with Her and as a result of this identification Her merits flow over to us. These merits which are now ours then counterbalance our bad karma and save us from calamity. The law of cause and effect still stands good. All that has happened is that a powerful and immensely good karma has overshadowed the weaker one ... (Lecture on Kuan-Yin by Tech Eng Soon - Penang Buddhist Association, c. 1960. Pamphlet.)

Transformation Body. See "Three Bodies of the Buddha."

Triple Realm (Three Realms, Three Worlds). The realms of *desire* (our world), *form* (realms of the lesser deities) and *formlessness* (realms of the higher deities). The Western Pure Land is outside the Triple Realm, beyond samsara and retrogression. See also "Pure Land."

True Thusness (True Suchness). Equivalent to Buddha Nature, Dharma Body, etc. See also "Buddha Nature," Dharma Nature."

Two Truths. 1) *Relative* or conventional, everyday truth of the mundane world subject to delusion and dichotomies and 2) the *Ultimate* Truth as taught by the Buddhas.

Pure Land thinkers such as the Patriarch Tao Ch'o accepted "the legitimacy of Conventional Truth as an expression of Ultimate Truth and as a vehicle to reach Ultimate Truth. Even though all form is nonform, it is acceptable and necessary to use form within the limits of causality, because its use is an expedient means of saving others out of one's compassion for them and because, even for the unenlightened, the use of form can lead to the revelation of form as nonform" (David Chappell). Thus to reach Buddhahood, which is formless, the cultivator can practice the Pure Land method based on form.

According to Buddhism, there are two kinds of Truth, the Absolute and the Relative. The Absolute Truth (of the Void) manifests "illumination but is always still," and this is absolutely inexplicable. On the other hand, the Relative Truth (of the Unreal) manifests "stillness but is always illuminating," which means that it is immanent in everything. (Hsu Heng Chi/P.H. Wei). See also "Ultimate Meaning."

Ultimate Meaning (Definitive Meaning, Foremost Meaning). "This refers to those teachings of the Buddha that are in terms of ultimate reality ...

relates to voidness." (Robert Thurman). This is contrasted to the conventional or relative truth of our everyday world. See also "Two Truths."

Unconditioned (Transcendental). Anything free of the three marks of greed, anger and delusion. See also "Conditioned."

Vaidehi. The Queen of King Bimbisara of Magadha. It was in response to her entreaties that Buddha Sakyamuni preached the *Meditation Sutra*, which teaches a series of sixteen visualizations (of Amitabha Buddha, the Pure Land ...) leading to rebirth in the Land of Ultimate Bliss.

Vairocana. The main Buddha in the *Avatamsaka Sutra*. Represents the Dharma Body of Buddha Sakyamuni and all Buddhas. His Pure Land is the Flower Store World, i.e., the whole Buddhist cosmos.

Vimalakirti Sutra. A key Mahayana sutra particularly popular with Zen and to a lesser extent Pure Land followers. The main protagonist is a layman named Vimalakirti who is the equal of many Bodhisattvas in wisdom, eloquence, etc. He explained the teaching of Emptiness in terms of non-duality ... "The true nature of things is beyond the limiting concepts imposed by words." Thus, when asked by Manjusri to define the non-dual truth, Vimalakirti simply remained silent.

Worldly Dusts. See "Dusts."

Bibliography

Asvaghosha, *The Awakening of the Faith.* S. Yoshito Hakeda, tr. New York: Columbia University Press, 1967.

Andrews, Allen A., "Nembutsu in Chinese Pure Land Tradition." In *The Eastern Buddhist,* Vol. 3, No. 2, October 1970, p. 20ff.

Birnbaum, Raoul, *The Healing Buddha.* Boston, Ma: Shambhala, 1989.

Ch'en, Kenneth K.S., *Buddhism in China: A Historical Survey.* Princeton, NJ: Princeton University Press, 1964.

Chih I (Patriarch), "Ten Doubts about Pure Land." In *Pure Land Buddhism: Dialogues with Ancient Masters.* Master Thích Thiền Tâm, tr. New York: Sutra Translation Committee of the United States and Canada, 1992.

Chihmann (P.C. Lee), tr., *The Two Buddhist Books in Mahayana.* Taipei: Corporate Body of the Buddha Educational Foundation [no date]. Originally published in early 1930's.

Claxton, Guy, *The Heart of Buddhism: Practical Wisdom for an Agitated World.* Wellingborough, England: Crucible, 1990.

Cleary, J.C., tr. *A Buddha from Korea: the Zen Teachings of Taego.* Boston, Ma: Shambhala, 1988.

Cleary, J.C. *Pure Land, Pure Mind.* (Unpublished manuscript.)

Cleary, Thomas, tr., *The Flower Ornament Scripture: A Translation of the Avatamsaka Sutra.* (Three vols.) Boston Ma and London: Shambhala, 1984-1987.

Cook, Francis, *Hua-Yen Buddhism: The Jewel Net of Indra.* University Park, Pa and London: Pennsylvania State University Press, 1977.

Cowell, E.B, et al., ed., *Buddhist Mahayana Texts.* New York: Dover Publications, Inc., 1969. (From *The Sacred Books of the East,* Vol. 49.)

A Dictionary of Buddhism: Chinese-Sanskrit-English-Thai. Bangkok: The Chinese Budddhist Order of Sangha in Thailand, 1976.

A Dictionary of Buddhist Terms and Concepts. Tokyo: Nichiren Shoshu International Center, 1983.

Dumoulin, Heinrich, *Zen Buddhism: A History*. James W. Heisig and Paul Knitter, tr. New York and London: Macmillan, 1988.

Foster, Barbara and Michael, *Forbidden Journey: the Life of Alexandra David-Neel*. San Francisco, Ca: Harper & Row, 1989.

Friedman, Lenore, *Meetings with Remarkable Women: Buddhist Teachers in America*. Boston, Ma and London: Shambhala, 1987.

Goddard, D., ed., *A Buddhist Bible*. Boston, Ma: Beacon Press, 1970.

Hsu, Heng Chi, *What's Buddhism? Theory and Practice*. P.H. Wei, tr. Hong Kong: Hong Kong Buddhist Books Distributor, 1989.

Hsu, Sung-peng, *A Buddhist Leader in Ming China*. University Park, Pa and London: State University of Pennsylvania Press, 1979.

Hsu Yun (Master), "The Ch'an Training." In *Ts'an Ch'an Yao Chih [Essential Tenets of Zen]*. Pamphlet. New York: Grace Gratitutde Buddhist Temple [no date].

Hsuan Hua (Master), *A General Explanation of the Buddha Speaks of Amitabha Sutra*. San Francisco, Ca: Buddhist Text Translation Society, 1974.

Hsuan Hua (Master), *Pure Land & Ch'an Dharma Talks*. San Francisco, Ca: Sino-American Buddhist Association, 1974.

Hsuan Hua (Master), tr., *Flower Adornment Sutra*. Talmadge, Ca: Buddhist Text Translation Society. 1982- [Issued in parts.]

Hui Seng, *The Buddha Speaks the Brahma Net Sutra*. Talmadge, Ca: Buddhist Text Translation Society, 1982.

Humphreys, Christmas, *The Buddhist Way of Life*. London: Unwin Paperbacks, 1980. (Originally pub. 1969.)

Hurvitz, Leon, tr., *Scripture of the Lotus Blossom of the Fine Dharma (The Lotus Sutra)*. New York: Columbia University Press, 1976.

Kato, Bunno, et al., tr., *The Three-fold Lotus Sutra (The Lotus Sutra).* New York and Tokyo: Weatherhill/Kosei, 1975.

Layman, Emma, *Buddhism in America.* Chicago, Il: Nelson-Hall, 1976.

Luk, Charles, tr., *The Vimalakirti Nirdesa Sutra.* Boston, Ma: Shambhala, 1972.

Mascaró, Juan, tr., *The Dhammapada: The Path of Perfection.* London: Penguin Classics, 1973.

Murcott, Susan, *The First Buddhist Women: Translations and Commentary on the Therigatha.* Berkeley, Ca: Parallax Press, 1991.

Narada Maha Thera, *The Buddha and His Teachings.* Singapore: Singapore Buddhist Meditation Centre. (Originally pub. c. 1973.)

Okazaki, Joji, *Pure Land Buddhist Painting.* Elizabeth ten Grotenhuis, tr. Tokyo: Kodansha, 1977.

Price, A.F. and Wong Mou-Lam, tr., *The Diamond Sutra & The Sutra of Hui Neng.* Boston, Ma: Shambhala, 1969.

Prince, A.J., "The World of Hua Yen Buddhism." Reprinted in *Phật Học (Ca, USA),* No. 6, 1986, p. 135-136.

Red Pine, tr., *The Zen Teaching of Bodhidharma.* Berkeley Ca: North Point Press, 1989.

Sangharakshita, *The Eternal Legacy: An Introduction to the Canonical Literature of Buddhism.* London: Tharpa Publications, 1985.

Saso, Michael and David W. Chappell, ed., *Buddhist and Taoist Studies I.* Honolulu: University of Hawaii Press, 1987.

Seki, Hozen, *Buddha Tells of the Infinite: the "Amida Kyo."* New York: American Buddhist Academy, 1973.

The Shambhala Dictionary of Buddhism and Zen. Boston, Ma: 1991.

Shao, Simpei, tr., *Discourse on Samantabhadra's Beneficence Aspirations.* Hong Kong: H.K. Buddhist Book Distributor, 1980.

Sheng-Yen (Master), *Faith in Mind: A Guide to Ch'an Practice.* Taipei: Tungchu Pub., 1989.

Sheng-Yen (Master), *The Sword of Wisdom: Lectures on The Song of Enlightenment*. New York: Dharma Drum Publications, 1990.

Shih Shing-yun (Master), ed., *Bilingual Buddhist Series*. Taipei: Buddhist Cultural Service, 1962.

Snelling, John, *The Buddhist Handbook: A Complete Guide to Buddhist Schools, Teaching, Practice and History*. Rochester, Vt: Inner Traditions, 1991.

Snelling, John, *The Elements of Buddhism*. Longmead, England: Element Books, 1990.

Sutra Translation Committee of the United States and Canada, tr., *The Buddhist Liturgy*. Thornhill, Ont. and Bronx, NY: 1983.

Suzuki, D.T., *An Introduction to Zen Buddhism*. New York: Grove Weidenfeld, 1964.

Suzuki, D.T., tr., *The Lankavatara Sutra: A Mahayana Text*. Boulder Co: Prajna Press, 1978.

Suzuki, D. T., "The Development of the Pure Land Doctrine in Buddhism." In *The Eastern Buddhist*, Vol. III, No. 5, Jan.-Mar. 1925, p. 285-326.

Suzuki, D.T., "Zen and Jodo, Two Types of Buddhist Experience." In *The Eastern Buddhist*, Vol. IV, No. 2, Jul.-Sept. 1927, p. 89-121.

Tay, C.N., "Kuan-Yin: The Cult of Half Asia." In *History of Religions*, Vol. 16, No. 2, Nov. 1975, p. 147-175.

Thích Thiền Tâm (Master), *Buddhism of Wisdom and Faith*. Sepulveda, Ca: International Buddhist Monastic Institute, 1991. (Reprinted by The Corporate Body of the Buddha Educational Foundation, Taipei.)

Thích Thiền Tâm (Master), tr., *Pure Land Buddhism: Dialogues with Ancient Masters*. New York: Sutra Translation Committee of the United States and Canada, 1992.

Thurman, Robert, tr., *The Holy Teaching of Vimalakirti: A Mahayana Scripture*. University Park, Pa and London: Pennsylvania State University Press, 1981.

T'ien Ju (Master), "Doubts and Questions about Pure Land." In *Pure Land Buddhism: Dialogues with Ancient Masters*. Thích Thiền Tâm, tr.

Realms of worlds in empty space might reach an end,
And living beings, karma and afflictions be extinguished;
But they will never be exhausted,
And neither will my vows.

The Vows of Samantabhadra